LETTERS HOME

Civil War Letters
by
Bishop Asbury Cook

Private in the 144th Regiment
of the
New York Volunteer Infantry

Compiled and Edited by
His Great-Grandsons

Donald R. Hunt, Sr.
and
Frank R. Hathaway

HERITAGE BOOKS, INC.

Published 2000 by

HERITAGE BOOKS, INC.
1540E Pointer Ridge Place
Bowie, Maryland 20716

1-800-398-7709
www.heritagebooks.com

ISBN 0-7884-1478-X

A Complete Catalog Listing Hundreds of Titles
On History, Genealogy, and Americana
Available Free Upon Request

Bishop Asbury Cook
1831-1874

FOREWORD

The following document is a series of letters that were written by Bishop Asbury Cook to his wife Louisa. They were written during his service in Company F, 144th Regiment of the New York Volunteer Infantry.

I have arranged the letters by the month written, as near as possible. It was extremely helpful that Bishop numbered the letters as he wrote them. However, sometimes he forgot the number or used the same number twice.

At the beginning of each month I have included two items before starting the letters. The first item is an outline of what happened during this particular month. The boldface type is what was happening nationwide in the war. The light face type is what the Regimental Historian recorded as happening with the Regiment. The second item is a History summarization which summarizes the historian's recordings. These histories are taken from the publication *Civil War Record of the 144th Regiment, New York Volunteer Infantry*. This publication was written by James Harvey McKee. It has recently been reprinted by Heritage Books Inc., 1540E Pointer Ridge Place, Bowie, Maryland 20716, ISBN 0-784-0007-X. The reprinting was done in co-operation with the village of Delhi, NY in commemoration of the Civil War Days in Delaware County, NY

There are many times when the outline, the summarization, and the letters do not seem to be talking about the same period of time.

As an Appendix to the document I have included his service record and his pension record from the National Archives. His wife received a pension after his death which was caused by a service connected illness.

I extend a sincere thank you to Frank Hathaway for all his help in putting this document together.

Donald R. Hunt. Sr.

AUGUST THROUGH OCTOBER 1862

The 144th Regiment New York Volunteer Infantry was formed at Camp Delaware, Delhi N.Y. They were at this location from August to September 8th.

History summarization, pages 33, 62

On September 4th, the sixth company (Company F) marched into Camp Delaware. This was the Hancock Company. **The first enlistment in the Company was August 12th, Bishop A. Cook** having enrolled himself on that day. At the time he was 31 years old.

Upon reporting to General Wool, Col. Hughston received the following orders:

Headquarters 8th Army Corps,
Hanover Junction, Md., October 12th, 1862

Col. Robert S. Hughston will proceed with his regiment, the 144th Regiment, New York Volunteers, to Washington, via Baltimore, and report himself upon his arrival at Washington to Brig. Gen. Silas Casey or the Adjutant-General of the army.

The men of this regiment are entirely "green," not having had the least pratice in loading and firing.

By Command Of
Maj.-Gen Wool,
E. Christensen
Major U.S.A. Aide-de-Camp

Camp Delaware, Delhi, N. Y., Aug. to Sept. 8th.
> **Aug. 9th, Cedar Mountain, Va.**
> **Aug. 28th and 29th, Groveton and Gainsville, Va.**
> **Aug. 30, 2nd Battle Bull Run, Va.**
> **Sept. 1st, Chantilla, Va.**

Walton, N.Y., Sept. 8th to 9th
Rock Rift, N.Y., Sept. 9th to 10th
Hancock, N.Y., and on Erie R.R. Sept. 10th to 11th
Elmira, N.Y., Sept. 11th
On R.R. to Baltimore, Md. Sept. 11th to 12th
On R.R. to Washington, D.C., Sept. 12th to 13th
Camp Seward, Va., Sept. 14th to 18th
> **Sept. 14th, South Mountain, Md.**
> **Sept. 17th, Antietam, Md.**

Camp Marcy, Va., Sept. 18th to 20th
> **Sept. 19th and 20th, Iuka, Miss**

Camp Bliss, Upton's Hill, Va., Sept. 20th to Feb. 12th, '63
> **Oct. 3rd and 4th, Corinth, Miss.**
> **Oct. 8th, Perryville, Ky.**

The first letter is dated October 12, 1862, and is not numbered.

Sunday, October 12, 1862, 4-1/2 p.m. We are about 15 minutes ride into Merriland. We are all rite and sound. We got to Elmira at 2 a.m. Saturday. Stayed in the cars till 7 a.m. and then marched to Camp. Took dinner with the Regiment that is there, then drew our belts and cartridge boxes. We then went to the depot and got our guns. They are nice. We then marched into the cars and rode all nite again.

It seems the country is full of soldiers. We have passed several encampments today. It is now 5-1/2 p.m. and almost dark. We are 15 miles from Baltimore and shall get there this evening. The people cheer us all along the way.

At 10 o'clock at Baltimore they furnished the Regiment a good supper. We marched through the city and took the cars for Washington at midnight. Some of the men lay down in the street and went to sleep while the rest stood in line.

Dear Wf, it is now Monday, 10 a.m. and we are 10 miles from Washington, having come 30 miles in 10 hours. The engine has given out and they have gone after another to take us to the Capitol. So you see we are taking it cool. We have had but little rest on the whole journey. I will write no more until I get another start in Washington.

Tuesday morning . We arrived here at Washington and got supper before dark. I seen Charley Dickinson, Dan Gardinier, and several others that I knew. The boys are 6 or 8 miles from here. Soldiers are coming in all the time. Where we are to go I do not know. but we shall go somewhere to drill.

Tuesday evening, October 14 . We are in camp at Camp Chase, about 2-1/2 miles from Washington. Our tent holds 6 men. Steve and two others are writing. The Captain has been around and ordered us to sleep on our arms and be ready at 3 minutes notice. I seen James Cook at Washington this morning. He came out of the hospital yesterday. J. R. Wheeler is in the hospital. Kilmer we have not seen since about the time we left Baltimore. Some say he went out of the car onto the platform and was not seen after. I hope he did not fall off the car and get killed. I tried to get the Captain to try to look him up, but he said he didn't know how to find him. He hated to go so bad maybe he has skedaddled.

There has been several men poisoned at Baltimore. Two soldiers that come from there this morning are dead and several others sick.

Wednesday, Oct. 15th, 10 o'clock We were called into line at midnight with 25 rounds of cartridges to meet the Rebels. It was done to try the grit of the soldiers. I smelt the rat, but some of them was considerably frightened. We got back in camp at 8 o'clock this morning. I have seen a good many wounded soldiers at Washington. There is no rebels within a good many miles of us. It is cool at nite and quite warm today.

3

Second letter (not numbered)   Camp Chase, October 15, 1862

Dear Companion,

I have given you something of a history of my journey. Here is how I will tell you of the fare. We have bread and a slice of boiled ham or a slice of cheese for our rations. I wish I could get into your potatoes. I have been to Sutlers and got a hunk of cheese and some cake and a coconut. We have to pay about 3 times for what we get here. 2 or 3 cents for an apple. Some of our Company went to the Sutlers and got a good breakfast for 50 cents.

It is quite a sight to see the fortifications and camps around here. You would think the whole world could not take it. There is some soldiers here you better believe.

I have stood the journey first rate and feel well, only I want to sleep. How do you get along? How did you get home from Hancock that rainy night? How are my sweet little girls? Tell them I think often of them. I wish I had their likenesses.

Dear wife, Edward Lake is dead. They say he died on the battlefield. We have prayers in our tent thank the Lord. I must close.

I suppose you must direct mail to Washington, D.C. in care of Colonel Huston, 144th Regiment, N.Y. State Volunteers, Company F. Or Captain Plaskett. But be sure and get the number of the Regiment and Company F and N.Y. State Volunteer.

How did your wood bin turn out? Give us the news. I don't know as you can read this for I sit on my knees and write on my knapsack.

I have spent only $1.50. That leaves me yet $7.50.

Yours in love,

B. A. Cook

3rd letter (not numbered)   Camp Chase, Washington, DC
                    October 17, 1862

My own dear Wife,

It is with pleasure that I attempt to write a few lines to let you know I am well and hearty and am learning to be a soldier very fast. We draw our rations regular. We have good bread, fried pork, and potatoes once a day. Also we have rice, beans and coffee.

We are in sight of Uncle Abe's house and a good share of the city. Can see about 2 miles on the Potomac River. There is 2 or 3 Regiments that come in every day. I had a good talk with a soldier from Alexandria this morning. He said there were a good many regiments there. There are forts and batteries all around us as far as we can see.

I think the fighting will be done in the course of 6 to 8 months, for everybody is preparing to fight. They must make quick of it I think. I am on guard today for the first time in Dixie. I have stood 2 hours, so don't have to drill.

I have $7.00 left and $1.25 let out. We don't know when we shall move from here, but you must write. Direct to Washington, D.C., in care of Captain Plaskett, 144th Regiment, Company F. They will find me somehow. I put a note in Steve's letter to direct to Camp Chase, but now I countermand that order. Steve Garlow has been here to see us.

Dinner is ready so I can't write more. You can write when you are a mind to and so will I. If you can't read this, send it back with all the rest of the directions. Be sure to put N.Y.S.V.

Yours in Love,

                    B. A. Cook

(This is a continuation of some letter. He notes that he will number the letters from this point on, so we can assume this is part of No. 1 Written from Camp Chase)

I number all the letters you see after this so you will know if you receive them all or not. I gave $1.00 for one plug of tobacco this morning. It weighed one pound 2 oz. We pay 30 cts. per pound for butter, 20 cts. for cheese, 2-1/2 cts. for potatoes, and 2 cts. apiece for apples. We have good water . . . better than I expected to get. Virginia the country looks desolate here. Hardly anything growing. No use for people to raise anything for the soldier to steal or destroy,

I went Sunday and visited 2 or 3 men that lived close to the camp. One of them said his neighbor had been a secessionist. A part of us went to see him, but he was away in the lot somewhere. He went to Washington and took the Oath of Allegiance, and got a certificate for the protection of his property signed by the General. We are agoing to register our names on the church book. We are to have prayer meeting tonite.

How do you get along? I have not heard from you since I left you, but I expect to get a letter this week from you. Write all the week and send it when you get a chance. I hope you are all well and doing well. I have not wrote to anyone but you yet. I want to write to all, but can't get time. I wish you had time to write for me. How are my little girls? Is the school out and are you all well? Do you think of Pa? Pa thinks of you often and would like to see you. Be good girls and try to do rite and be God's children.

Now Louisa, you must pray with the girls and do for them the best you can. The Lord will assist you. I think the rebellion will soon come to an end. How happy I shall be to get home and meet my little family if it be the Lord's will. But if otherwise, I want to meet you all in Heaven.

There is some here that have been in service a year and have not been in action. So you see, everybody don't fight that is in the service of Uncle Sam. I must close.

Yours,

B. A. Cook

No. 3, Mount Upton, Camp Bliss, Va., October 21, 1862

Dearest Wife,

I take my pen to talk to you a little, knowing that you are anxious to hear from me often. I am well. I will tell you of our travels since I last wrote.

We pulled up stakes at Camp Chase last Saturday at 3 o'clock and marched 8 miles to some place. Got there about 7 in the evening. Took a lunch out of the haversack and lay down on the ground to sleep. Got asleep and were called up at 9 o'clock for roll call. Answered to our names and lay down again until morning. Got up at daylite and found it Sunday morning and rather chilly. But the sun come up and made it pleasant. We had to carry water, wood, and put up tents and dig all forenoon. In the afternoon, we met on the field and our Chaplain preached us a short sermon. Then we met in the evening, 7 of us in our tent, and had a good prayer meeting. The orderly was with us. There are 5 of us with tents together, all praying men. Two brothers named Gould, Silas Parks, and Steve and me. We all share alike.

Well, I have not told you that we moved to this place yesterday. After having worked and brought straw, and fixed ourselves comfortable, we had to leave it in one day. We started about 3 o'clock yesterday and marched about 6 miles to this place. We pitched our tents without orders after we were halted, determined not to lay on the ground without shelter again. We slept first rate after having family prayers.

This morning I see a little frost for the first in this country. I suppose we are about 8 or 10 miles from the Capitol. I can see the top of the old White House yet. We are where there was a battle last summer a year ago. I suppose there are rebels within 15 miles of us now, but not in large numbers. There was one captured Sunday near our camp. He was dressed in gray. When they hailed him, he ran like an Indian, but they stopped him by sending a couple of bullets close to him.

We don't get our ration regular. All the ration we drew this morning was a cup of coffee. But I had some bread and got some cake off the Sutler, so I had a good breakfast.

We have to carry our knapsack, blankets, overcoats, haversack, canteen, cartridge box, and gun. It makes quite a load, but it is nothing after you get used to it. I got wounded last nite. I sat on a brier and scratched my thigh, but did not draw blood, so I am all rite.

The news has come that the Rebel Braggs army is whipped and cut to pieces. One whole regiment come over to our side, so I guess Kentucky is sick of fighting against the Union. It is near 12 o'clock and we have been taking up our tents and putting them in line, so we have quite a village. To see the fortifications, forts, and cannons that are planted here is astonishing. There is men enough too. Regiment after Regiment. I am not discontented in the least. I see no hardship but what I can endure for the good of my country. I would of thought it would of made me sick to lay on the cold ground exposed to the nite air. But the Lord protects and I am thankful for his protection. I cannot write more, but as this cannot go to Washington until tomorrow morning, I will write more then.

I have shortened this in all points, but I will tell you I wrote to you a week ago what my business was on Monday. Well, on Tuesday the Orderly sent me to the Colonel's tent to wait on him. I will tell you what I had to do. I had to carry a pass to one of the Captain's tents in the forenoon. Then in the evening, the Colonel sent me to call the Captain. That is all my day's work.

Breakfast is ready, so I cannot write more. I was glad to hear from Charlie and it was such a good letter. He is the only one that has written to me except you. I will write to him soon. Are my girls well this morning?

Good bye for this time,

B. A. Cook

No. 4, Camp Bliss, Mount Upton, Va., October 26, 1862 (Sunday)

Dear Wife,

I am thankful that I have another opportunity of writing to you. I received your welcome letter Friday nite. How pleased I was to hear from home again. Sorry you are all sick. Hope you are well now. I am well and fat . . .weighed 151 lbs. yesterday.

Last Thursday, Company A and F went out on picket duty. We went 2 or 3 miles from camp. We had a first rate time. We came back to camp Friday nite. I am on guard today. It commenced raining at 8 o'clock this morning and continues to rain. I have stood for 2 hours, and go on again at 3 this afternoon. I guess I shall have a wet time of it.

When we were on picket, one of our boys accidentally shot his forefinger off. There is another sick with typhoid fever, and one of our tent mates sick with the mumps. There is considerable talk about a good many of our Regiment joining the regular army for 5 years, but I don't know as they will. I think they will miss it if they do.

I heard Kilmer had been home. Is it so? Some say there is snow up there. I don't believe all I hear. Kate did not write to Steve about the apple cuts. I am glad you have got so many apples. They are worth 2 to 3 cents apiece here.

We live pretty well now for soldiers. We have plenty of meat and bread, some potatoes, beans, and rice. We can get pie and cake if we buy it. I got a little round pie yesterday for 10 cents. If I had some of your pumpkin pies here, I could sell them for 25 cents quick.

There is talk that we shall move from here tomorrow, but I don't believe it. We have prayer meetings in our tent 3 times a week and enjoy ourselves first rate. There is 2 that have resolved to seek an interest in Christ. I hope in God we shall see many seeking Christ.

God be with you Dear Wife in your lonely hours and sustain you in your days of trial.

I think you had better kill the pig as soon as you can. Get it fit to kill, for it will not be profitable to winter two pigs. Get it so it will cook itself. It will make good meat. You must not work so hard to make yourself sick. Be careful of your health.

I dreamed of you nite before last. I shook hands with you and kissed you. If it had been real, it would have been better. If we are permitted to live together again on earth, we shall know how to appreciate the blessings of each others society. It is a long time since I have seen my girls. I would like to hug them. I hope in a few months I shall be with you. If I live 6 months here, I shall get a furlow and come home. That is the doctrine.

No. 4 (continued) (Monday)

Dear Louisa,

I have a few spare moments to pencil a few lines to you. I feel better today than I could expect after standing on guard in the rain yesterday. They tried to get me out in the nite, but I was wet enough. The wind blew and it rained until 10 a.m. today. Some of the tents blew down in the night. We could not get a fire to cook breakfast, so we eat some clear bread. For dinner we had boiled pork, potatoes and coffee, and I have got my clothes nearly dry.

They are drafting in Penn for certain. Thousands of drafted men are coming to Harrisburg and other places for encampment. So if they get all the men in service, we shall soon know our strength, and the rebs will feel it too.

We got some boards and hay and put a floor in our tent, so we shall have a comfortable bed tonight. We are on the mount, so the wind has a fair chance at us. We have got to go on dress parade pretty soon. I will finish this tonight and send it in the morning.

I tell you I wished myself in Cook's house beside the old stove last nite and this morning to warm myself and dry my clothes. If I had been there, I guess I would eat breakfast with you. There were many homesick men here this morning, but they have forgot it all now the sun shines again.

You may be thankful you are as well off as you are. Take all the comfort you can. I would if I was in your place (and had a man). I hope to be with you and my little girls before many months, for we shall either whip the rebs, or brake the government down, for the army is constantly increasing.

There is a prospect of some fighting pretty soon. It is rumored that they are fighting now at Harper's Ferry, some fifty miles from here.

If you can read this, you will do well for I set flat down on my blanket and write on my knee. Chairs and desks are our of fashion here. I must close. Give my respects to all inquiring friends. I am looking . . .yes, here they come, two letters from my own wife. Thank the Lord all rite.

B. A. Cook

11

No. 5, Camp Bliss, Mount Upton, October 30, 1862

Dear Wife:

I will scribble a few lines to let you know that I am well and fat as usual, and enjoy myself first rate. Last night I received the letter you sent to Delhi. I dreamed I see you and the children together. Oh, wasn't I glad, but behold, it was a dream. But I live in the hopes it will not always be so.

We have to drill 2 a day besides dress parades. We go to bed every night at 9 o'clock and get up at daylight. There is 10 or 12 in the hospital from our Regiment, besides a number that are not fit for duty. But I am all rite yet, Thank the Lord. We had prayer meeting last nite. We had a good meeting. How thankful I am that we can have prayer meeting.

Uncle Brainard is about 5 miles from here. I shall try and get a pass and go and see him. He has not joined his regiment yet. He is not fit for duty, but he can take care of himself.

You want to know how much a hogshead holds. It holds 9-1/2 bushels. If you find the head you will see it marked 9-1/2. You wish to know what that hundred men came to camp near Kingston. Probably there was a prospect of some resisting the draft. But they must come when Uncle Sam calls.

There is no danger of England siding with the South yet. There has been another battle in South Carolina near Charleston. Our men drove the rebs across the river and burned the bridge. We get N.Y. papers every day here for 5 cents apiece, so we get the news. I went to the Sutler and got some cheese and butter. Butter 35 cts. and cheese 20 cts. I toasted some bread and cheese and had a good breakfast.

I have wrote a letter to send to Almus today for the first. I would like to come and dig potatoes for you, but Sam has something for me to do at present. I can't even eat all the bread he furnishes me.

If you was close by, I could send you two loves of bread every week. I could get all the meat gravy you want for one cent per lb. at our cook tent. Some pay 6 cents apiece for washing, but I choose to do my own. We have soap and candles, so you see we can keep clean and see to write to our sweethearts. That is rite, is it not.

I cannot write every other day, but I shall write often. I suppose you feel highly honored to have a soldier address you from Virginia. And I assure you I am glad to hold correspondence with a lady in northern Pennsylvania.

It is September weather here, a little frost most every morning. I would like to step in and stay with you tonight and see them little girls. I hope you are all well. How is Mr. and Mrs. Terrel? And Br. Jakes folks? I must close and go to roll call and then go to bed. Give my respects to all inquiring friends.

From your old boy, ever yours

B. A. Cook

NOVEMBER 1862

History summarization pp. 68-72

The camp of the 144th known as Camp Bliss was pleasantly situated on the eastern slope with a very good water supply near at hand. It was at Camp Bliss that the 144th, using the expressive words of Kipling, began to "find itself." Up to this time the Regiment had been simply a structural organization. Guard duty that had seemed irksome and unnecessary when no enemy was near now began to assume a new importance. Little by little the relative importance of obedience, implicit obedience to orders, to ensure prompt results in the movements of the army was seen to be necessary. There was the "finding" by which knowledge was acquired as to how the soldier could best be cared for in the sanitation of the body, the tent, and camp. The matter of the food ration and how best to use it was another of the problems, and not the smallest "finding". Few will forget the first issue of the "hardtack" ration in place of soft bread. Another and large factor in the "finding" of the Regiment came through the experiences on the drill ground. Thus far the Regiment had been quite free from sickness, except that the mumps had a short run; but after a few weeks at Camp Bliss negligent sanitation on the part of companies and men, together with changed conditions of living brought consequent result in long lines of men responding to sick call and a large number in tents not able to respond in person. November 17th was marked by the first death in the 144th on Southern soil. Curtis Fagen of Company B died on that date in Regimental Hospital after only a few days illness. On this occasion the entire Regiment followed the escort in the order of companies to Fall's Church, where the body was buried. The Government furnished an A tent, 7 x 7' but without bed or bedding or other furniture. The tent squad put the tent in place and then scrounged up other material for comfort. Scrap lumber and bricks were used to make a floor and fireplace, etc. The special service aside from the regular drill and camp duty performed by the 144th was picket duty in the defense of Washington. The line extended from Fall's Church to Rose Hill (on the Alexanderia Fairfax Turnpike). The night of December 28th was marked by special wakefulness. At about half-past ten P.M. the long roll was sounded in the camps. Orders were given directing that knapsacks be packed, haversacks filled, ammunition distributed and the men ready to form a line in fifteen minutes. After a march of a mile or so a battle line was formed after reaching Annandale. The 144th on the right, the 143rd on the left and the 127th in reserve. Pickets were posted, arms stacked and the men directed to lie down and secure what sleep they could. In the morning the cavalry pickets brought in six Rebel cavalrymen and this was all the enemy in sight. The expedition went down in the memory of the men as "Bloody Annandale". During these months of adjustment to soldier conditions quite a number of men grew restless and thought to better their condition by deserting to and enlisting in the regular army. Early in 1863 February 12th the Regiment moved into the vicinity of Alexandria.

No 6, Camp Bliss, Fairfax County, Va., November 4, 1862

Dearly beloved Wife,

I seat myself to tell you that I am well and in the same camp that I was when I last wrote. I received your letter No. 4 in due time 4 days ago. I think your new dress is very nice for winter. How much flour did you get for 14 shillings a sack. . . . enough to last you all winter? I think 22 cents is a fair price for your butter. I see by yesterdays paper that in Philadelphia it is worth from 20 to 24 cents the highest. The school is out and the girls are at home all the time now I suppose. It is strange that you have so much stormy weather there and such nice weather here. I have not seen but one storm since I left Hancock and that I wrote you about.

Last Sunday we had a sermon, after which I wrote to Mother and a few lines to Uncle Jim Cook, and sent in it Russ' letter. I wrote to Al last week, so they will hear from me.

You heard about those women being poisoned. That was a rumor. The women were very suddenly taken ill but the doctors said it was not poison, so they survived. We had prayer meeting last nite. I gave the orderly your respects as requested. He made a bow and said all right. This morning he came to me and told me to go if I would and get a hatchet and go to the Colonel's tent, for the Colonel wanted something done. I told him I would go to the Colonel's tent. The Colonel wanted some poles cut to fix a bunk. He gave me a job to go to the woods. I got some little poles and come back and got some straw and made him a nice straw bed. He thanked me very kindly. The regiment had gone to drill when I got through, so I spent the rest of the afternoon in writing to you.

I do honestly think this war will close by next spring. There is only 3 of our tent fit for duty. Two are sick with the mumps. Stephen stands it like a tiger and is fat as a bear. We get up in the morning at the beat of the drum, put on our equipment, and form into line. The roll is called and we are dismissed. We go and wash and then to breakfast. We then wash the dishes, sweep the avenue between the tents, and prepare for drill at 9-1/2 a.m. We drill until 11 o'clock, then prepare to eat dinner. We then drill for 2 till 4, and then have dress parade about sundown.

Tuesday evening, November 4th. I have had my supper, got a new pen, and washed the dishes. There is prayer meeting tonite, but I must write. I looked for a letter tonite but none came. So I will wait patiently and maybe I will get 2 at a time. You have not wrote anything about Jenny. How does she get along and all the rest of the things? Oh how good it is to read those lines thy hand has traced. I read them over and over with interest. I know the anxiety and love you have for me, no love for man purer than thine, and yes Dear I am thine although far away. But I trust the day will come when we shall meet and enjoy each other's society again.

I went to the Sutler and got a pint of molasses to eat on bread. It was so good, the rest of the boys went in with me and we bought 3 pints for 12 cents a pint.

7-1/2 o'clock in evening, November 4th . You are pretty good to do business I guess, for you went to Susquehanna and got flour and things. You can do as well as I can. When I come back, you and Jenny can go after things and I can tend to my work.

I am glad Aunt Harriet wrote to you. I must write to her before long. I have got a paper here with something in it you will like to read. I think I will send it to you. I have marked some of the pieces as you will see if you get it. I think you ought to get this next week. If you lived close to the railroad, you would get it Friday nite.

George Wheeler is in the guard house for ill conduct. He has been there most of the time for 5 or 6 days. There are 5 or 6 others in that can't behave. John Garlow has got the gout(?). I guess his knee is swelled considerably.

I must close soon. You must write all the news. I see Wesley Dickinson on Sunday. He is in the 43rd Regiment that is encamped close by us. He came over to see us. He looks natural. I don't know what else to write unless I tell you that I went to the Chaplain and put my name on the Church Book. Yes, one thing more. I have got 2 dollars and 50 cts. yet and $2.25 lent. I may get all of it and I may get half if payday comes soon. If not, then all rite for I shall send home for 2 or 3 dollars. But don't send until I order it. I wish I could kiss you and my girls and go to bed.

Good nite wife and children Dears,

B. A. Cook

No. 7, Camp Bliss, Monday, November 10, 1862

Dearest Companion,

This evening finds me sitting on the blanket in the tent trying to converse with the one I love. What a blessing it was I received No. 5 of Nov. 2nd in due time. Glad to hear you are doing so well. You said the corn was husked and beans thrasht (sic). It is too bad for you to have to work out doors so much. I hope Charles will help finish up. Has Almus come?

I spoke about a furlow. Some said after we had been here 6 months we were entitled to a furlow, but I guess it ain't so. I hope the war will end in 6 months or a year at longest. I have not written to you in one week, that is too long, but I had to go on picket duty last Friday, and came back Sunday.

You may be surprised if I tell you it snowed all day Friday. The snow was 4 inches deep here even if it is down south. I slept about an hour Friday nite and like to froze on Saturday nite. It was freezing cold. We had a fire and we could freeze one side and burn the other. At daylight Sunday morning I laid 2 rails . . . . one on the ground and the other on a log by the side of the fire. I lay on them and went to sleep. The first I knew I rolled onto the ground. I gathered up pretty sudden and we all had a hearty laugh over it.

Steve and I went out Sunday in the woods. The tracking snow was good. We captured one gray squirrel. My gun shoots first rate. I dressed the game and put it in the pan with some salt pork and cooked it for dinner. It was the sweetest meat I ever eat. Steve got some cabbage for supper, so we had boiled pork and cabbage and I tell you it was good. I have not went hungry yet and have not stole anything. I am afraid them starving ones are inclined to steal for fear they will want. I have told you what we had to eat. Each man has 1 loaf of bread per day. With the rest we have, it is all any man can eat.

I got a pass today and went down to Alexandria to see Uncle Bane and cousins. Was about 6 miles. But I did not see them. Al Cook died last week. James Cook got his discharge and Uncle went to Washington with him, so I did not see him. Too bad. Russel went with me. He is not very well. It is roll call and we have no light to write.

Tuesday morning, the 11th. It looks like a fine day. The snow is about gone and it did not freeze last night. I got a snotty cold when on picket. Most every body have colds here. I expect to hear from you in a day or two. I am in a great hurry to finish this and send it this morning.

B. A. Cook

No. 8, Camp Bliss, Upton Hill, Wednesday, November 12, 1862

As I have a little time, I will improve it in writing to you Dearest of Earthly Friends. I received yours of the 5th last nite. It reassured me that I am not forgotten by those I love.

Glad to hear that the boys were there doing the work up. If they come back in the Spring and I don't, they can help you. You are anxious to know when I am coming home. If I knew I would tell you, but no man can tell. We hear one thing one day and another the next. McClellan was ready to move a month ago so he said, and he has hardly moved yet. That is the way it goes. Now he is superseded by Burnside. Now just as soon as an officer gets in shape to do something, he is superseded. The paper today states that McClellan will run for the next President. Likely he will. The paper talks that the war will soon end. It says we have double the men to fight this winter than the rebs have. And we know that they are better fed and clothed and can stand the winter as well as they can. I think quite likely we shall winter near here, but we may have orders to move from here in 3 days.

I did not tell you what I seen in my travels the other day. I saw many soldiers that had been through battles. Some sound, but weak with disease and some crippled from wounds of all descriptions. They were in the hospital. It is a very nice large brick building the rebs once used for a school. It comes very good for the soldiers for it is all roomed and very convenient. I have not seen a reb that I know of yet and don't know when I shall. We have got brick and built a fireplace in our tent, and a chimney. So we can have fire to keep us warm. My cold is loose and I guess will wear off in a few days.

I stood guard yesterday and last nite, so I don't have to drill today until dress parade. That comes off at sundown. I went to the creek and done my washing this forenoon. I traded watches the other nite and got a new watch. It looks like the one I let Barns have. I got 60 cts. and am to have 40 more. I paid 75 cts. for repairs and it runs good now.

That Rose that was at Delhi went to Washington to the hospital today. He borrowed 50 cts. off me several days ago. I guess I will not get it again. I have got $2.00 left yet, but I have got to get my boots fixed and that will cost 75 cts. likely. There is lots of men that are out of money here. I have lent them over $2.00 and can't get it off them until after payday. I think the paymaster will be here in a few days. If he don't, I shall have to send to you for some next time I write. There is now 2 months pay due . . . $20 to you and $6 for me. If we could get it, it would be very nice. It looks as though it will rain tonight.

I told you that Jimmy got his discharge. He got as far as Uncle Brainard's and died. Russ got a line to that effect. Ain't that too bad. If they had discharged him in Washington he would get well. But no, they let him go to camp again and the dysentery carried him off. It is hard thus to fall.

You talk about my not telling you what to do. First, tell me what you have done, and then ask what you wish to know about. Then I will tell you the best I can being so far away. I want you to keep

Jenny, if possible, for I think so much of her. If she acts ugly, you must gad her about the stables and make her know who you are. She will not hurt you. If she wants to play, you can let her out to play a little occasionally.

You would like to hug your old boy, would you. Well, I think I would like to get hold of you too. I thought last nite during the dark hours that I was standing on guard how I would like to bend ever those little girls and kiss those sweet sleeping faces, and then surprise you be getting into the warm bed with you Dear Wife. I wish for that time to come, but I will wait patiently and trust in God. That is the best I can do.

Is the grain all thrashed and how much do you have? You know we must save some of that spring wheat. About 1 bushel is enough seed. If we can't sow it next spring, it will keep 5 years if the mice don't get it. Have you put the cows up yet? Do you manage to keep the sheep and cattle from the orchard? Those nice trees must be preserved if possible, for they will be the mainstay of the family in 5 or 6 years when they get to bearing. If your rye and wheat don't turn out pretty well, you will have to get more flour. I tell you, you have got to look out for yourself, for the people are going to see hard times there as well as here. Things are so high, it will cost a good deal to live. And if you get short, you can't start out and sponge your living as some can. If the Government pays me as they ought to, you can live comfortable. But if I should not get pay in 4 months from now, you and I would both suffer for the necessities of life.

How much money have you got. You have not said anything about money, only that you had paid Lions. I have got my boots fixed and paid 75 cts., so I am reduced to 76 cts. and 2 postage stamps. I have got tobacco to last 3 weeks yet, so what money I have got will last some time if I don't buy anything. Next time I won't lend money . . . that is so. I don't know but I have wrote enough, but I won't stop yet. I thank you for your good long letter. Do so again.

I want you to write how Jenny gets along, and if she gets enough to eat. Tell her I would like to see her. I see a great many horses here . . .cavalry and artillery horses. There are batteries and forts in every direction. There is one fort by the side of our camp that covers acres of ground, and lots of others that we could take shelter under if the rebs should come. But they can't get here.

E. W. G. told the truth doing as he did I guess, for I see him with some fresh pork. There is some in the company that will steal. He has not forgot his boyish tricks and he finds enough to go with him here. I think that one-half of the company will not steal, but there are some that will steal even if they steal from someone in their own company. When I went our on picket our tent was alone part of the time. I had a cigar box with one doz. cigars in it with 30 sheets of paper. When I come back, half the paper was gone and all the cigars but one. They steal dishes and blankets if they can. We have to guard the Sutler's shop to keep them from robbing that. They stole 3 or 4 dollars worth one nite. For my part, I can get along yet without stealing and so can my tent mates.

Some of this company I believe have went so far as to have connections with wenches. White women are scarce here you see. I think any man, if I may call them men, that will make beasts of themselves ought to be shot in the ass or head. I don't know why it is, but I have no desire for women now so far from you, unless you were here.

I have not been homesick in the least, which I expected to be. As long as I am well and can hear from home often and things are rite there, I shall be contented I think.

How much corn did you have? Tell me about the other grain. I hear you have plenty of snow up there. It makes bad work for you having to take care of the stock, but I hope you will be careful of your health. I don't know what Turrell will hear next . . . maybe that York State seceded after this I guess. The call comes for supper.

We had coffee, rice and bread. And I got a motherly letter from Mother. I tell you it was a good one. She wants to get home again where she can get cows milk and oven bread. She says it is cold and snowy. She feels for her son in them cloth tents. But we are comfortable and we shall have different quarters before long for winter. It is most dark and all is well. I did not know that I thought so much of my girls, and I guess they didn't know they thought so much of Pa before.

From yours only with love,

B. A. C.

No. 9, Camp Bliss, Upton Hill, Fairfax County, Va., November 19, 1862

Dear Wife,

It is 10 minutes past twelve and I take my pen to answer yours of the 15th, which I received last nite, and tell you that I am well and no rheumatism about me. I feel like a buck. I am sorry it was so long before you got a letter. It was partly my fault and partly on account of the snow. I answered Mother's letter and wrote one to Elijah Reynolds. I intend to write to you as often as once a week and oftener when I can. Steve got a letter last nite too. Kate says Mrs. Wheeler is the same as Mrs. Greenman and Mrs. Gates.

If all works well, our school will be larger one of these days won't it. You may think I am coming back in the spring, for I think things shape that way now. The election will make but little difference with the war. The war news we get lately is pretty good. I think Burnside will set the rebs to thinking. The papers say he is within 6 days march of Richmond and the rebel army 12 days march from it. We are under marching orders and may go tomorrow. I have not learned when or where we are going to hunt rebs. Maybe into some fort or into winter quarters. These things are not for us to know until we get there. This living in Virginia without you is not very pleasant. But when we meet, what a meeting it will be. I think the war will end soon. I put the time inside of 8 months, and I should not wonder if the fighting would be pretty much done in 3 months.

Well, it has rained a little drizzle for the last 24 hours. I stood guard last nite. My oil cloth kept me dry. It is warm. There is an apple tree here in camp that has got blossoms on now. The snow went as soon as it came.

Well, I am glad the boys done a good job. Just in time too. It is best to get the hog killed if you have fed it the corn, for is will not pay to buy meal to feed her if she is eatable now. You talk about my scolding about the hog. Keep still, for I shall not see the pork it will be eat up before I get there likely.

I hope you will not have the rheumatism all winter. You must be careful and dress warm this winter. There are two of our regiment dead. One died Monday and one last nite. One died of dysentery and the other of typhoid fever. There are several sick in the hospital. Al Cook died of dysentery. His wound was well.

> No treasures from the ocean
> Or from the shaded mine
> Can make no such emotion
> As one short note of thine.

I have received 2 letters from thee lately . . . dated 9th to 11th and the 15th. No. 6 and 7 respectively. I wish you to correct the number of my letters as I have kept no record of them, and have become frustrated as you will observe. But I have put this down, date and number thus . . .Nov. 19th, No. 9, and got it in my pocket. If it is not rite, correct it. Now comes dress parade.

I have dress paraded and eat my supper, so now I will finish writing. We may not march in a week. Let that be as it may, you can direct as before and the letters will find me. Our pickets captured a rebel cavalryman today. They say that the pickets were fired upon last nite, but no one killed. The reb cavalry are trying to find some spot to crawl out, but they may crawl in where they can't get out so easily. I tell you, the papers are looked for with eager eyes, for we expect that they are fighting the decisive battle if our troops are victorious. If the rebs gain ground, it will prolong the war. The southern soldiers are in poor condition for winter. Thus I end yours with love.

B. A. Cook

No. 10, Camp Bliss, Fairfax County, Va., Sunday, November 23, 1862

Dear Old Girl,

It is with extreme pleasure I attempt to converse with you with my pencil. I received two letters from you last week. Oh what a blessing it is to hear from those we love so dearly. It is worth everything to me to read the good long letters from you. If they were as long as the Potomac River, they would suit me. And the language I find no fault with.

You dream more than I do, but I dreamed last Wednesday nite that I was back 15 years ago. I thought I was home on furlow for 2 days to Aunt Harriet's. My furlow had run out and I had not seen you and I made up my mind I would not come back until I went and seen you. But in my trouble about my furlow, I awaked without you . . . but not until I had filled myself with johnny cake and butter. But, in the morning I ate my breakfast just as well as tho I had no johnny cake. Thus you see, dreams do not amount to much.

I wish I could comply with your wishes. Last Sunday nite, if it had not been so far, I could of run the guard and come home. But it is too far to walk. I think I shall have to wait a few months and then come by railroad. I am glad you got to meeting once more. Br. Smith thinks the war is likely to last a good while you say. But if there is any truth in what writers say that have been in many of the Southern States for the last 6 months, there are many of the Southern men that were strong advocates of secession who are now sick of it. North Carolina is considerably Union. Kentucky, Tennessee, and Missouri too have a good many Union Men, and most all of the south are sick of the war. If they could gain a victory or two, it would strengthen them. But I hope that they will get enough of the war in a couple months to come.

I suppose it is no use writing you what I read in the papers about the situation of the Army of the Potomac, for you get the papers once in a while don't you? We shall leave this camp before long. I expect we are to be ready to march at an hours notice. Most likely we shall go into winter quarters soon.

You can get a sheep next month. A hog goes 16 weeks, so you can count for yourself when you want your pigs. If you can get a cutter to use this winter, do it. If you can't, you can get some fills put to the bobsled and a box on it. You will want some way to get around. I am glad you have got the cattle in the stable and everything so nice. Have you killed the hog yet?

I have no news to write worth writing. You can send me 2 dollars if you have it to spare, for some think we shall have no pay until January. If that be the case, we will want some change. Steve is not very well, as he has a cold. It is hard finding one in camp that has escaped a cold. Two of our regiment died last week. One of them was Andrew Fagan's brother.

Our pickets have captured a few rebs but I have not seen any of them. I suppose Charles has gone home, hasn't he? I am sorry for Brother Lake, the way he is afflicted. Mrs. Turrell would like to see me no doubt. I would like to see her too, the kind old lady. I think the ladies are doing something for their country according to all accounts. The orderly is in here . . . you can see how he hit my elbow. I told him I would tell you how he acted.

Yours in love,

B. A. Cook

No. 11, Camp Bliss, Fairfax County, Va., November 27, 1862

Dear L. M. C.

Your kind letter of the 21st reached me last nite. I wrote to Mother yesterday and told her I expected a letter from you last nite. So I got it. Well, you had all your trouble for nothing about that battle. Yes, it was an awful day, the day we parted. Our feelings the pen cannot describe. But Dear Wife, our trust is in God. He is able to support on all occasions. Glory be to his name.

Louisa, I know you. When you write, you must write just as you feel. That is the kind I like. You are not to be blamed for feeling interested in my welfare. for we are near each other. I feel for you, for you have a double portion. First your mind is on me, then you have the cares of the children and the business to see to. But I am glad to see your faith in God. He is just as able to sustain us as we are as though we were together, although it is trying to be separated especially under such circumstances.

Well Dear, I wish I could of been there and eat dinner with you the other day. To eat something cooked by a woman once more would be quite a treat. But what a treat to look upon you once more and those dear children. Well. I do expect to see you all in less than a year. If our armies are successful, I expect to be home in the spring. I know we are strong enough to take Richmond if our forces are concentrated. I believe it is the intention of Burnside to take the rebel capitol. We and all the rest of the troops about Washington are under Stegel, the little Dutchman, and his forces are held in reserve. Bully for us.

There is a man here in camp that is taking notes of the different regiments. He says the war will all smash up when Congress sits. That will be next month I suppose. If Congress does settle this war this winter, there will be thousands of merry hearts, won't there. Well we must not swallow all we hear, for if we do, it may physic us.

The reason why I write today is because I have time. We don't drill today. It is only 4 days since I wrote to you, but I thought I could not improve the time better than to talk to you a little while. I have to get wood for our fire and wash our dishes, as one of our tentmates is on guard and gone on picket, and Steve has got a bad cold. He can't eat much. Colds are plenty down here. The two Mr. Goulds are our tentmates yet and have ever since we have been in Virginia. They are good men. Mrs. Lamkasky and her man tent within a few feet of us. I see her most every day. I guess she is a good woman.

I have had a bad cold ever since I was on picket, but I am most over it now. I have laid off duty one day in consequence of my cold and that was day before yesterday. One more death in the regiment. That makes 3 in 3 months, I think. That is not very bad considering the number of men. We expect to go into winter quarters soon and then if we want any socks or eatables we will send for them. But we may have to go and reinforce Burnside if he has not sufficient forces to take Fredericksburg. But I guess he has. I don't see any signs go getting our pay very soon, but never mind, we will get more when it does come.

Thursday evening, November 27th. I have just received the letter you wrote on the 19th. It was mailed the 25th. The one I got last nite was written and mailed on the 21st. I suppose you sent the first one, and the other one you carried. That was the difference. Well, I must proceed to answer the other letter. I am glad you have enough to eat and wood to cook it with. We have the same here and a good appetite. We had for supper rice boiled in water not sweetened, and a cup of coffee sweetened, and bread. In the morning it will be coffee, meat, and bread. For dinner, pea soup and bread. That is the way we live. Sometimes we get beans, and sometimes a few potatoes. But we get fat. I weigh 152 . . . 15 more than when I was a farmer.

There was as much wheat as I guessed . . . I put it at 5 bushels. The oats were nothing. Anyhow, Jenny will need no grain until spring of any amount. Two quarts of oats is a good mess for her when she works, and when she is idle, she needs none. Be careful and not let her drink when she is sweattie, or eat grain, for it will founder her. That coupling chain was around the shed, or on the drag behind the shed I think. The log chain Bill Evans borrowed also the yoke, staple ring, and bows . . . until he could get some of his own. But never mind them now. If he tries to pay the boot in some way this winter, then all rite. If he don't, I will write to Chas. Greenman to see to it.

I cannot think of your moving away from your home. Stick to it. If you can live off it, you can live on it. You can get someone to put the fence up and plow the garden. Then you will have pasture for the cows and everything. The cows help you a good deal. If you go to the river, you can't take any of the stock with you, for there is no place to keep them. Without somebody on the place, the place would be worse off than if you stay on it and do nothing. If you have money, you can get the haying done, if I don't get there to help you. But this is looking good ways ahead. We will talk this over after this.

The grain you have . . . if it is but little, it is still worth considerable, for grain is high and butter is high. Have you sold your butter yet? You had better buy flour now, and save your wheat and rye to grind next spring when flour is higher. Have you killed the hog, and how dose the spinning go off? Can't Mrs. Turrell help you? You can't spin, work outdoors, and do housework too,

Friday morning, November 28th. This morning we have got to go on brigade drill, so I can't write much. One poor fellow on picket last nite accidentally shot himself. The ball went in above his ankle and passed thru his foot, tearing his ankle and foot horribly. He was sleeping on his arms according to orders. Some men can't think that guns are ugly things.

Friday evening . Well, we went on brigade drill at 10 a.m. and come off at 3 p.m.. This drill is where 5 or 6 regiments get together and drill. I got another letter tonite, the one you wrote last Sunday. So I have to answer 3 letters in this. I am glad you are in good spirits and courageous. You have to be man and woman. I wrote to E. Reynolds because he is a pretty good fellow, and I wanted to see if he would answer. He has not yet.

A man ought to board himself for 50 cts. a cord. Around here they cut 4 foot wood for 5 shillings and board themselves. If you can't get it cut at that rate, that is 50 cts., and they pay for their board, then let me know before you get out of wood and I will send word to Uncle George Cook and see if he won't take a job to cut you some wood. The blanket on Jenny will make her hair look slick.

You can use your own judgment about paper, but I should prefer a city paper. I am sorry for Hattie poor girl. You must be careful and not exercise too much and you may outgrow it. If you don't, you will have to wear a truss. My little girls, I am glad to hear you are kind to Ma and think often of Pa. The Lord bless and protect you and help you to be obedient to your kind Mother. I hope to kiss you before many months.

Dear Wife, I will not write much more as I am tired of sitting flat down and it is getting near roll call. That is half past 8. Then we prepare for bed. Steve is writing tonight. Kate wrote him one last Sunday too. Russ was in here this evening. He had a letter last nite. He has got a berth to drive an ambulance wagon at $18 a month. That is a good berth.

I am pleased to hear from you so often. I have now 5 and 2 are 7 postage stamps and 20 cents. I am all right yet. If I don't get any money in 2 weeks, I can stand it well enough.

From your own dear boy B.A.C. with all the love this envelope will hold.

B. A. C.

DECEMBER 1862

History summarization, pages 77

The night of December 28th was marked by special watchfulness and wakefulness on the picket line. At about half-past ten p.m., the long roll was sounded in the various camps of our brigade. Orders were given directing that knapsacks be packed, haversacks filled, ammunition distributed and the men ready to form on the color line in fifteen minutes. About midnight the brigade moved out on the Alexandria and Fairfax Turnpike and matched twoard Fairfax Court House. A line of battle was formed, the 144th on the right, 143rd on the left and the 127th in reserve. Pickets were posted, arms stacked and the men directed to lie down and secure what sleep they could. In the morning the cavalry pickets brought in six hungry Rebel cavalrymen that they had captured, and this was all of the enemy in sight. About six in the afternoon orders were received directing a return to out camps which we reached about ten o'clock.

The Regiment is still stationed at Camp Bliss

Dec. 13th, Fredericksburg
Dec. 28th and 29th, Chickasaw Bluff, Miss.
Dec. 31st and Jan. 1st, '63, Stone River, Tenn.

No. 12, Camp Bliss, Fairfax County, Va., December 1, 1862

Dear Companion,

Your letter of the 27th, No. 11, reached me last nite. I did not expect it in a day or two, but I am glad to hear from you at any time. That is so. The little 2 dollars will last me some time I hope. I feel sleepy today, for I was on guard last nite. Had a very good time too, for it did not storm. It is storming today. The rain comes pattering on the little tent as I am writing. Steve is layed down on the blanket, for his cold don't agree with him. William Gould is reading the paper. James Gould is mending his breeches. This is the way it goes.

No drill today if it rains all day. We have fire in our tent, so we are comfortable. For breakfast we got some pork, put it in some water and boiled it a little. Then broke up of hard crackers, put them in, added a little salt and pepper, and let it boil until the meat was done. This is what we had to eat.

Messers. Gould's wives sent them a box of dried fruit, butter cake, and nice things. They have given me butter to spread on my bread and a piece of cake. It was very good. The Deposit boys got a box yesterday with butter cake and chickens. They had a good time I tell you. When we get into our winter home, I will get something for New Years home too. Don't you say so?

If you can't sell your butter for 20 cents or upward, send it down here. I can get 30 cts. for it here and the express charge would not be more than 5 cts. a pound I think.

I am glad you are getting to think that you are quite a man to do chores. If you can have health, you can do it. George Thomas done big things about the beef. But never mind about trifles. He don't say anything about paying anything does he? Kate has paid him all they owe him.

Well. how are my little girls? I hope you are all well. Your Pa wants to see you as bad as you want to see him. But my little pets, I hope the war will end one of these days and Pa can come home and see all of you. Then we will have a good time, won't we . . . eating ham and eggs.

I am glad Brother Lake and wife have made you a visit. He is a good man. I think I must write him. Well, did you have a good ride with Mr. Gates and get back safe? That pain in your stomach what is the cause of it? You must eat regular and keep some pills on hand to keep your bowels regular and avoid those spells. I think it is a derangement of the stomach that makes it.

I think I will see the Colonel to ask if I can get a berth that will pay better or that suits me better. I will try. If Mr.Thompkins wants them runners and will manage to pay for them when he gets them in some way, then that should suit you all right. I suppose they are worth $1.50, but he is a poor paymaster to be trusted.

I wish I could have been with you in your dream. I have no more news to write.

To my dear Wife with all love,

Bishop A. Cook, the Soldier

No. 13, Camp Bliss, Fairfax County, Va., December 7, 1862

Dear companion of my youth,

I was happy to hear from you once more. I fear you are not very well, but I hope you are not sick. Your letter of the 30th, No. 13, I have just read. It was mailed the 1st of Dec. and reached here the 6th which was last nite. But I was on picket duty. I went on Friday and returned today. We had pretty nice weather until Friday when it commenced snowing just as we got on picket, and did not cease until 10 in the morning. The snow is about 4 inches deep. When the storm ceased the wind blew and grew cold and last nite it was pretty cold. The snow squeaket (sic) under my feet as I walked up and down on guard. It was cold enough to freeze the bread in my haversack. I kept warm for I had my overcoat on and the cape turned up over my ears and my blanket pinned on my shoulders. We would stand for an hour and then be off for three hours. When we were off, we went into our wigwam. It is constructed of poles and brush with a hole in the top. We had a big fire in the center which we could lay or stand around. We use rails for wood. As a result, the fences are getting burned up pretty well around here. The smoke goes out the hole at the top of the brush house and the fire can not be seen. The pickets are not allowed fire or lites at night, so this is a very good contrivance. A person could not see anything of the fire when on the outside.

Well I tell you, we had something good Friday nite for supper. I and one of our company went to a house a short distance from where we were stationed and bought a quart of milk, and we got the woman to make us some mush. So we had mush and milk for supper and paid her 25 cts. It was the first time I have been in a house since I left Washington. It seemed strange to go into a house and set down in a chair and eat at a table. There was a little girl there with black eyes. She said she was 9 years old. She made me think of my little girls. Well, we have good times here.

I have got over my cold and feel first rate. We can stand the winter in our tents, for we shall build a sort of a log house and set the tent on the top. Some think we shall get our pay this month. If we do, it will relieve our families at home. I think you will not be able to pay any debts with my wages, for things are so high you will need it all to keep you comfortable. If you think Jenny wants a little grain, get it for her. For if she eats grain, she will not require so much hay.

> This is a continuation of some other letter. No indica-
> tion of date. He speaks of it being very cold and the hay
> going fast. He also mentions the Emancipation. Since
> the Emancipation Proclamation was written Jan. 1,

1863, I think we can assume this letter was written during January 1863).

You say the hay goes fast. It will go fast this cold weather and it will go fast off the top of the mow. It will not go fast after it gets down where it is solider(sic).

Dear wife, what a flame of love it kindles in me to read your lovely letter. Yes, we were friends in childhood. What a comfort we have been to each other even when we thought we had hard times. Yet as you say, if we ever get together again, we will know what comfort is and how to prize each others society. I trust in God that we shall meet and live together again. I believe it.

Greely thinks the war will be settled in less than 6 months. I think that Lincoln's message is very good, and if Congress works rite they can do much to restore the Union. But is we have to fite it out, it will take all of next summer at least. But I think the states will come back into the Union. The South seems to feel discouraged and tired of the war in many places where they were strong secessionists just 6 months ago. Our armies are not going into winter quarters, but intend to harass them all winter. The Emancipation will weaken them and bring them to terms I think.

We get mail every day from Washington. It is almost a week since I wrote to you. I should of write, but I went on picket. So I have more to write. I am sorry you live so far from the office. It seems useless for me to write twice a week with you so far from the office that you can't get them unless you get 2 at a time. I had 8 postage stamps and 3 makes 11.

I think you must send and get that paper and wine. He must owe us about $1.00. We sent $1.50 and the paper ceased to come in 3 or 4 months. So you can send to him the money and state the case to him and see what he will do. The paper is worth the money, and the grape wine will be very nice. I am a great lover of fruit you know.

I like soldering pretty well. I am well at present and hope to remain so. I want to see this rebellion put down. I am getting wages all the time and at the end of the war we will have our bounty, and it is cash. I hope that you will have your health. They talk of raising private's wages to 15 dollars instead of 13 dollars. I hope it will work. It is dark and I must close. I will rite again this week.

Those verses were very nice. I send the picture to the girls and the card to you.

From yours only with love.

B. A. C.

No. 14, Camp Bliss, Fairfax County, Virginia, December 9, 1862

Dearest of Earthly Beings,

The picture I carry by my side looks good and I have just stole one kiss from your left cheek. No harm done I suppose. I would like to be by the side of the original about now, but distance prevents at present. But Wife, I do expect to greet you one of these days in your quiet home.

It is hard to be a soldier, but I truly enjoy it better thus far than I expected. We have every day for breakfast, bread and bacon and coffee. For dinner we have a cup of soup and a hunk of boiled pork to eat with our bread. For supper we have boiled rice sweetened a little and a cup of coffee and good bread. I thought before I was a soldier that they had to live on beef and bread and coffee, but we don't.

One reason I am writing tonite is because I have some room. The two Mr. Goulds are on picket, so Steve and I have the tent to ourselves. We are both writing. We have not drilled much this week, but have been making preparations to fix our tent for winter. It freezes quite hard at night and thaws a little during the day. It has been clear ever since the snow storm.

Well, I went yesterday forenoon over to the 43rd Regiment to see Wesley Dickerson and to read the letters I had received from Kingston. He let me read a letter from Charlie Dickinson and one from Will Thomas and 3 from Hattie Dickinson. We had a good visit. I then had a little visit with Russ.

In the evening I went and made Colonel Hughston a visit. I went to his tent and knocked. He said come in, so I stepped in, raised my cap, and saluted him. I then felt a little streaked for I saw his hostler there. But as good luck would have it, he went out immediately, and I was alone with the Colonel. I then told him that I had a request to make. Well said he. I then told him that I wished to get a berth where I could get a little higher wages. He said he did not know of a chance at present. I then told him that if there should be an opportunity present itself, I wished to be remembered as I had a wife and 3 small children. And with everything so high, my present wages was not sufficient to make them comfortable. He looked at me and said your countenance is familiar, but I can't call your name. I told him I would give him my name Bishop A. Cook, Company F and he took it on a card. I told him I tented in the first tent above the Orderly's. He asked if we were comfortable in our tent. I told him we were, we had a fire in our tent, and had prayer meetings once or twice a week, and enjoyed ourselves well. Thus I bid him good evening, and come to my tent and no one knows it but the Colonel and yourself and me.

Wednesday morning, December 10. I had to stop writing last nite for the candle burned out. I have just eat my breakfast and now I will talk to you a little. I almost think that we shall not be called to fight at all. I hope Congress will try to settle this was without fiting it out, that the Union may be preserved, and we return home.

Wife, how do you get along this cold weather? Are you comfortable in your boots? How is all of you? I shall look for a letter tonight. I can't send this til tomorrow morning.

Yesterday I drew a pair of cotton and wool shirts, so I can wear 2 shirts this winter. I fixed my socks so they will last me a month yet. If you send a box, you can send near 50 lbs. because a box weighing over 50 lbs. the express calls 100 lbs. I would like some socks as the Government socks are poor things, and a little dried fruit and so forth. Steve wants some butter and I too. He talks of having his Mother-in-law send some butter and things. I should think the folks mite fix up a box. Mrs. Gates could send some butter, a hunk of cheese, and dried apples. If she would, it would taste good to soldiers. Each bundle can be marked who from and who to, so when the box is opened here, we will know which is whose and who from.

I write to Charlie some time ago and have had no answer. Do you hear from them? It is pleasant today. I never was so close to the Congress before. We can hear what they are doing every day. Now I will wait till evening and see if I don't get a letter so I can have something to write about.

Wednesday evening, December 10th. No letter tonite and I shall not wait longer. I will finish my letter. Steve and I are alone, but the other boys will be in tomorrow. We had fried onions for breakfast this morning. I got 2 lbs. off the Sutler. I got some sausage tonite for breakfast in the morning. 3/4 of a pound at 20 cts. a pound. We enjoy ourselves first rate. But I feel for you this cold weather with so many chores to do. I hope God will give you health that you may be able to struggle through the war and get your bounty about 5 ft. 9 inches high. Then I suppose you and I will feel happy and give God praise.

Paper says today that there has been a battle in Arkansas and our loss was 600 and the rebel loss 15,000. I hear it is too good to be true, but there may be something in it after all. I guess we shall get pay in 2 or 3 weeks. Then we shall have money enough to carry us through the winter if we have our health. Has Jenny got shoes on or barefooted? How is the girls? Do they read any? They must learn some if they don't go to school. You must give your stock salt. If you take the T.B. paper, he will give you some hints about matter and things likely.

Steve Garlow was here yesterday. He is pretty smart, but he is done for a soldier. I think he will be home before long. I felt his heartbeat. He has a heart disease undoubtedly and will get his discharge. (*Paper torn*) ran away from here last week and I suppose he is at home now, so the Government won't have to board and pay him this winter.

I must close for it is most time for rollcall. I hope you will receive this in due time. Here is a picture for one of my girls.

Yours truly Wife from your husband,

Bishop A. Cook

No. 15, Camp Bliss, Fairfax County, Va., December 17, 1862

Dear Wf,

I now seat myself to answer your letters No. 13 and 14. I went on picket Monday and returned today all sound. One of your letters came nite before last and the other last nite, so I must answer both at once. I tell you I looked for a letter 3 or 4 days before I got one, but I got two so quick I feel pleased. I tell you, to hear from you once more and to hear you are all well, the good Lord is good to us. I am well and doing well. It is cool today and spits snow a little, but we have a good warm tent and are all rite.

Steve is better of his cold. I expect you have cold weather there. We have very cold weather here for Virginia. Some think we have had as cold weather as we shall have this winter. I think often of you this cold weather, having the chores to do and everything to look after. You must dress warm. You write lots of news. The hog is killed and the spinning most done.

About the whiffletree. There was none on the little wagon Mr. Lakes was on. You know Kilmer had the wagon and put their whiffletree on. Steve couldn't get it off when I went to Brant, so he took our big whiffletree to put onto Lakes wagon the day I went the rounds to settle before I went away. So the big whiffletree is probably down to Lakes and they have come and got theirs off of your wagon. But there are 2 or 3 more whiffletrees laying around that might be fixed with hooks so you could use them. Furthermore, I got a little one purposely for the little wagon and left it in Turrell's shop to get it ironed sometime, so as to have one purposely for the little wagon.

Well, the orderly has been in here but has now gone with his company on dress parade. We pickets don't have to go on parade tonight, so I improve the time in talking with my dear ones so far away. I tell you, it is reviving to read those lines those dear hands have traced. I think Hattie's letter pretty good. I know it was the sentiment of her little heart truly. I am glad my little girls think so much of me, and the old one too. I must go to supper now.

Well, I have eat my supper now of rice, coffee, and bread and it is most dark. I am sitting by the side of our fireplace writing, so you need not wonder if it is not wrote so nice written by firelite.

Willie Dan was in here this afternoon after I read my letter and asked if you were going to send a box. I told him I guessed so. He said his wife said you talked of it. She wanted to send some things to him. I suppose such things must be directed the same as a letter and taken to Deposit and sent by express, for if it comes by freight, it will be a good while getting here. There aint money to pay freight on a box in the whole company. I have 90 cts. left yet that will do for me quite a while. If you can sell your butter, sell it and get the good of it. Butter is in good demand there aint it? 20 cts. in trade our Sutler says it is worth in Delaware County 25 cts. at the dairy. He pays 28 cts. in Washington for butter and sells it here for 40 cts.

Well, Uncle Brainard was here last week and made me a visit. He is not very well, and expects to get his discharge and go home this week. He has never been in a battle, but he has been in the hospital. What Will Dan wrote was correct about the guards, but they got a comfortable tent for them now with a fire in it.

Pete Garlow I suppose told the truth about the bitches. I suppose they do the washing for those that want it done. I do my own. I have never spoke to one of them yet and presume I should not if I were to stay here 3 years. I don't know but they are all right. I never seen anything wrong in them and never expect to if I keep proper distance.

I hope your pork is eatable. We have pretty good times in our tent. It is so warm here I am sweating this cold nite. If I don't get paid before long, I shall growl, for my family must not suffer. I shall write to the Justice to collect something for you if necessary. It is hard enough to do the work you have to do and have everything you need without being pinched. Kate has depression has she. Well, poor creature, she don't take as much comfort as you do I don't believe. I have not heard from Kingston in a good while. Do you hear from them?

Well, is is most roll call and I must soon close. This is a short letter, but I want to send it in the morning so you will get it soon. Mrs. Dan wrote that you was coloring yarn for Will's mittens. That is right good. Good nite to all little and big ones from your Husband and Pa.

B. A. Cook

No. 16, Camp Bliss, Fairfax County, Va., December 19, 1862

My Dear Old Wife

4 letters from you this week . . . I tell you, what is going to happen? What has broke loose? I tell you, I am glad to hear from you every nite. I feel pretty good tonite for I got a letter from you last nite and one from Kingston.

Today, J. V. Whittaker came here and gave me a paper of tobacco. He said he saw you the other day and you were well. I got a letter from you tonite with the $2 in it all right. I hope you did not rob yourself. I am sorry you have so much trouble about me when I am all rite. You had quite a job to get the box rigged and expressed. I hope it will arrive safe and when I get home, I will pay you for all your trouble.

I have wrote an answer to Mother's letter today and this evening, and I am now writing railroad speed to get this so it can go in the morning. I'm sure you are anxious to hear from that letter with the money in it.

Well I enjoy myself pretty well. The Captain was in our tent this evening for the first time. He thinks we have the nicest tent in the company. Burnside has fallen back across the river. What is to be done now I don't know, but time will tell. The 2 Mr. Goulds are on picket.

Tell Hattie that I burn up my letters after they get 3 or 4 weeks old and read over and over again. Dear Wife, I hope I shall not have to apply gun powder very soon to stop the effusion of blood. I am proud to know that I have so worthy a wife at home. You are worth everything to me. The lines I get from you are love to me. I would that I could be by your side tonight Dear Wife then I would not have to lay on a board until my bones ache. I don't sleep more than 6 hours on an average. I do not require the sleep I did when at home and I don't think any person would if they had to sleep on the bed we do. But it is nothing after one gets used to it.

I hope Congress will raise the pay of soldiers. Our families need it, for things are so high and no prospect of their being lower. But the Lord will provide. I tell you, I trust in the Lord for I know he will help in time of need. I feel he has been very good to me all the days of my life. Therefore, I am not afraid to trust in him.

I have been out to roll call and shall soon have to put out the lite and retire. So you must excuse this short letter. Will Dan was here today and said that his wf and you were going to send a box to us. I have not seen him tonite. Did you pay all the express charges out of your own money, or will they pay their share?

Yours with love,

B. A. Cook

No. 17, Camp Bliss, Fairfax County, Va., December 23, 1862

Dear Wife,

I was discharged from guard this morning at 9 o'clock. I went down to Munson Hill and bought a pound of good tobacco for one dollar that will last me 2 months I guess. I made Russ a little visit and came back and found that box all sound in the tent. What a surprise. I was going to have the Quarter Master look for it tomorrow. Steve went and found Willie, and I opened it and he took his things to his tent. I am very thankful for the nice things you have taken so much pains to send me. I shall take comfort eating and think often of you. The popcorn is very nice. My little girls are often thought of by their Pa.

The official report of Burnside is 1100 killed and 9,000 wounded. Most of the wounded only slightly . . . only 1600 sent to the hospital.

Oh I have eat my supper and how good it is. We all pronounce the cake very good. I ate bread and butter, chicken, a piece of that pork and beef. It made me think of eating at home. A nice lot of fried cake that will keep some time. I should like to get hold of you tonight and pay you for your trouble. The Lord bless you and protect you Dear Wife and children. How about the freight on the box? You said you paid $3.00. Did they pay their share to you or not? If they didn't, Steve and Will will pay me after pay day. But if they pay you, let me know.

Almus and Mother and Charles wrote me a good letter and I answered it immediately. It has been very pleasant here today. I have no news to write. How does Mr. Terrel and his wife get along, and Mr. Lake's folks? Do you have things comfortable and do you and Jenny agree well? Have you made any preparation for lambs?

Now little girls, are you well and do you learn something this winter? You must be good to Ma and help her all you can, for she is good to you and ever was. It is not every little girl that has as kind a mother as you have. From your Pa.

Dear Wife, as I am writing by the lite of the fireplace this evening, I believe I will close. I wish you a merry Christmas and hope this will reach you soon after Christmas at least.

Ever yours,

B. A. C.

(Louisa apparently sent this letter on to someone. Probably her mother. She added the following note to the letter.)

Well, here is another of Asbury's letters for you to read. It is written with a pencil and rather poorly. But I guess you can study it out. I received a letter from you last week. I have got wood. Have got a good cellar or about middling. Have water rite by the door. Asbury dug a well in the fall after we moved here. The horse is gentle. The barn is not far off. The pig pen is by the side of the backhouse. The wood shed is on the hind end of the house. So don't you think I have things handy? You must excuse this short letter, for it is late and the fire is most out. Hattie and Emma want to come and see you very much. Write soon.

Yours with great respect,

Lousia M. Cook

No. 18, Camp Bliss, December 26, 1862

I seat myself to write a few words to let you know that I received yours of the 21st last nite. Glad to hear you are all well. Yesterday was Christmas here. I took one of my chicks and put it in the messpan and warmed it and got ready for dinner, and 4 of us had a good dinner out of it. I have treated the orderly and one or two Corporals to some cake. They pronounced is very good as well as myself.

We had some fun here yesterday, or some call it fun. There was some grog here somewhere, and some of the officers and some privates drank too much and were pretty tight. They acted so we had to put extra guard around the Sutlers shop to keep them from upsetting it. Some of the officers got in a gangle and got knocked over, so they paid dear for their whiskey.

Rufus Howk, a man in our Company, left a wife and 5 children at home, the oldest 13 years of age. Last nite he got a letter informing him that his wife was dead. I tell you, he is a forsaken looking man this morning. Out Lieutenant is going to try to get him a furlow to go home a few days to get places for his children and arrange business. It is a hard thing to think of 5 children that need a mother's care and no mother or father at present. I understand their grandparents want to take them and keep them together.

How did you get cheated out of 2 dollars when you sold your butter? I thought you said you took out 14 pounds to make the tub come under 50. If so, it would not come to 10 dollars as the weight of the tub would have to come out of the 50.

You want me to write just as I feel. I think I do. I feel pretty well and have enough to eat and a good appetite and a good place to sleep. But no warm woman to sleep with and no little girls to amuse me in the evening. But all this I can endure patiently for my country if need be. I honestly enjoy myself far better than I expected, far better. I have to drill just enough for exercise. Standing guard is the worst, and picket duty. But I am careful to keep as warm as possible when out on duty in the nite. You must not worry about me, for I think I shall come out rite. My eyes bother me some lately. I guess it is caused by writing by firelight the other nite.

Well, one more man dead out of our Regiment. They must die wherever they are. It don't save your lives to enlist. I find there are many here who did not enlist to serve their country, but enlisted for the bounty or to evade the draft. And such of course are sick of the business and wish themselves home if the country went to the devil they say. That is not my sentiment. I wish the war would end in some honorable way and have the Union preserved. And some way devised to root out slavery if it takes 40 years to do it, for I see no way that we can have permanent peace without slavery is done away with.

I have not changed my mind as to the duration of the war at all. I think it will not last longer than June 1863 at the longest, and hope it will end sooner so I can come home to help you farm it. I would like to have the war close, but to give up whipped by the rebs and give them their independence I cannot do until forced to, which I think can never be.

David Allen wrote a letter to Aaron Travis and I read it yesterday. He said the Abolitionists were very quiet since the election and he could breath a little purer air now. He said he thought we would not have much fighting to do for foreign powers would interfere in the Spring. So that is his views on the matter. You have it as cheap as I do. I must go and get my dinner.

Saturday the 27th, 11 o'clock AM. Dear Wife, I was detailed to go on guard this morning. I have stood 2 hours, so I am off 4 before I go on again, so I have time to write a little and eat dinner. I tell you, I live high now days. I have just eat some of them apples. I am alone in the tent at present. Steve is on picket and the Goulds are on drill, but will soon be in. We suppose 2 of our company deserted last nite. One left the guard house. The other was our fifer, so our fifer and drummer have both left. The other was a gambler scalawag, a disgrace to the Company.

I will write a little more before dinner. I enjoy very good health lately. I don't drink coffee of late. I think it best not to drink it at all. I think I feel better to let it alone. You know it never did agree with me very well. Cold water is better.

There has been no papers in camp for sale in 3 or 4 days so I don't see what is up. We used to get papers every day. I see Congress has adjourned until the first Tuesday in January, so they are doing nothing more than we are. I mistrust that some of our armies or fleets are fixing to strike on the rebs somewhere and it is the reason we don't get papers. They want to keep the news from the rebs. I don't care if I don't get any news in 3 weeks if then it would come that we had got Richmond or some other strong place.

E. W. G. said Mrs. Gates has got a girl. I think that is pretty good. I think they must try again and get a pair, and then they will have 2 pair. I suppose they feel proud enough of their luck. Well I will go and get dinner.

Sunday morning, 10-1/2 o'clock. Louisa, I was discharged from guard at 9 this morning and have washed myself and changed my clothes. The regiment have gone out for inspection. The orders of the Captain is for the old guards to go to, but the army regulations say that the guard has 6 hours free from duty after coming off guard. Although I would of went if I could of got my things packed.

We have had nice weather here the past week. I hope you have as nice weather up there. You must not get the blues if you hear discouraging news, but trust in the Good Lord. You see, you hoped and prayed that I was not removed to Fredericksburg. Your prayer was answered and your wishes granted, but your hopes were too much mixed with fear. Exercise more faith with your hope and not so much fear and you will be all rite, thank the Lord. Think of how good he has been to us all the days of our lives. How can we but trust in him, or how can we distrust him.

I should like to this day be with thee to chat with you and hold my little ones and eat popped corn with you. But I have to eat corn without you and you eat without me, but I trust we can sit down together and eat and talk our fill one of these days. You say the time seems long to you. I know it does. But the time passes very fast to me. It does not seem to me that we have been in Virginia 2-1/2 months. We came across the Potomac the 14th of October.

Old Gerry is cross. It is natural for her to toss her head when you do to untie her. She used to do it. If she don't stop kicking, I would not stable her. You need not bother to send any butter to me for it is too much trouble and expense. The box was directed as you ordered precisely. It came in 5 days. I hope you will have more than one new milk cow in the spring. I think Mary is quite sharp at making speeches. I'm glad Sire could come and see you once more. I think Hugh McCready must feel cheap and it is good for him. Our dinner is ready.

Afternoon, 4 o'clock. I have just got back from washing my clothes. I washed 2 shirts, a pair of drawers. Now I will finish my letter so as to send it in the morning. It has been one of the nicest days that you could ask for. The sun shines like September. I wish you all a Happy New Year, hoping this will reach you by that time or this year at least. I have most of the last 2 dollars you sent me yet in money and postage stamps. I think it will last me until payday. Tell me if you are in need of shoes or anything for yourself or children. If so, I will write to somebody to collect something for you or fix so you can get what you need. I think some of writing to Brandt Schlager to let them know where I am and what I am doing.

I will close and fix for dress parade. Good day for this time.

Your true and affectionate husband,

B. A. Cook

No. 19, Camp Bliss, December 30, 1862

Dear Companion,

It is with extreme pleasure I attempt to converse with you and answer your kind letter that I received last nite at 9 o'clock when I arrived at camp. I suppose you got those pencil marks that informed you we were on the move. Now I will give you the particulars.

At 9 c'clock in the evening we went to bunk as usual suspecting nothing. But between 11 and 12 the drums beat the long roll and we were all ordered to fall in and march with everything packed up. I couldn't take everything for my washing was wet and I could not take my dried fruit, so I left it in the box. We took our shelter tents and blankets. For my part, I did not care about taking everything for I expected to come back in a short time. A great many said we never would see the old camp again, and some were of the same opinion as me. The sick of our company were left to guard what was in camp.

Well, we marched about 6 miles and then lay down with our blankets on our arms, in line and ready to jump and fire at a minutes notice. It was cold and frosty but we lay till daylight. We then got into line and moved a short distance and stacked our arms and unslung our knapsacks. We done what we had a mind to, only we must keep within hearing. We were kept all day. The cavalry brought in 3 prisoners. The story was that a raid of cavalry had come within our lines and our brigade was after them. We didn't see them. They say they about faced and left, so at dark we left.

Some said we were going to Fairfax Courthouse, but I thought we were going to camp. So at 9 o'clock we were here, pretty tired. We were accompanied to Annandale, the place where we were, by 2 batteries with 12 cannon each, our surgeons, all the ambulance wagons, and everything ready for battle. But not a gun fired. Thus ends the battle with no one hurt.

Sid Dimmick told me this morning that his letter said David Bressee is dead of fever at Fredericksburg. It seems hard don't it, but he thought he never would come back when he went, by the way he talked.

I took all the cake in my haversack instead of bread. Ate what I wanted and fetched the rest back. I have half of the fried cake yet and the baked goods also. It seems to be it is the best cake I ever see, and the roast beef is so good it is like chicken.

Maybe everybody wouldn't think so much of them as you do. I prize the good long letters I get very much. You know it too. Well, about that Judgment that was given for $131. $100 within a few cents has been paid with the 30 you paid. You must find when the Judgment was given. Then reckon the interest up to this time. Then deduct what is paid with the interest. If I knew the year the Judgment was given, I could tell, but I think it less than 80 dollars. You can figure it as well as I can, but write me about it.

I hope Bill will cut you some wood. I think you had better get everything you need, clothes and everything, as soon as you get the means and keep yourselves as comfortable as you can.

We have got straw now and sleep comfortable. I am a happy man. When we were marched out to meet the enemy, I was cool as you please. It annoys me much to hear my fellow soldiers find so much fault with the victuals they have to eat. What will they do when they get where they have to live on 3 or 4 crackers for 3 days and have to fight as some have done.

I think we are all good friends here. We don't know when we shall leave here again. Maybe in less than 24 hours and maybe not in 3 months, so we don't know anything. We are in good spirits and hope to remain so.

How many swarms of bees has Mrs. Garlow got? Didn't she take up some? She must have had some that wouldn't winter. Maybe she has taken up some and said nothing, as they did the first year.

I will close. You will excuse this brief letter. I would not of write today if I had not known the anxiety you would have to know how we came out with the march. I haven't time to write more today. My little girls, I have got corn yet and I am glad you enjoy yourselves so well. Don't make much noise when Ma is writing. Russ had been in here a little while. Give my respects to all and save the love. This must go in the morning. Yours truly with the writers best and kindest regards. I haven't time to read this for it looks like rain.

JANUARY 1863

Camp Bliss, Upton's Hill, Va., Sept 20th to Feb. 12th 1863
January 11th, Fort Hindman, Ark.

History Summarization, pages 79, 80

During these months of adjustment to soldier conditions quite a number of men grew restless and thought to better their condition by deserting to and enlisting in the regular army. Unfortunately for the service there was a provision, or rather a construction of army regulations which made such an enlistment a bar to any punishment for desertion from volunteer organizations. This unfortunate and anomalous condition in military affairs was corrected later; but in the meantime it led a number of men to make the effort to change conditions. In the interest of more thorough drill and discipline the following order was issued by the Division Commander:

"Headquarters Abercrombie's Division
"Arlington, Va., Jan 3d, 1863

"General Orders, No. 21.

"Commanders of brigades will require the field officers of their respective brigades to drill in person their regiments and such as are found incapable of doing so will be brought before the Board of Examiners. The same test of capacity of company officers will be made by their respective regimental Commanders as far as it relates to company drill.

"By order of Brig.-Gen. Abercrombie

"Samuel Appleton, Lieut. and A. A. Gen.

"Official: W. B. Dean, Lieut. A. A. A. G. Headquarters 3d Brigade, Jan. 4th, 1863."

Army Regulations and Casey's Tactics were in more demand and consulted oftener, indeed there was compulsion in this matter in more ways than one. To many of the volunteer officers it was a startling revelation.

No. 19-A, Camp Bliss, Upton Hill, Fairfax County, Va., Sunday, January 4, 1863

Dear Wf,

I thought I would write a few lines to you tonite and tell you that I am well and feel like a tiger. I would like to come and spark you tonite. I have got on my clean shirt and new breeches . . . wouldn't you like to have me come? But hold on, we are under marching orders and I can't come tonite, but I will come as soon as I can.

We may have to march at an hours notice, and we may stay here all winter. It depends on the movements of the rebs, but we are ready for them if they come too near. Our forces are giving them all they want now days. They are skedaddling.

Well, I have not got that letter from you. I looked for it last nite and tonite, but it will be here soon I think. I had a letter from Kingston last nite and answered it today. They all wrote to me and filled a big sheet. It was mailed the 1st. They said they received a letter from you telling of the kick you got.

I don't know any news to tell you, but we were mustered on the 31st of last month and I expect we shall get pay this month.

Monday After Dinner.   I had to stop writing so we could have a prayer meeting. We had a good meeting. The Orderly attends out meetings regular. The other morning he came into out tent and began to rub my ears in play, so I arose from my seat to play and he pulled 4 or 5 letters out of my coat pocket and started to run. Hold on said I, there is one letter I want you to read. It was the one I got from Kingston. But he tried to get outdoors. He could not do it, so he called to someone outdoors to give the letters to him, but he didn't feel disposed to take them. So the Orderly tried to get from me, but I had my arm around his neck and he got his lips against my cost and hurt his lip a little. He then said hold on and gave the letters back to me. He seemed to be mad. I handed the letter to him that I wanted him to read, but he started off and said he had played with fools before. I spoke to him 2 or 3 times through the day, but he wouldn't notice me, so I let er rip. He seemed to be cross to everybody. But Saturday nite he said he had felt very disagreeable the week past, and had been angry more then he had in a good while. Last nite when he spoke in meeting he owned up like a Christian and asked forgiveness and said he would try to govern his temper. He is very quick tempered, so say them that are acquainted with him. But he is all rite now he is better. He come to me this morning and said he would have to put me on guard today. I said fine and put my rigging on. So I am on guard today. He detailed men enough without me, but one refused to go. So I went. The one that refused to go the Captain ordered him to put on his knapsack and take his gun and march 8 hours with a guard by his side for a punishment.

Tuesday the 6th. Good news this morning. I have come off guard and got a paper to read. Murfreesboro is taken and Vicksburg is in our hands, hundreds of rebs taken prisoner, and a good many cannon and horses taken. Our forces are successful on every hand lately. The Mississippi open for our vessels. Etc. Etc.

I wanted to finish this letter to send this morning, but there were so many in our tent, I couldn't write. I want to do my washing today and I have to go on drill. We have to carry knapsacks on drill now. The Captain is in want of a clerk. I don't know but if I urged the matter but he would take me. But I guess he has another one in view. But my turn will come by and by at something. well, the company has gone to drill. The Company consists of only 14 men, the rest on guard yesterday and today, and some on picket.

I feel a little sleepy today, sleeping only 3 hours last nite, but have no time to sleep today. I dreamed of being with you last nite, even if I didn't sleep long.

No signature

No. 20, Camp Bliss, (no date probably Jan. 1863)

Dear Wife,

I hope you will pardon me for not sending a letter sooner. I have been and got some wood and built a fire and got some apples soaking to cook for tea. I am trying to get the good of them for if we march I can't carry them. I have finished my cake. I have got a little corn yet. You better believe I live well. I am fat on the ribs. I think I will weigh near 160. I am quite a man but that don't help you any, does it?

Well how do you get along this year of 1863? I have not heard from you this year but expect to soon. We had a shower last Sunday nite but it is nice weather. No snow, no mud and not very cold. Is it cold up there and have you wood and things comfortable? Have you got bread and timber to last til spring? How is that matter with Brandt? Has George paid anything yet? How does your neighbors treat you? Are they kind and have you seen Mrs. Gates' girl yet?

Mother wishes me to send her my likeness and I intend to do it. I can have it taken and send it in a letter and must do it as soon as a good hand comes here to take likenesses.

Louisa, I have eat my dinner. I had bean soup and bread and meat. And it is raining a little. I don't know as we shall have to drill this afternoon. Steve has come in off picket. He is not very well. He had a letter from Kate. She said she promised to write to you but she hasn't had time yet.

I long for the time to come when we can do away with this writing and talk it. I often think of the days that are past that we have spent so happily together when we were free. But now I am not free but belong to Uncle Sam. But I hope I shall be free once more and enjoy your company as I thought I did last nite. I should like to be by your side, dearest of earthly beings. This you well know, but it will do no hurt to tell you of it.

I have been and got some water and stewed the apples. No drill . . . it rains too hard. I guess we shall have quite a storm. A lady named Manson sent this Regiment 5 barrels of apples for New Years. That was 1/2 barrel for a Company. We had two apiece and they were nice.

The mail has come and no letter for me. It must have gone astray or something is up. I hope this will go straight to you. I don't know what to write. We did not have to drill New Years. There is dress coats here for those that want them but I won't want one for my little coat is good yet. And if I don't get one I won't have to pay for it or carry it if we should march this winter. I believe our Regiment has lost 8 men. There are several sick in the hospital and some grunting around in camp. The climate don't agree with some men here but I think it agrees with me this far. How the warm weather will agree with me I can't tell, but I hope coming south will improve my health.

Have you got tired of doing chores? I would like to be there to help you tonight. How are my little ones? I hope you are all well and doing well. If you are only well and have enough to eat and wear, you will stand it. I am writing as fast as I can for it is getting dark. So I will bid you all good nite. Be good girls all of you.

From your own Husband and Pa,

B. A. Cook

No. 21, Camp Bliss, Fairfax County, Va., January 9, 1863

Dearest Wife,

I have a little spare time, so I will write and inform you that on the 7th I received 2 letters from you dated Dec. 28 and Jan. 1st. They were not mailed until the 5th of January. Your letters found me well and you better believe glad to hear from my love once more.

I am glad you have got some papers to read and are pleased with them. I have seen two copies of the Deposit paper and read some letters from those you spoke of. Charles Hathaway belongs to Company A. He is a clever fellow and has a clever father. He is the man that kept us over nite when we were on our way to Delhi.

G. W. Wood is in Company F with us. He is naturally smart, but he is a profane, reckless man, so his smart don't amount to much in my estimation. But some of his writing is good. You would think him a servant of God, if not a clergyman, when you are reading his writing. You should hear him swear and hope that the Almighty would open the ground beneath his feet and engulf him if he ever put his knapsack on again. Then the next day he will put it on again, and there is more of the same . . . and such horrible oaths I cannot repeat. He is a brother of old Lib Wood that was over the river at the big shanty when the railroad was being built. I think Mr. Judd sent me quite a letter.

I am glad your hens are laying. I should like to help you eat john-nycake and butter and mush and milk and potatoes, for we don't get such things. Here it is bread, meat, beans, rice, and coffee and sugar. We don't drink coffee in our tent, but we draw it before it is steeped and sell it. We have sold 4 pounds at 15 cts. per pound. We have also sold meat and grease to amount to as much more, so we can buy our paper and envelopes with coffee and grease. We sold 2 bars of soap that we drew more than we needed for 8 cts. a bar. I wish you could have a chance to buy the soap grease and soap we sell, for we don't get more than 3 cts. per lb. for meat gravy.

Have you had a sleigh ride yet? The ground was just covered with snow, but the sun is making it disappear. Steve had three letters last nite . . . one from Kate, one from Mr. Lake, and one from C. Bryant. Kate said she wrote to you New Years eve. Gene has been sick she says. She has hard times to take care of the boy nite and day, and wishes Steve would come home. I don't doubt it at all, do you?

Your letters contain so much love, I hate to burn them. I read them over 3 times, then put them in my pocket and read them when I have leisure time. I keep them til I get 5 or 6 on hand, then look them over and burn the oldest ones. That way I keep 3 or 4 on hand all the time.

I am glad you have a chance to keep your letters. I hope I shall get home soon and help you read them. Home I say, for if any man has a home, I have. For a good wife and children make home attractive. I am sorry you feel so lonesome without me the 4 months that are past. I hope in 4 months more the prospects will be that we are soon to be reunited again. Let us trust in God and be faithful and all will work well.

The war news is more flattering of late. Now I have to go and drill until dinner time. We did not drill long, so I can write more before dinner. I hope it won't be long before we will have some money.

We owe Mapes not far from $60.00. I gave him a note for $32.00, and the one I gave Almus for $20.00 makes $53.00. I traded a little perhaps near $3.00. So when the interest is added to the principal, it will not be far from $60.00

George Thomas done big things didn't he? Bill was correct about the work . . . there was some 3 days work due us with the team. You know we were to have the team to work 10 days, and I only had them 7. I think him very selfish and unmanly in asking the $2.00 of you. When he has paid the team work and the note, then pay him the $2.00 and not before. I think this is justice, don't you. Bill may be in need of money, but I think he ought to look some-

61

where else for it. I think Turrell is short out of whiskey money, aint he. But never mind, the old fellow needs all he can get.

Have you got the tongue and liver eat up yet? If Jenny acts mean, you must train her in the stable so she will fear you.

Well, I have eat my dinner and resumed my writing. Dear Wife, it is hard to be thus parted when our hearts and minds are so united. But never fear, we shall meet I think on earth. But if we never meet on earth, let us live together in Heaven. What a hope this is . . . is it not worth living for? The Lord is very good to me, and I am bound to praise Him, let me be called where I will. I feel contented with my lot and do not feel like complaining. If I live to get out of this war, and gain my dear little family in praising God, I shall be a happy man.

The sun is shining warm and the flurry of snow has disappeared. Three of us are writing. You need not think that I am here without friends, for we are friendly to each other. As a general thing, we are bound to stick by and help each other as far as we can for we are all soldiers here together.

Yes, I remember last haying time. I hope Mrs. Gates' baby will keep quiet after this. I hope Bill has got you some wood. It is worth 6 shillings per cord if he won't do it for less and board himself. You know I cut and piled 4 foot wood for Steve for 6 shillings a cord. I also cut and drawed stove wood to Brunig for $1.00 per cord. I honor your judgment in having the wood cut at the door to save the chips.

Your lambs will come late and I am glad of it, for they will all live without much trouble. I think James Robinson's face must feel sore. Well, I had to stop writing to put my blanket in my knapsack to be ready to drill and I must go and drill.

Well, I have come off drill and will write until dress parade which will be soon. We fired blank cartridges that are fired without balls. But some shot balls, so the Colonel made us stop shooting.

There have been 6 or 7 officers sent in their resignation. Capt. P. L. Burrows and our Lieutenant Cole and several other Captains. I guess we had better all resign.

Your lambs will come about the first of June, won't they. How is my girls? I would like to see you tonight. You must be good girls and try to learn something. I want to get home to see your little faces. When spring comes, I want to come home, but maybe I shant get home until summer. Dress parade now.

I have been on dress parade and eat my supper. The mail has not come yet. Maybe I will get a letter when it comes. If I do, I will be pleased, won't I. I want to you to write all your affairs. I think the young people are doing great things up there. The war must soon end for the Union is so strong in the North. The war debt is now estimated at 720 million dollars . . . aint that quite a pile. Well, I must close, having wrote all I know. So good nite Dear Wife and children.

I remain your own.

B. A. Cook

No. 22, Camp Bliss, January 15, 1863

My own Dear Wife,

I will write a few lines to let you know that I am all rite and sound. Just came off picket. I went out the 12th. I got two letters from you the first nite I was on picket. That makes twice in succession that I have had 2 at a time. I had to delay answering them until I came in.

We had a good time on picket. No storm and it was warm enough so we could lay down and sleep. Yesterday morning I heard a robin sing. That was something I never heard before in the middle of January.

Last week we had visitors to our house. Saturday, a Lady visited us with her husband Mr. Garison. They belong to the battery about 4 miles from here. In the evening it rained and there was a little bird came in and dried himself and then went out again. So I think we had visitors. And we had a nice dog come in to see us Monday morning.

Well, thank you for writing so often. It shows that I am loved and often thought of. I have read the last letters over 4 times and think I shall read them more than once before I burn them. I am glad you and the girls take so much comfort together. I hope the Lord will spare your health and lives.

The sore throat is raging in many places I hear. One man told me last nite that he had lost a boy 8 years old with it, and his wife had it now. What trouble people have in the world.

Well, you thought about a change to let me be at home and you off down here. You thought exposed as I am that I would feel pretty streaked. I believe you. I don't know how I could stand it. But as it is, I think of you at home and well with enough to eat, and I have the same. So I am contented and want you to borrow as little trouble as possible. And if anything happens to me, I will let you know it at the earliest practical moment.

I rather think you will get some lamb yet. What cow was it that you turned into Turrels' lot? I dreamed last nite that I saw the cows and 2 of them had calves by their side. One of them was near a week old and the other was one day old. I thought they were nice. How much milk do you get and which do you milk? Is the red heifer coming in? Have you had a sley (sic) ride yet. I can't tell how much you ought to pay for fixing the whiffletree . . . from 2 to 6 shillings according to how it is fixed. I have got a dollar yet and as much as 12 stamps and paper enough to last a month.

The paymaster is around here paying. I saw some of the money a few minutes ago. I think it will be our turn to get some soon, but I guess we shant get but 2 months pay instead of 4 which we ought to have. I see something in the papers about a bankrupt law. If they go in for that, all individual debts will be paid. But I hardly think it will become law. You can get Chas. Greenman to make out a new note for George to sign, or you can figure the note and interest and make a note for him to sign. I don't know but you had better let Charlie have it and try to get it into a judgment note so it will be secure. You can do as you think best. I don't know but it is safe enough as a common note.

Now as to political matters. The North is divided and that is what has prolonged this war. I think myself that the Republican Party have allowed themselves to mingle too much with the Abolitionists for the good of the party. That is I think this war should have been a war to put down a rebellion, or in other words restore the Union. But they are trying to make it a war to abolish slavery. My plan would be this . . . to restore the Union as it was and abide by the Constitution as it was, knowing that every state has a right to make its own laws if not in violation of the laws of the united States or Constitution. I mean to have the South come back into the Union as they were and then try to get them to do away with slavery in a certain length of time, even if we have to compensate them for their slaves. That is what Lincoln spoke of in his Message. I believe Missouri is going to do it that way to get rid of her slaves. If all the south would do it that way, it would be far better than fighting. If we have to fight until the rebels are whipped, it will be a good while for they can fite some time yet. But I think the war will smash up before many months and a compromise got up in some shape. But time will tell. If our nation has become so wicked that they don't regard the lives of men, then let them fite until they learn better. I think if we had the leaders of this war together and let them fight it out alone, it would soon be settled. But how many thousand will lose their lives to please them.

Well, I must close for it is time for dress parade nearly. Tomorrow I must wash if it don't rain. This letter is not very long, but I want to send it in the morning. We don't get much news of importance lately, but I hope there will be something done before long.

65

I have just eaten my supper and got a letter from Kingston and there is a meeting here tonight. Our folks are all well. Tell Mary the Goulds are kind to me and I would like to see her little face. I think the girls are getting big if they can clean stables. I am glad you have some help. When I get home you will have more. I hope your colds are better and you are all well.

Good nite dear ones,

B. A. Cook

No. 23, Camp Bliss, Sunday, January 18, 1863 10 o'clock a.m.

Dear Old Wife,

I got a letter from you last night--number 23 of January 10th. I guess I have gotten all your letters, but sometimes they are a long time on the way. That is what's the matter.

I was glad to hear that you are all well and in good spirits. I am the same. I have the rose in my cap this morning. It looks like something from home. I layed awake a good while this morning thinking of you and wishing the time would soon come when I can encircle you all in my arms once more. That will be a happy day for all of us.

I had another letter from Kingston last week which I have not answered yet. They seem to feel much pleased to hear from me so often. They are having a great revival and Charlie is in the hall helping Mrs. Smith.

Yes wife, when you write too often I will tell you of it, for I am glad to hear from my little family often.

I shall send Mother my likeness and some money after payday. I am glad Wilbur has made you a visit and I hope Allan Bane will come over and see you. He can tell you about soldiering if he hasn't been in a fight. I am glad Mr. Lake has gotten rid of his horses.

There are quite a good many deserters and I expect some more of our Regiment will try it after they get their pay. But it won't be me. I think I can march and carry my load as well as the most of the Regiment. Yes, I think two-thirds of the Regiment would fail before I would march now and leave the sick ones in camp. That is about one-third of the men. We have only about 60 in our Company that are able to do duty and I am one of them. There has been one die in our Company and a good many are grunting around. Elias Garlow is one of them.

I went and done my washing yesterday, and we had knapsack inspection this morning. The sun shines pleasantly today. Friday and Saturday nights were pretty cold, but I slept warm. We have to go after wood a good ways--about a mile--to burn in our tents. The cooking is done at the cookhouse where they have a great big cooking stove and tin boilers to cook in. Thomas Whittaker is boss cook. He is Fred's brother, the one they used to call doctor. He is a good cook and a good fellow too, so we have our cooking done in nice style. The stove and furniture cost $50, and the Captain proposes that every man pay 50 cents and he will pay the rest and make it a Company stove.

We have news and hear that a Union force in Arkansas has taken 6 or 7 thousand prisoners with their arms and everything. That is a pretty good haul, ain't it. Bully for that and keep a-doing so.

We have now got a floor in our tent. I am cooking apples for supper. The Gould boys had some sausage sent them and Steve and I get a share when they cook it. We have not spent much money since our box came. We now sell about 40 cents worth of coffee every week. That is 10 cents apiece that will buy our paper and postage stamps, you see.

When you sent me that last two dollars, I gave one for a pound of tobacco and I loaned Jim Gould 25 cents and have about a dollar yet. If nothing happens, is will last me a month easy enough for I have got a good lot of tobacco and postage stamps. If you are bothered to get stamps, let me know and I will send you some.

Friday I went and bought 3 pounds of corn meal for 9 cents and a quart of milk for 10 cents and made some mush for supper. It went pretty good and I had meal enough left to make mush again. I am going to get some more milk and have another dish tonight.

Captain Burrows has gotten his discharge and gone home and left his Company. When he was getting up the Company, he pledged to stand by to the last minute. The boys don't like his leaving them at all and I don't blame them either.

I believe I have told you all the news. Now about sparking. It's hard for some to spark without screwing ain't it. Especially in the dark. Well, I will bet they will be married for they know their business. I guess Mant wouldn't own she liked him. You know, no more than you would own you liked somebody once. I wish them good success, don't you? Did you ask them to go to bed, and what did they do after 4 o'clock? I am quite inquisitive. I would have thought it would have made you feel rather galish when they were performing. I had 3 legs this morning and I thought of your pretty strong hand. After a liberal discharge I was not bothered with the third leg.

B. A. Cook

This is a continuation of letter No. 23, written on January 18, 1863

We have company this afternoon. There are 3 or 4 from the 143rd Regiment here and we are having some fun. Bully, here is another letter from my own Dear Wife, No. 24. I am so glad to hear you are not sick. I am sorry you have no wood. That is too bad, but you can't do without wood this cold weather. I don't think Bill is very punctual in fulfilling his promises, but I hope somebody will get you some wood. If they don't, they will hear from me, and that is so. If you have got to freeze, I will come home and keep you warm.

I hope you have got to Deposit and got home safe. Jenny feels pretty good laying still. If she feels like playing, be careful and don't let her get the start of you and upset you. I thank you for your good long letter and for your dreams of me. It is most dark and I shall have to close though I must talk to you as long as I can see. We are to have prayer meeting here tonite, thank the Lord. We serve him here and our country too. The good Lord bless my little family . . . trust in him.

These good letters do me so much good to read them. It makes me think of old times. I must bid you good nite altho I hate to stop. But we have to get wood and prepare for meeting. We don't hear as much about marching as we did a spell ago.

Yours,

B. A. C.

Sunday evening . We had a good meeting. I thank the Lord for the comforts of life we enjoy here in our little tent. We can serve God here. I would give a good deal to be with you tonite. Last nite I took off my clothes, but I don't do it every nite.

I remain your affectionate husband,

B. A. Cook

I suppose I have wrote all I know, but here is some more:

> Always look on the sunny side
> > And never yield a doubt
> The ways of Providence are wise
> > And faith will bear you out.
> If you but make this maxim yours,
> > And in its strength abide,
> Believing all is for the best,
> > Look on the sunny side.

I love thee and that thou dost know.

How much I love thee I am bound to show.
When I get home I will be your beau
In spring, summer, autumn, and winter, that's so.

Bishop A. Cook to L. M. Cook
January 18, 1863

No. 24, Camp Bliss, January 25, 1863

Dear Wife,

I seat myself to write a few lines to the one I love, best hoping you are all well. I never felt better in person than I do here. I am fat as a bear. I weigh 160 without my overcoat on. I was on police duty yesterday fixing up the guard house. We have had a very rainy spell last week so we didn't drill two days at all. So I went to making rings out of beef bones. I made 4. One for you and I don't know but I shall send it in this letter. One I got on my finger and 2 for Em and Hat. I shant send them yet, for I calculate to make one for Mate soon and another one for you. I guess this ring in pretty near the rite size for you. It is rite for my little finger, but you know I am fleshy. You can rite me and tell what finger it fits and what one you want the other one made for.

It is very warm here since the storm. I saw Mr. Ford of Deposit today and shook hands with him. It is one week since I received a letter from you but I expect one tomorrow. There is talk that Burnside is about to move. I saw a letter today from Mr. Gould's brother dated the 23rd. He said they were under marching orders but the roads are unpassable, but as soon as it dried off, there would be stirring times on the Potomac. Some say our regiment is to go to Washington for a city guard, but I hardly believe it.

There has been several regiments paid off near here but our turn hasn't come yet. But I hope it will come soon for the sake of my family. I have got 60 cents worth of stamps and 50 cents in money.

I will send you two or 3 stamps for you maybe are bothered to get them.

Steve had a letter from Kate last nite. The boy is almost well. We are all well here in our house. I seen George Wheeler last week. He has enlisted in the cavalry near here.

I enclose some miserable verses that were printed here in camp. I think I could do better myself, couldn't you? We have a printer in our camp and he prints a little paper. I guess I will buy one and send to you before long. E. Garlow don't go on duty yet.

Well I had to stop and go on dress parade. I hope you have as warm weather as we have here. I have no news to write. I seen Wesley Dickinson this afternoon and he is well. How do you get along for wood. I wish I was there to cut your wood for you. Do you have salt for the cattle and sheep? I hope you will have good luck with your stock. Do you have milk yet? How do you get along eating the hog and potatoes? Have you a plenty of flour and things to eat?

There is a good many visitors here most every day to see the 144th Regiment. I wish the war would end so I could come home and dwell with my little family. I think we shall get through this war one of these days. How do they think up there? Do folks think the war ended or do they think it just begun. There is a good many here that want their discharge and are trying to get it. E. Garlow wants to be lieutenant in Coles place, but I don't think he will get any higher than he now is. I have not been promoted yet and don't expect to be very soon. I must close now for we are to have meeting tonight. Excuse this short letter.

I remain you own husband,

B. A. Cook

No. 25, Camp Bliss, January 28, 1863

My Own Dear Wife,

I have just come off 2 days guard in this snow storm. 6 of us were down to the railroad guarding commissary stores. The order is that we have got to pack up and march, not to meet the enemy but to pile and load wood at the railroad. But I guess I shant go today for I have just come off duty and I shall stay til tomorrow. I shouldn't wonder if it snowed all day. I suppose you have sleighing up there, but we shant get sleighing here.

I am glad the Elder drew you some wood. I guess you had better let him get your wood for Bill acts so about it. I got your letter of the 27th numbered 25. I was very glad to hear you were all well. I hope you may be well for time to come. I think we are blessed with good health. Thank the Lord for that. I wish we could live together this winter. If we had no children, you should be here with me, for Lamcowsky and his wife are taking all the world and making money too, They board 5 or 6 officers for $4.50 a week. If you was here, you could stay until we marched and then you would have to go home.

You say you are lonesome. I suppose you are in the dark, gloomy days of winter, but spring will soon be here and I wish it would bring peace with it. I suppose there are a good many deserting from the Army of the Potomac. Our Second Lieutenant went to Washington and got on citizens clothes to go home, but got arrested and is in the old Capitol Prison. I think that is big business, aint it? I think if I was Leiutenant I wouldn't desert, would you?

We live first rate now days. We have fresh beef and pork and beans and good bread most of the time. What do you have to eat? Pork and potatoes and johnny cake I suppose. I think the soldiers here can't find any fault with their living, but some will find fault anyway.

There is a good deal of dissatisfaction in all the regiments around here, partly because we don't get our pay and partly other reasons. I think this was will bust up soon, at least there will be a change before long for better or worse.

I think we ought to pay Smith 4 or 5 dollars if we can get it to pay him. I am glad you got what you wanted at Deposit. They will trust soldiers wives for they know they will have money some time or other. You can have some nice dresses. When you get them made, you can send me a piece to look at in a letter.

That young man's name was Arad Lakin. He lay around here some time and then went home discouraged. But I want to have a hand in settling this rebellion, and then I want to come home honorably to dwell with my little family. I don't know but I shall go with the company this afternoon. If I do, I can't write much more. If I don't, I can write a good long letter. It snows, so I don't like to go, but if the captain says go, I have got to. That is the way it goes here. I have read your good long letter 3 or four times over. Where did you get that hand Bill that was in the letter? I see Birds name was on it.

I guess I shall send and see what I can get, and after payday, I shall try to get some to send. I will act as Agent according to his request. I believe it will pay.

I want to finish the girls rings before I go from my tent and send them in this letter. Well, the company is gone and I am the sole occupant of out tent, so I have a good chance to write you a good letter.

B. A. Cook

Continuation of No. 25, January 28, 1863

Thursday, Jan. 29th. Wife, the storm continues and it is very tedious and I am in my tent writing to you. I think it has been a hard stormy time for you. I wish I could of been there to done the chores for you and I hope you had wood to last you through the storm. The mud is about 4 inches deep here, and snow is near a foot deep, and the wind blows. But the sun is coming out and I hope the snow will soon disappear.

The boys that went down to the railroad yesterday had a hard time of it yesterday and last nite. One of them came up here this morning. He says they were all covered up with their blankets, and the blankets were covered with snow.

It is now about noon and I have got to go and get some wood soon. I expect to go about a mile through the snow and get a rail from a rebel's fence. They make good, but it is as good ways to carry it and it is such awful going that the teams can't do much.

I tell you I hear complaints from all quarters of hard times in the north. Everything is so high, it costs twice as much to live as it used to. But I guess we will get along some way. We had good beefsteak and tea and bread for breakfast. We ate pretty late for I had to go and get water before I could get breakfast. We didn't get up very early for we don't have any duty to do in the weather but take care of ourselves. I have got the last of my dried apples soaking to cook for tea. The little bag of dried fruit you sent me I shall keep some time for I can carry that if I move.

I seen Russ last nite. He said Ruth Cook was married and he thought likely they had been to see you for they had been over to Orlows. She was married the 18th to Mr. Kidder, a man that the rebs had catched and paroled, so he is a paroled prisoner. Well, I must go and get some wood now.

Well, I have got some wood and washed the dishes and got the apples stewing for supper. I shall not go to the railroad today I suppose. We get 25 cents per day extry (sic) while there. I hope we shall stay there some time for we don't have to work very hard, and I had rather do it than drill.

You need not think of hearing of my being in battle very soon for I suppose we are here for the defense of Washington, and probably shall not leave here very soon. It is likely that our armies will not do much for 2 months to come, for the roads will be so muddy that an army cannot move. Therefore, I think there will be but little fighting until warm weather comes. Burnside is superseded by Hooker and the army is quiet near Fredericksburg.

Now I believe I have made up for the short letters I have wrote and told you all I know. But I will say that I expect to get some pay most every day. Maybe the government has not got money so plenty that they can pay us all up. And as near as I can learn, they are in the habit of paying part at a time. I hope this may reach you soon. I sent one last Monday and this will go tomorrow, which is Friday, if the road is not so bad that it can't go. The sun is shining very pleasant but the wind blows. Now be good girls and keep comfortable if you can.

From your unworthy Husband and Pa.

B. A. Cook

Continuation of No. 25, January 28, 1863

Now dearest Wife, I can converse with you a little while if no one comes in to interrupt me, and the wind don't blow the smoke down the chimney too strong which it is inclined to do at present. When I am alone, my mind goes back to my loved home and brings to mind the many comfortable and happy hours I have spent there with my dear companion and my prattling children. Oh I sometimes think I didn't prize my treasures as highly as I ought, for few men have the standby of a wife that I have.

Accept my thanks for the language you used in your letter concerning deserting. Yes, better die on the battlefield with honor in defense of our government than to live a coward, a deserter, a traitor. This is my mind and shall be as long as there is one ray of hope. For I love my country, I love my family, and I love the government as it once was. And I will strive to protect all as far as I can. I think the Lord will protect and bring us to meet again, and if we do meet, his name shall be praised.

I expect a letter soon from Kingston and from you too. I am glad the children enjoy themselves in some way even if it is in building pigpens of stove wood. Dear little gals, I would like to see their faces tonite.

I will stop writing and fix the sealing wax in their rings if I can find any to put in. Well, I have got Hat's and Em's rings fixed so they will please them I guess. So I will write a little more.

George Tiler, one of our company, is going to stay with me tonight. He is not very well and has no wood, and it storms too bad to go and get any. But I have got wood in the tent to keep the fire tonite, but the wind blows down the chimney and smokes the fire so we can hardly see. I tell you this is a pretty hard storm. The wind blows and it snows like fun. I hope it will abate by tomorrow. I expect it will be nasty wet and muddy weather here for 4 or 6 weeks to come.

I will stop writing soon for the present for I may possibly get a letter from you when the mail comes. I can finish this after supper. Well, I have eat my supper. I had fried pork and bread and sugar and might of had tea if I had of made it. I have got plenty of black tea . . . much as a teacup full.

Elias Garlow is here talking about the war. He thinks just as he used to about it. He thinks it ought to have been settled before it commenced. I must hurry and finish this before the candle goes out. Be good girls all of you.

From your boy,

B. A. Cook

FEBRUARY 1863

Camp Bliss, Upton's Hill Va., Sept 20th to Feb. 12th, '63
Camp California, Va., Feb. 12th to 14th
Camp Cloud's Mills, Alexandria, Va., Feb. 14th to 28th
Fall's Church, Va., Feb. 28th to 29th
Vienna, Va., Feb. 29th to April 11th

History Summarization, pages 82 through 85

In Camp Cloud's Mills the 144th met an enemy that it was never able entirely to subdue in all the years of service. The old proverb, "Misery loves company," was in this case proved signally true, for there was something most humiliating to the individual to find out that he was lousy and his tent mate likely to find it out and charge him with it, but it was quite another thing to know that not only his tent mate but the entire Regiment suffered with him, and more to know that it was through no fault of his but because this vicious enemy had possession of the camp ground before we came, having held it after another regiment camping there left.

Time at Camp Cloud's Mills came to be divided largely between camp duty, military drill and work on fortifications. Occasionally there were details for other work. Company F was sent out to assist in securing supplies of wood for military use in Alexandria and for our camp.

The Regiment's first pay day in Dixie came on February 8th. These visits of the paymaster were always most welcome and

77

helped very much to brighten all the camp or field surroundings. Large amounts were reserved from the men's wages and sent direct to families at home. The 144th Regiment sent $100,896. "Moving day " came on February 12 when orders were issued to "break camp" and move into the vicinity of Alexandria. Accordingly, we were marched out near Fairfax Seminary where we commenced to put in order a camp designated, Camp California: but the next day another order took us to Camp Cloud's Mills, near Alexandria.

No. 26, Camp Bliss, Upton Hill, (Down in the woods 3 miles), Sunday, February 1, 1863

Dear Wife,

I seat myself this morning to write to you again. I am well and did not come into the woods until yesterday. We have to load wagons with wood and then load it onto the cars. We have some poles laid up from the ground and some cedar brush laid on them to sleep on. We have our canvas stretched over some poles for a shelter. Thus with out blankets over us we sleep comfortably.

The letter you wrote a week ago I got last Friday nite. One from Mother too saying they are all well. Is there a prospect of getting that post office to work? I hope it will.

About the note. Has Bill got the lumber to Allen's Mill or made any move towards it? If he has, then it may be sold to Allen and his Note taken for it. But if he has not got the lumber, then we have got to look to Bill for it you know. If you can ascertain whether he is trying to do as the Note says or not. I will tend to him if he don't try to get the lumber, for I will write to the Justice to fasten the cattle and make him pay it if possible. But don't you threaten or let anyone know anything. Only find out by Bill if he has got or is getting the lumber. If he is not, let me know and I will put somebody after him.

Yes, if you can get anybody's Note and anybody will take it for what we owe, then let them have it. We can use money when we can't notes if we can get it to use. Don't trouble yourself about the debts for I guess they will all be paid in time. And do not do without things you need when you can get them.

Your views as to political matters are purely Abolitionist and just as such as we who want to put down this rebellion.

I think Jerry will come in in March. I know she comes in in good season. The red heifer ought to be farrow this year for she is so young. I guess she will make a good cow won't she? I should like to see you today. Maybe you and the children have got on your new dresses. I expect you shine with them on.

If Mapes and Deal aint married, maybe they will be. Clarry hopes to see her fellow in a year. Well, I hope she may. Captain Plaskett said yesterday he would bet $50 that we would all be home in less than 6 months. That is what I stick to all the while. I suppose he knows no more about it than I do, but time will tell.

I like the place we are encamped and drawing wood better than drilling. These are lovely verses and I will send them back so they can be preserved. I sent a paper to you yesterday morning and hope it will reach you. The snow has gone in some places, but it is 3 or 4 inches deep in most of the fields yet. I hope Wife that you are not snowed under. I don't know but we shall have to go and load cars this afternoon, but I hope not.

I believe I have wrote all I know and haven't time to write what I don't know. While I am down here in the woods, you must not look for long letters. But I will write often and try to answer your good letters up to the handle. From your old boy,

B. A. Cook

Continuation of No. 26. Written on Friday, February 6, 1863

Dear Wife,

I hope your dream will come to pass about my coming up the lane. I hope that day will come in less than 6 months. I am sorry that you were so uneasy about me when you didn't get a letter from me. I have neglected writing to you 7 or 8 days 2 or 3 times. I will try to write once in 6 days and no oftener unless something turns up very special.

Yes, the time we spent at Delhi together was very agreeable to me and I hope those good days may return again. I hope I can come home and let you rest. Oh, if I had my arms around you, you would think that my love had not turned to coldness, but that it had increased as much as I have in weight. It continues to rain and we are not called out to work, so I hope to get a long letter for you this time.

There may be something in your Mother's dark hours previous to your birth and I think it has a great deal to do with the offspring. I believe I wrote to you in one of my letters that Ben was reclaimed. Jerome is all right . . . Will had a letter from him since the battle.

I think our young friends had better be a little careful or they will be talked about, and more than that, unless they understand their business pretty well. But don't you talk to anybody about it, unless it is someone concerned in the matter, or you may see trouble. I need not caution you for you know enough to keep cool.

Tell Em that Mr. Hawk went home to see his little ones and has returned. Phil Fitch is in our company and gets letters from his wife. They have not been married long. I have been told that she was a ho_e (sic) when he married her, but she is good enough for him. He has no learning except what the Devil has learned him.

Steve and I stick pretty close together nite and day. Steve said the other day when we stood in ranks together that he wants to be by the side of me if we ever went into battle. I can't ask Dan when his wife is coming home for he is up in camp and we are down in the woods. We may stay here 20 or 30 days and maybe we shall go to camp next week. I suppose we get 25 cents extra every day we are here. I would like to stay here as long as the war lasts if the Government wants me here.

Em thinks Pa rites short letters She is right. I have rote some short ones and some long ones too, but if you can get a letter from me stating where I am and that I am well, that is something. I generally write according to the time I have to write in. Sometimes I am anxious to get a letter started and don't wait until I get more time to write.

I am glad to get my fingers on some hair that belonged to my little girls. I think that Em's and Mate's hair is some darker than it was when I left home. I am glad they sent it to me. I shall try to keep it to look at.

You must have fun in the snow wading around up to your cheeks if you have had as cold weather there as we have here. It has been cold enough to freeze everything up unless you have kept it warm. I had to cover my ears up with a blanket to keep them from freezing at nite. One end of our tent is open, but we keep a good fire at that end of the tent and lay with our feet to it. So we sleep nicely beneath the covers.

Do you suppose you can sell the wood that is over in the hollow? Is there much teaming done up there now days? You say you are out of buckwheat flour and sweetening. I suppose you have buckwheat to grind, so you can have all the pancakes you want. I hope to send you some money before long. Cotton goods are awful high and will be higher no doubt, but the sheep will help you a good deal. I am sorry you had such luck with your meat.

I wish I had bought a good lot of cotton cloth before I left home.

Well, I will close, and if I get more time before this goes, I will send more in the same envelope.

From your soldier boy,

B. A. Cook

Later that same day he wrote . . .

I think Mrs. Ferrel done pretty well for her. It sounds very much like her. I don't think you will see me until I am honorable discharged, unless the war lasts a good while and I should get a furlow and come home. I believe you when you say these verses were your sentiments. They are very nice and good. You have not sent me a piece of your dresses yet. When did you send the paper? It has not come yet.

The Goulds and Steve and I are all writing today for we haven't been called on to work. Dinner is most ready, and after dinner I expect we shall have to go and load the cars with wood. It doesn't rain now and I hope we may have nice weather now for a spell. But the mud will be deep enough here.

People die up there as well as here. There is not much sickness here at present but E. W. G. does no duty yet. And some others are up at camp that think they are not fit to handle wood. Aaron Travis hasn't drilled or done anything in 2 months, but he looks as well as ever. Here he comes from camp with his knapsack on his back, so I guess he is better.

I won't cut this sheet in two for you can write on the other half and send it back. Dinner is ready and I will stop.

Good bye Wife,

B. A. Cook

No. 27, Camp Bliss (In the woods) Thursday, February 5, 1863

Dear Wife,

I thought I would write a few lines and let you know that I am well and in the woods yet. We don't have to work very hard for it is storming quite hard and has snowed all day.

The news is today that the rebs have broken the blockade at Charleston. So says the daily paper. And I heard yesterday that our regiment was going to Baltimore to do patrol duty at that city. I hope we may go. I tell you it don't look much like whipping the rebs. And I tell you further that the North are sick of the war and many men are trying to do something to get it settled without fighting it out. I think it will be settled yet in some way.

I suppose you know that France is as war with Mexico. I think they are trying to get a foothold here so they can help the South. It may not be so, but I think that is the game. Time will tell. Well, they were at work on the Bankrupt Law this week in Washington, but they voted the Bill down and I am glad they did.

Old Wife, I think of you often this cold weather. It is hard for you to do so many chores this cold weather. I hope you can get through all rite. I expect a letter from you tonite. It is about time for one to come. I broke the glass in my watch. How does your watch perform? I have got one or two keys that will fit your watch. I guess I have got 3 keys, and one of them only fits my watch. So I guess I will send you the keys in a letter before long for I may lose them.

I have got sixty cents and plenty of paper, stamps, envelopes, and tobacco. I will send you 50 cents. It will come in handy for you and the little soldiers. Paper that is printed in camp says we are to be paid next Monday or Tuesday. If that be the case, I can send you something that will help you to whatever you need and that will be very gratifying to me. But I don't expect a very big pile.

I have seen a great many negroes of late that have come from the land of the rebels since Christmas. One of them told me that he had seen about 2000 that had escaped from their old master's homes since Christmas. Some of the darkies are quite intelligent. They are Chopping wood for the government at one dollar per cord. And some are driving teams at 25 dollars per month. They can make money at that rate. They buy meat and corn meal and coffee. They fry their pork and bake their hominy cake in the ashes.

Friday morning after breakfast. It rained all nite and the snow is nearly rained off. Now we will take the mud. But we are comfortable. Steve got a letter last nite and I got 2 from my old wife of the 27th and 31st. I tell you I expected one and they were both mailed the 3rd and arrived the 5th.

No Signature

No. 28, Camp Bliss, Monday AM, February 9, 1863

I think I will write a few lines this morning and tell you I am well and got some pay yesterday, Sunday being the day that they pay us. We got about one and a half months pay. Some didn't get one cent in money, but a check for the whole. There was no private in the company that got more than I did for my date of enlistment was back the farthest of any except 2 that were the same day. Well, I got a check of $20.00 for you and one dollar and 23 cents in change that will last me a good while if I am well. And the $20.00 will last you until I get some more. I guess we will be paid again in about 2 months. We are paid up to the 1st of November, so you see there will soon be 4 months pay due us. All you have to do to make this check good is put your name on the back and it is as good as any $20.00 bill. You must not try to pay any debts out of this unless some that you have contracted yourself that you see fit to pay. But get some things to make yourself and children comfortable. If you have any to spare you may send me 2 or 3 dollars so I can send Mother 2 dollars and my likeness.

We are in the woods yet. It is Monday noon and I have been loading cars this forenoon with wood. It is hard work to handle green oak wood, but we work about as we are a mind to. It seems like spring now. The snow has all disappeared and the birds sing like spring. But I expect you have good sleighing up there.

I got the paper in due time. I think the verses are very nice. The boys are copying them off. They are lovely verses and I will send them home soon. I have read the paper all through. Did you get the paper I sent you? The Captain is hollering hurry boys, but I set on a stick of wood writing to my old gal, the one I love best. I think such letter as I get are worth having. I get the worth of the money every letter I get. I hope I may get home to enjoy your company a few more years.

There is not much prospect of our getting far from here very soon. They say we are in the 27th Army Corps and for the defense of Washington and the territory we now hold. We are under Hintzelman.

The teams are unloaded and it is not quite sundown, so I will finish this sheet before supper. I think by the papers the Reb soldiers are sick of fighting. I see that some of Bragg's men threatened to shoot him the first time they get in battle. Congress has passed a bill to raise 2 or 3 hundred regiments of blacks to put in the field. Let them fight for their freedom, that is the doctrine. A negro is no better than a white man. I think if the North dose the fair thing and hangs together, the war will soon end. But there will be hard times after the war is ended. It will be a good while before things will be as they were before the war. I may never be in a battle if the war lasts a year, but I don't think it will last long.

Supper is most ready and this sheet is full.

Louisa, I have eat my breakfast and seize my pen to write a few lines before I am called to go to work. there is nothing new to write this morning. But the new things begin to show among the soldiers, such as boots, new knives, and pipes and tobacco. A great many have sent their allotment home, but some drew all money and in 3 weeks time won't have as much money as I will for they will spend it all.

I saw Will Dan Sunday when I was up to camp after our pay and had a chat with him. He said his wife would be home according to what she wrote in about 2 weeks. Kate is coming too, so I suppose then you can see them and talk about your boys that are at war. We have to ask each other when we heard from home and how the folks are when we meet.

I suppose I shall have to go to work soon, but I will write as long as I can. I hope this letter may find you well and in good spirits. I feel thankful that I am blessed with health. I have been very lucky since I have been in service and always was. That you know as well as I and the Lord be praised for it. I wish to see my little family, but I haven't been homesick since I have been here. And as long as everything works well I shall not get homesick.

I suppose Mother will come home in the spring. She talked in her last letter that she was going to farm it alone next summer. I thought by that that the boys were agoing into something besides farming.

Well, a great many think the rebellion is in its death struggle, and I hope it is for I want to get home to help you do haying. We are talking about getting home by the 4th of July. If we do, what a time we will have, won't we? I would like to be home now to take a sleigh ride with you and the girls. Have you heard from Aunt Harriet lately? I have things that I would rite to her, but I have not got at it yet. I would like to write to a good many, but I can't get at it. I wish I could have time to sit down and rite without being interrupted, but I can't write but a few minutes at a time, and when I am writing there is so much talk going on you can't write.

Tuesday noon, Feb. 10th . I have eat my dinner and got to writing. that handbill I got, I have got 5 names on it that I got this forenoon. I intend to send them to Philadelphia this week if nothing happens, and see what we will draw. I will let you know what success we have.

We have the nicest weather here that you can imagine. We loaded the cars this forenoon and had a nice ride on the cars for about a mile.

I have looked at the girl's hair since dinner. Em's and Mate's hair are of a color, one is as lite as the other. I expect a letter from you soon. It is about time to look for one from my Ever Faithful Companion. I send you my love if you have not already got it. No more at present.

B. A. Cook

No. 29, Monday Morning, February 15th, 1863

Dear Wife,

This morning finds me well and I will try to answer your letters No 29 and 30 which I received day before yesterday. I was glad to hear from you and find you ware not broke up. I was glad you had been down and seen Deal and Mr. Mapes, his debt is correct

I am glad you got down to the office to get the letters and papers when they come and wish you lived nearer to the office to get them some times but we can't have all we wish.

The note of George (illegible line) and I had (illegible) grass seed and he paid N. Gotinmer(?) near $15 and help to log the (illegible word) and everything is credited to him in one of them Account

Books. I guess if it is not addressed on the note I think I wrote on the note what was due on the note at that rate and it is correct $125.85.

I am pleased to think that I have sent you something to help you to a little money. I hope you have got your 20 dollars before this time. I hope your potatoes didn't freeze for you need them. I had 6 for my breakfast this morning they were all I wanted. I wish I could of had some of them fried eggs that the girls wanted so bad. I think Deal is very kind to our girls and hope they will always respect her for her kindness to them. Lincoln must of patched your boots and shoes a good deal to come to $1.25 when you found sole leather. He ought to of fixt both pair for 50 cts when you found leather. So he must of done 75 cts worth of patching he owed you 25 cts. it is on your books.

I am sorry you are afflected with your neck. I hope you can get something done for it immediately if it is not already better. I cannot see into its being sore on the out side and enlarged so.

It has rained all the morning a little. The cars have just gone past, it seems good to have the cars running here. We are in the wood business yet but out regt with the rest of the Brigade have moved about 6 miles from the (illegible word) hill to near Alexandria. We may stay here to work at getting wood a good while if our Regt don't go to the front. But if they are ordered to go any great distance we shall probably go with them. Some of the old troops have come back the 4th Pa. Regt. are encamped where we were on Upton Hill. The regt numbers about 1180 men the rest have been discharged disabled or killed in skirmishing, or died of disease. (the rest of the letter is illegible),

No. 30, Camp Bliss, February 22, 1863

I seat myself this Sabbath afternoon to write to you and answer your letter that I received last nite which had $3.00 in it. It was written last Wednesday, the 18th I think (No. 32). I got it quick, but No. 31 I haven't got. I suppose it was in our last Friday's mail and that we haven't got yet. There was a mistake. They sent our regiment the 144th Pa.S.V. mail instead of our own. It will have to be exchanged.

This is a tedious day. The snow is about 6 inches deep and still falling. We had 8 or 10 inches last weekend and it rained off. The Potomac was very high last Friday for I was on the hill where I could see the boats running. We are getting wood yet. It has been very muddy this week past.

Now Wife, I think it a shame that you have to get your wood yourself. It is enough to make anyone mad to think that the Abolitionists of that place will let the women get their own wood or freeze. If anything would make me desert it would be to know that my family were suffering. I have a good notion to write to Gates and put something in his ear. But now that you have got money, maybe you can get wood without cutting it yourself. I hope so. At least I am glad Mate is better. I didn't know that any of you were sick, except you said you all had bad colds. I hope you are all well now. I have been well and hearty. Have felt a little rheumatism from this wet stormy weather, but nothing serious. I hope you will be careful of your health for my sake and for the children's sake. I would gladly be with my family this gloomy Sabbath. This you well know. But my country claims my service and I am bound to serve to the best of my ability.

Have you seen Gen. Butler's speech delivered at Baltimore, M.D. He is the man the Rebs hate so bad. According to his statement, one half, yea more than one half of the territory occupied by the rebs one year ago is now in our possession. And I think the summer's campaign will make the rebs hunt the hole. It makes the Northern Secessionists tremble to think Congress has authorized the President to enroll all between 18 and 45 and draft if necessary, and the drafted men are to fill up the old regiments. I see in the paper the rebs say that for the first time since the war commenced, our forces are superior to theirs at almost every point. That is acknowledging a considerable for them, but they say they are determined to fite to the last.

I see an account of one man's resisting the Conscription Law unto death. The rebs tried to get him into the army and he said no, he would not fight against his country. He tried to get away, but they told him they would punish him if he didn't fight. He said he never would raise a gun against a Unionist, so they were bound to kill him. But he with a knife cut his own throat and thus freed himself from their hands.

I went to the Sutler's the other day and got a quire of paper and a pack of envelopes and some stamps and 25 cts. worth of tobacco. I paid out the last shinplaster except one 5 ct. one that I gave to a boy for apples. A quire of paper for 20 cts. is cheap. It is better paper than this. This is some I had left from the pack of envelopes I got for 16 cts.

I was pretty near whipped for money, but I had everything I needed. Now I have got 3 dollars and I must get my likeness taken if I can for Mother. I'll send her a dollar and get a crystal in my watch. How did you get this 3 dollar bill if you hadn't been to Deposit? Oh, you went to Deposit and got your check changed and put the money in and sealed the letter (I guess).

I sent to Philadelphia for my breastpin. But it has gone along with your letter No. 31. But I guess they will come after a while. I want to know if you have got the paper I ordered him to send you. Did you get the shinplaster I sent you? Well, I suppose I am asking questions that you have answered in No. 31.

I was glad to read Aunt Laurie's letter again. She was a good soldier and she gave me some good advice. Thank the Lord and trust Him Dear Wife, and all will be well. I hope you will hire someone to cut wood, for it is too much for you. Do not undertake it. How is your throat and is it better? Have you had anything done for it?

I have your likeness and the girl's hair to look at. This is some satisfaction, but if I could see you all over, all of you, I would jump up and down. But I live in hopes of seeing my home and all that is dear to me. If you have time, tell me how your watch and revolver look.

Be good girls and think of

B. A. Cook and Pa

No. 31, Camp Bliss (In the woods) February 26, 1863

Dear Wife,

As it is raining this morning, I thought I would write a few lines to inform you that I am well and in the wood business yet. The snow has settled, so it is about 6 inches deep. We expect to muster in again next Saturday, the last of this month.

I went to camp last Monday and put a letter in the office for you. I went into the 143rd Regiment and saw Wesley Dickinson. I read a letter he got from Hattie Dickinson and he had her likeness. I also saw a letter from Aunt Harriet Cook. She said she had been and took dinner with you. I was glad she stopped to see you.

I have not got that letter No. 31 yet. I hear that Charles Greening's wife is dead. That is a great loss for she was a good wife.

I had conversations with several slaves that have got away from their Master and are in the service of the Government. They have left their wives and children and are now earning money to go and get them away from their Masters. The other day I stood on the railroad track talking with a young man that belonged to the 7th Pa. Reserves. He had seen hard, hard fighting. While I was talking with him an aged man came down the track and asked if there was any train that would be down soon. I told him that there would be a train down soon but I thought it would not stop so he could get on. He said he was chopping wood for the Government and had broke his ax and had to get a new one. He seemed to feel bad. He said man is full of trouble. I asked him if he was born in Virginia. He said he was and had always lived about 13 miles from Washington. I should think he was 50 years old. I asked him if he had lived so long in the world and never experienced religion. He said he never had. I told him that it was something that would make a man happy under all circumstances. He said he wished he might have it for he thought it a good thing if it was the right kind with no hypocrisy about it. He said further that he had always been poor and worked hard. I asked him if he ever read the Testament, and he said he never had any learning and couldn't read. I told him it was a great comfort to Christians to read God's word. He then said that maybe I had got religion. I told him that I thought I had for I felt that Christ had forgiven my sins and blessed me every day and that he was my hope for days to come. I told him Christians had nothing to fear but offending God. I told him that the Lord said in the day thou seekest me with all thy heart I will be found in thee. And I told him that the poor had great promises in the word of God. I told him I hoped he would give himself to Christ and ask forgiveness of sin, and he would obtain pardon and be happy in Christ. He said he wished he mite. I told him I hoped he would. So he give me his hand and said God bless you. I told him to trust in God and he said I had given him the best advice he had had in a long time. He was a poor white man and the poor whites are no better than the blacks. They have no chance of education, but are kept under foot by the rich.

The half has never been told of the evils of slavery. Uncle Tom's Cabin and all we have ever had to read does not begin to tell what I have learned from the slaves that I have talked with. If I had time, I could write volumes that would be interesting to you. But some of our neighbors would think it false. I say Death to Slavery and Treason.

B. A. Cook

Thursday afternoon same day. It has not rained much and James Gould and Steve and I have been out shooting at a mark. We can shoot pretty good. Close enough to hit a reb as far as we could see one in the woods. Day before yesterday, William Gould, Steve and I went hunting rabbits. There was so much snow, they couldn't run fast as I could. They would skulk under logs and brushheaps. I succeeded in getting one started from under a log, but the brush was too thick to pursue him. We tracked him to his hole under another log. Steve saw him under the log and said he could grab him, but when he grabbed, the rabbit was not there but had jumped out in the snow. I struck him with a cane but he jumped from under it and ran under another log. We soon found the hole, so William Gould placed himself at the hole and fixed for a grab. I punched the rabbit out and he slipped out of his hands and ran under his leg to hide. So he jumped up to look for the rabbit and the rabbit made his escape. Then we surrounded it and got it in a brushheap. Steve drove it out and it ran directly to William Gould and he struck it with his cane and killed it for we had no guns with us.

We got another started from his hole and I pursued it so close it got under more brush. We surrounded it and Steve drove it out and I killed it with my cane. So you see we had lots of fun and we sold them for 25 cts.

Dearest Wife, I have told you of some of the events of the past week, but I must tell you something more. I have thought of you and my Dear Children often, and imagined how you look at home and wished I could come and surprise you some day. But I shall have to dream of being there for a while yet. I live in hopes of seeing you at home one of these days, but when I am unable to say. When I think of the happy days we have spent together, I wish them back again. I hope our lives will all be spared to live together again.

Well, I have eat my supper and it is about dark, I suppose we shall move from here in less than a week. We shall probably go up the railroad to get wood. I think our Captain is trying to get us detailed from the regiment to get wood for our business.

I am now writing by firelight. The boys have had fun snowballing. I have got my breast pin. It is a good pin and I will send it home in this letter for I have no use for it here. I will finish this in the morning for I may get a letter when our mail comes. That letter No. 31 has not come, but the paper has come. It is quite a paper aint it. Steve got a letter from Kate last nite. She is at home now. I suppose you will see her before you get this. I must bid you all good nite.

From your own,

B. A. Cook

MARCH 1863

Vienna, Va., Feb. 29th to April 11th
March 14th, Spring Hill, Tenn.

History summarization page 85

As the month of February drew to a close rumors prevailed in
camp that the brigade was to be called´ to active service.
Taking advantage if these rumors some waggish punster
caused to be circulated on the last day of February, as coming
through the Adjutant, an order to have by twelve o'clock three
days rations ready for March. It created quite a ripple of excitement at the time and later no little amusement when the
joke came to the surface.

No. 32, Vienna, Va. March 3, 1863

My Own Dear Wife,

I seize my pen to answer yours of the 22nd, No. 33, which I received today. It found me well and in the woods getting wood
some 15 miles from Alexandria. We moved up here yesterday on
the cars. We have taken up quarters in a large depot house, so you
can see we have a nice place for our company. There is such talk
that Company F is to be permanently detached from the Regiment
for this business. I should not be surprised if it should be so. for

there are 5000 cords of wood to get here. There are 200 darkies cutting now. The Colonel over this business is much pleased with Company F's work. His name is Green.

On our way here we saw where the rebs tore the track up, burned the ties, and lit the rails and bent them around trees. They burned several cars. This was done before the first Bull Run fight by a South Carolina regiment that was here. Most of the folks here are from the North and Union. But there is one old reb here who has a son in the rebel army. The old fellow has been taken to Washington 4 times and been kept in prison quite a while, but he's quite clever now and he better be.

I got that long letter No. 31 2 or 3 days ago. I was glad to get it and that ring of hair. I have got all of your hairs in the likeness. I think a great deal of the hair for it is something you have wore. And as you say, I think a great deal of what you had your hands on. I got the paper all rite and I guess I will send it home soon. I sent the pin in the last letter, No. 31, and hope you have got it safe. If you find a gentleman that wants to give $1.50 for it, you can let him have it if you are a mind to. I think it is a good pin. No brass. It was priced $6.00.

I was glad to hear that you were all well again. I know you are lonesome, but spring is here and I hope when warm weather comes you will not be so lonesome. I think you had quite a run of company. I am glad if the neighbors have made up their minds to not let you freeze to death. Don't talk to me about drafted men. I had rather be a volunteer by all odds.

Do not think wife that I would not be contented if I were with my little family after being in a large company so long. For home sweet home is the place for me and I have often told you that I expected to see that home again. Give yourself a little rest for awhile, and don't borrow trouble about me for I am a wood drawer. I aint a fighting rebs, so keep cool awhile.

I haven't see E. W. G. but once in 5 weeks for we have been getting wood and I haven't been to the regiment but once. I don't see any difference in him. I have nothing to say, but some say he is trying to play off. He and John are both in the hospital. Willie D. has been bad off but he is better and is fleshy, but he is not well yet.

It is spring here. I saw a man plowing yesterday. Today we had a snow squall, so we quit work about 3 o'clock this afternoon. This gives me a good chance to write you a letter. It thundered and lightning twice this afternoon in the squall. I suppose you expect some calves before long, but I don't know what to tell you to do with them. I suppose we ought to raise one for Jerry if you can get a good heifer calf. But if you think it will be too much trouble, you can get someone to take them or you can veal them, and when you get a good chance next year, buy a yearling.

You must try to make things as easy for yourself as you can and even then you will have all you can do if I don't come home. When is Mother coming home? I wrote to her a few days ago, and also wrote to Brandt and Uncle Orlo Cook. It is dark.

Now I will finish my letter. The boys have got a fiddler here and there is plenty noise but I must finish this so it can go tomorrow. There is all kinds of wicked (illegible words) God is just and I want to live in his plan. How thankful we ought to be that I have been so favored. Many that enlisted last summer have fared hard and many have been in battle and many are now dead. I talked with Rodney Smith when you came to Delhi about enlisting but he thought he rather be at home. But I hear he was crossing the river at Little Falls and fell through the ice and his body has never been found. Thus we are not safe or free from death, at homme.

Wednesday morning the 21st. I could not finish this last nite for I was called on to go on guard. So I went to bed at nine and at eleven one of the centuries (sic) come in out of breath and said get up quick for there was cavelry coming. It was A. B. Cook so we roused up and made inquiry he said be quick for Alfred Cole was shot the 2 above named were at one post and were to be relieved by me and Charles Cook. About one o'clock this morning well we all got up and put on our straps and loaded our guns and out we went. The Capt. took 12 of us and left the Orderly in command of the rest. We went down to the camp of our Cavelry only a short distance and the Capt. asked them if they had shot at one of our men. He said one of them had shot accidentally. The way it was one of the boys see 2 cavelry men coming and he ran and said they are coming. And the cavalerymen saw them and thought they were rebs, not knowing we had guard out there. So they persued them and one of the boys see no use in running and stopted. But the other one got the start and come in. Well when the cavalryman stopt his horse he stoped so sudden that his rider pulled his gun off but the charge went up into the air. But the one ahead thought surely his comrade was shot. Great times and no one hurt. C. C. and I went and stood the later part on the nite all we see was one big dog.

It is quite cool this morning and squally. I dont have to go in the woods this forenoon because I was guard last nite. It was fun to see the excitement last nite.

We had fun the first of March. One of the boys accused the Orderly of pissing in the spring. But he denied it. He said it was so and he could prove it. The Orderly said he couldn't. Finally he asked him if it warnt the first day of Spring and if he hadn't pissed, he owned up, sold.

If Uncle wants that wheat let him have it for we have no place to sow it, on the proposition he made. When is Kingston coming up. I suppose it is about time. Tell my little girls to stick to my coming home and we will all stick to it and the Lord willing I will come in due time. Some of the English are offering large bounty to someone to run our blockade. They want to pick a fight. Be good girls.

Here is one kiss for you.

B. A. Cook

No. 33, Vienna, Virginia, March 8, 1863

My Own Dear Companion,

Love prompts me to write to you again and tell you some of my thoughts. This morning before daylite, I waked and thought of loved ones at home. I wished myself by your side in bed, I presume if I could of been there I would not of been an unwelcome visitor. Oh wife, how many happy hours we have spent together and how sweet their memory still. How we enjoyed our visit to Delhi. One week ago today you was writing to me those precious lines that No. 34 of March 1st contains. None but thee could pen those. I was glad to hear you were well and in as good spirits as circumstances will permit. I have received all the letters you have sent and everything.

As today was Sunday, after inspection one of the Goulds and Steve and I went out to see what we could see. Went about 4 miles towards Drainsville and went to a house and found 3 dogs there. Dogs are plentiful here. And old grey-headed man come out to stop the dogs barking and we talked a while with him. We bought some eggs and left, but we were sure he was a reb. He told us how far it was to different places and where our pickets were stationed. Well, we left him and come towards home about half a mile to a bridge over a run that the rebs burned when they were here a year ago last summer. Well, after we crossed the creek, we saw a woman cross the railroad and go up to a house. So we thought we would see who lived there. We went to the house and she came to the door and asked us to come in. We went in and took a seat and she asked where we got our eggs. We told her and she said that the man was her father. She had two little children, one aged 3 and the other about 8 or 10 months old. And also her sister about 12 years I would judge. She said her brother came and stayed with her nites and cut her wood. We talked about the Yankees and the Confederates and found out her sentiments. She said her man had been in the rebel army most 2 years. I asked her if she heard from him often. No, she had not heard from him since last summer. He was home at the time the rebs crossed into Merryland and got whipped.

99

She said he got hurt once by the explosion of a shell, but had not been shot. She has not seen or heard from him since last August.

She said she wished the war would end, but she believed the rebs were foolish enough to fite as long as there was a man left. But she thought the best way was for Abe and Jeff to get together and fight it out alone. She said she was a rebel. We told her we did not blame her for that for she lived where most of the people were secessionists and her man was in the army. But we told her that we were going to get 600,000 more men and if we needed more, we could get a million more. She wondered where so many men come from. She allowed that we couldn't take Richmond and Vicksburg. I told her that Vicksburg would be taken soon. She allowed if we got that and Richmond, the rebs might as well give up.

She cooked 16 of our eggs and we eat part of them and some corn meal and water stirred up and baked, which was ready when we got there. So we can say we eat dinner with a rebel woman.

I feel sorry for the women and children here, for they must suffer without the necessities of life.

I have said enough about the rebs, but she allowed when Jeff got into Washington she would get there and get things cheap. She said when the weather got good we would see the rebs coming here and all such trash. She really believed it, poor creature.

Steve is writing to Kate. I suppose he will tell something about the above. I must say we have the nicest quarters here that can be and plenty of wood to handle. We have got 10 days provisions on hand and everything is lovely, for the frogs are thawed out and spring is here. We have everything to eat . . . potatoes, beans, rice, coffee, tea, sugar, molasses, pork, fresh beef, and good bread. And we can buy milk and eggs if we have the money.

I have got almost 3 dollars yet. I haven't had a chance to get my likeness taken yet, so I guess I will wait until near payday. I hope you have got that little pin, and I sent you one of the keys in my last letter. Tell me if it fits your watch. If it don't, it is of no use to send the other for it is the same size. I have got my watch yet. There is a darkie that wants it after he gets his pay. I told him he could have it for $8.00.

I am glad you had such good luck to get the promise of turn to pay Mapes something and get the pay for Bill. That's perfectly satisfactory to me. And I hope G.T. will pay something. I hope he won't have to press Br. Leonard to get the pay, but what will a body do. We can't wait always. It is nine o'clock and I have got to go to bed.

Monday morning, March 9th. This is a beautiful morning and I have got through breakfast. I had 3 good potatoes and a good lot of steak and bread and coffee. I drink coffee now, for it is made fit to drink.

I think it is too bad for Elenora to act so redickalous (sic). How must Wal feel if he knows it. It is enough to break ones heart if he thinks anything of her. I am grateful to God that I have a true wife, one that loves me and regards my feelings. May God preserve us that we may meet to make our home lovely. If I should not get home until the 3 years is up, the girls would almost grow out of my knowledge. But I think this rebellion is near a close. Time will tell.

I have got to go to work, so I must close. I will send that paper with this letter and you may be surprised by getting something else before this month is out . . . from Philadelphia. Give my respects to all the good folks at home.

And excuse this short letter, Dear Wife.

From your

B. A. Cook

No. 34, Vienna, Virginia, March 13, 1863

My Own Dear Wife,

I received your No. 35 yesterday. I was glad to hear from you again and hear you are all well. I had a letter from our Mother this week and Al wrote you a good letter. I will send it back for safe keeping. I am happy to say to you that I am well and doing well. The weather is quite cold here today. The wind is piercing. It feels as though it comes off of your snow up North. You must have very severe weather now, but I hope it won't last long. I suppose Mother will be up in a few days. Then she will be company for you. I feel for you this severe weather. You have had a hard job this winter, but I hope I can be with you next winter and relieve you of some of your cares.

I have no news to write to you except for the rebel raid at Fairfax Courthouse last Sunday nite. They captured some of the pickets and got into the village. They got a number of officers and horses and left. I heard yesterday that they were nearly all captured by our forces near Leesburg. Fairfax Courthouse is 4 miles from here.

Steve has not paid that dollar so you and Kate can make it. If you can get Wry for all they owe us, it will help you a good deal. I think Joe has got his foot in it at last, if it can be proved against him. I have said nothing to Steve about F. and M. Only that they had been to our house, that is all.

I am glad you got the pin. You are to have the paper a year. You will receive a set of Ladies Jewelry from the same place if you have not received it already. I ordered Mr. B. Dean this week to send you a set, so I suppose they will reach you before this does. I expect they will shine.

Borrow no trouble about me, for I have good quarters. Now I sleep and eat upstairs. It seems odd to sleep so far from the ground, but it is better than sleeping on the ground I tell you. I guess I won't write any more now.

Saturday morning, March 14th. This morning finds me well and trying to talk to you again. It is not so cold as it was yesterday. Last nite before dark, I took a ride. 7 of us got the trucks of a car on the track. From here there is a little downgrade all the way for 3 miles. So we got on and let her rip the distance in about 10 minutes. Then we went and got some boards and put on the car and pushed it back again.

How long we shall stay here I don't know, but I would like to stay as long as the war lasts. I long for the day to come when you can get your arm around my neck. If I could get a furlow and come home I would, but there is so many applications made and refused that I won't try yet awhile. There has been 2 furlows granted to our company since we have been in Virginia.

I am glad you got your pay on Bill Evans' note. You never told me whether the girls got their rings or not. I have got one most done for you, a little larger than the other one. And I want to make one for Mate when I get time. I wish I could be with you today and take Jenny and have a sleigh ride, don't you, for I suppose you have good sleighing now. There is no snow here. The folks around here are sick of war, even the secess think it won't last long. So Say I. Excuse this short letter. I will write again soon.

B. A. Cook

No. 35, Vienna, Virginia, March 20, 1863

Dear Old Girl,

I have time to write you a few lines. I have the line that come in Steve's letter. I am glad you are all blessed with health, and I am well. I am going to send Dean 6 more names for jewelry. That makes 15 that I have sent. I hope you have got your jewelry before this time. Now it's time for another letter from my wife, but we don't get any mail today. But I expect one when it comes.

We didn't get any pay yet. Have you any money left, or are you moneyless. If you are let me know and I will send you some, for I have sold my watch for $8.50 in cash. I have lent one dollar and sent for your jewelry and sent 25 cents to see what I will draw again. I have $8.65 left.

We have cold sour weather yet, but I hope it won't last long. There was an accident on the Orange and Alexandria Railroad yesterday. There was a mule on the track that threw the car off and killed 6 or 7 men and injured several others. They were soldiers belonging to the 143rd Regiment I believe. They were going up to load the cars with wood. I stood guard last nite for 3 hours and maybe will stand again tonight.

Nite before last I went to a house a short distance from here and had a chat with a northern lady that had lived here 2 years before the rebellion broke out. She told all about the rebels attacking the cars at this place a year ago last summer before the Bull Run battle. The rebs were in line right in front of her house, and the general had his headquarters there. She said she was as near crazy that day as she ever was. But when our forces retreated from Bull Run, she and her family went with them to Washington and left everything.

The rebs took 6 or 8 hundred bushels of grain and 20 head of cattle that they got nothing for. She used to live near Rochester. She went there and spent a few months, then came to Washington and stayed until this week. Her husband is doing business in Washington. She expects him home Saturday nite to stay a few days. They have a nice situation, but they were drove from it and dared not stay when the fighting came so close.

Her man had fled before the rebs came for he was for the Union, but she stayed as long as she could. She said she cooked all nite for our forces when they were going to Bull Run. When they came back, she went to Washington with them, but she hopes to live in peace now. She has no one with her but one daughter at 16 and a colored servant to do her housework.

She said she is well acquainted with Jackson that shot Ellsworth at Alexandria. Jackson's wife tried to get him to take down his secess flag, but he would not do it. Ellsworth took it down for him and he shot him for it. But Brownell shot him and thus avenged Ellsworth's death.

I don't know any more to write at present. I would like to get a letter from you before I send this, but I guess I shant wait. Will send this to our regiment in the morning. I hope you will have hay enough. I have sold 2 loves of bread this week and 20 cents worth of meat, because I can't eat all I draw. So I sell it to the darkies rather than throw it away.

Friday evening. No more news to write, so I will try and ask a few questions. Has old Jerry come in yet? I am much obliged to Mr. Bruning for his best respects, and return the complement. I would like to travel up the Shad Pond Creek (he spells the middle word "pound") next Sunday. There is someone up that way that I would like to stay with. But hold on a few months, and then I will be around. Tell all my friends that I think of them often, and would like to hear from them. I have written to 2 or 3 and got no answer yet, but when I write to you or Mother I get an answer. There, the letter is on fire from the candle. Well, it won't be of much consequence, so let her rip.

It is time to go to bed, so good nite. Don't scold much about this short letter. I will write soon again when I get your next letter.

B. A. Cook

No. 36, Vienna, Virginia, March 25, 1863

My Own Dear Wife,

I take up my silent pen this morning to inform you that I am pretty well and have received your letter of the 15th. Glad I was to hear that you are well and had been to meeting. I have not heard a sermon in a long time, but I hope to hear one in the Union Schoolhouse again one of these days if it be the Lord's will. It is quite warm and pleasant this morning, but we had a hard rain last nite. I hope some of your snow is gone before this time, for your hay is running low and I find that hay is going to be scarce up there. I think you had better get a ton off Kate instead of half a ton, for you will have to feed until the 10th of May quite likely.

I suppose ere this Mother has arrived. I will write to her as soon as I find she has come to town. We are in Vienna in the wood business yet. It is almost 2 months since we went to getting wood, and I suppose we shall get no extry pat as we are supposed to. But I would rather be here than with the regiment, for it is far healthier than in camp.

I am glad Clarry Dan's boy has been home to see her, for I wish everyone all the comfort they can have. I think if we could have a visit we could be as happy as the best of them. It would take all the time to write and tell all we would like to tell each other. But it is a great comfort to us to write what little we do if it is a slow way of exchanging thoughts. I suppose Kate is all right. She has got a silk dress. Well, if she can afford it, I am glad. Steve thinks he has got the nicest woman in the world. Every man ought to think so, I suppose. But I guess few women have done as you have this winter, and I hope you can have me to help you next winter. And I think it will be so.

Aunt Rachel is a great woman ain't she. She won't take comfort herself, of let anyone else if she can help it. I bet she thought strange when you told her what you did about men being away so the woman could take comfort.

As to getting a furlow Louisa, the Commander of regiments and divisions can grant furloughs not to exceed 30 days at 5 per centum at a time. That is 5 out of a hundred at a time. And then it is subject to the approval or disapproval of the General. And they don't grant furlows longer than 10 days. A fellow don't stand a very good chance to get one anyhow, and I should hate to ask and be refused. And I should hate to take a 10 day one for I'd rather have a 10 year one, wouldn't you. But I may try to get one by and by.

I wrote to Brandt to find out how much we owed him, and have got no answer. Perhaps he didn't get the letter. Your new dress is nice. I am glad he sells calico and factory so cheap. That is the place to buy. I have the money I got for my watch and will send you part of it if you want it. But I will wait until I hear from you, for I hope we shall get some pay before long.

I hope you have got your jewelry all safe. I am sometimes fearful that you won't get it. I guess I will do without a watch and see if it won't agree with me as well as it does to do without a woman. You weigh 9 lbs. less than last summer. I have forgot how much you weighed then. How much do you weigh now? You always wished yourself poor, so maybe you will get your wish. If you only feel well, it don't make much difference poor or fat. But if you are like to get very poor, I shall have to come home.

Well, I am looking for a letter from you every day now, for it is about time. I won't finish this until tomorrow and maybe I will get some news to rite.

Thursday morning, March 26th. Yesterday afternoon there were 300 cavalry came here and they are here yet. We were all on guard last nite. If the rebs come here, we will know it before they get here for we have patrol guards out all the time. How long this cavalry will stay here I don't know. They belong to the 6th Michigan Regiment.

One of our neighbors here is agoing to leave. He has a little place here, but he used to live up north. He is going to leave Virginia and go to Erie County, Pa. His name is Bingham. The old man was taken to Richmond by the rebs and kept in prison 55 days. They treated him shamefully and he is sick of living here.

I was on guard 6 hours last nite and I am a little sleepy today, but I do not have to work today. But I have got to go on guard again pretty soon, so I must close. I guess you are tired of reading this trash, but if I had time I would write more.

B. A. Cook

No. 37, Vienna, Virginia, March 29, 1863 (Monday)

Dear Louisa,

I take a few moments to write to you and let you know that your letter of the 23rd is at hand. I received it Saturday. I was sorry to hear that you was sick. Don't you think you could get some pills that will help you and bring things regular. I have seen such advertised. You must do something for it if you are agoing to cut up in that way. But I hope you are better and all right now. I was very glad to get the news from Danville and that Mother has arrived.

I have lots of news for you. Yesterday, what should appear to us but the 144th and 127th Regiments. They have followed us up here. The report was last nite at 11 o'clock that the rebs were at Centerville. But we hear so much there is no use thinking of what we hear . . . how long the regiments will stay here or how long we shall stay in he wood business. Some think there will be a battle at Bull Run again, but we can't tell how that will be. The rebs are getting the worst of it every day for they are running short of clothing and provisions. They have got to get out and get something or do worse.

A stood picket on picket last night, but I suppose our company won't have to do nite duty any more while the regiments are here. Our business will be to handle wood every day and sleep nites. Our company had more men fit for duty than any other in the regiment. It has been a very sickly in the regiment since we left. There are not 500 men in our regiment fir for duty, officers and all. Some have been discharged, some have died, some are sick in the hospital, and some are grunting. I am told that Thadius Sterling is dead. He was sergeant in our company. He died of fever last Saturday. We thought a good deal of Thad, as we called him, but he has left us. There was 6 of our regiment to be put in coffins yesterday. That is taking them pretty fast. March is a bad month for soldiers, the worst in the year I think. The weather will soon be settled here and the men will be healthier.

I have no good news to tell you only that I am well. That is good, aint it? Yes, health is everything. You have written good long letters most every time. I am ashamed of the short letters I have sent you, but I will try and do better in time to come. Sometimes I don't get time to write all I want to.

Well, I have eat my dinner and returned to converse with you my Dear Wife. Yes, how good it is to know we are not forgotten by those we love. What a consolation it is to read a few lines of love and kind regards when they come from one we know is true. It is gratifying to me to think of the days that are past and think how much comfort we have taken. We did not disagree, but were bound to regard each others feelings. I regret being deprived of the privilege of being with you when you were sick, and I hope the Lord will give us all health that we may see our family as it was last July. Oh how much comfort I have taken with my little family. It is a trial for us to thus separated, but we trust it won't be long before we can say peace is with us.

The truth is the rebel soldiers want peace and are discouraged. I hope you will be careful of your health and don't go to wading in the snow to make sugar. I hope I can spend you some money before long so you can buy sugar and everything you need. I will send you and Mother each 2 dollars now. It will be better than nothing. I am afraid you won't get the jewelry for I don't hear anything from him. I have wrote to him twice and sent him 3 or 4 dollars, and have got no returns as yet. But it may come out rite yet. The cost of your jewelry, or what it cost me is $1.25 . . . valued at $8.00. I am sorry you have not got them.

My little girls, how are you. Tell Ma to write something for you. Tell her something to write. If I can't see your faces, I want to hear a speech from you. You must be good to Ma and mind her and do what you can to help her. Your hair I keep very close, and was pleased to get it. From Pa to Hatty, Emma, and Mary.

Now Wife, this letter is long enough, is it not? If it aint, I guess it will take you long enough to read it at least. I will write to Mother tonight if I have time and send it with this.

Your ever,

B. A. Cook

Unnumbered letter, Vienna, Virginia, March 29, 1863

Dear Mother,

I will now try and answer your letter which I was very glad to get. One reason why I did not answer it before was because I thought it would hardly get to Kingston before you would leave. But now I have a little time and will try to improve it by telling you some of the events of the day.

There is a good deal of stir around here for there are 2 regiments of infantry here and a regiment of cavalry. Also a battery of 6 guns and more close by. The news is now that the rebs are in considerable at Aldea some 25 miles from here. We are about 15 miles from Washington and 5 miles from Fairfax Courthouse and 14 miles from Bull Run at a place called Vienna. We have been here 4 weeks today, and it is 2 months since we left the regiment. Some say we are detached from the regiment, but I hardly believe it. We hear so many things that there is no truth in that one don't know what to believe. But Colonel Green in Washington gives us great praise for getting more wood than any other company, and wants to keep us. But Colonel Hughton and all of our regiment tried to get us back a month ago, but they did not do it you see.

Now I want to hear all about the boys and where they are and what your plans are for this summer, and everything in general. You must take time and write to me, for you and Louisa are the only ones that will write to me. I hope you will pardon me for neglecting to answer your last so long. I will try and be a better boy for time to come.

How things change in a short time in our neighborhood. Some have gone the way of all the earth since you and I left there. Thus we see that Death is not confined to the army, but Death will find us where we are. And may it be our lot to be found prepared to meet it at any hour, that we may meet in Heaven with those that have gone before.

We have no snow here. It is quite nice weather yesterday and to-day. Saturday it rained all day and it was very muddy. But the mud is pretty well dried up now. I have had a good roof to sleep under and have enjoyed myself very well. I guess that I am as heavy as I was 2 months ago.

Monday eve. Everything is quiet here. We have eat our supper and I can write a few lines more and close.It is now time the troops were moving. And they are moving and we will hear of some fighting before many weeks. I think the fighting will be all or nearly all done the following summer. The darkest time is just before day and I hope the day is close at hand when the old flag will wave in every state both North and South.

Good nite Mother,

Bishop A. Cook

Here I enclose a little greenback for you. B.A.Cook

APRIL 1863

Vienna, Va., Feb 29th to April 11th
Camp Cloud's Mills, Va., April 11th to April 15th
On Steamboat *Hero,* April 15th to 16th
Norfolk, Va., April 16th to 17th
April 12th to May 5th, Siege of Suffolk, Va.

History summarization pages 86 through 87

In the early morning of the last day of March a severe snow storm visited us, the snow falling to a depth of one foot. On April 10th orders were received directing the division to move back to former camping grounds, and on the 15th further orders were received directing it to be embarked on transports at Alexandria and by twelve o'clock of that day we were on board the vessels provided and moving down the river. On the afternoon of the 16th we were so far down the Bay that we could look out upon the Atlantic and at six we were at Fortress Monroe, where we stopped long enough to receive orders which directed us to proceed to Norfolk. At Norfolk we found our destination was Suffolk, Va., where the Confederates under Longstreet were just now making a special demonstration with the intent to open up a way for the Confederacy to the sea. That portion of the Regiment that came on the transport *James Lewis,* debarked and bivouacked on the dock, waiting the coming of the rest of the Regiment. The next morning the balance of the 144th having arrived in the night we took the cars to Suffolk. About three o'clock in the afternoon we reached Suffolk and went into camp on the north of town. The continuous roar of cannon, the frequent bursting of shells and the desultory firing on the picket lines indicated that the siege was on and both sides intent on doing the other harm. Our encampment was so near the rifle-pits of the enemy that the bullets would whistle pst the tents, sometimes entering them. In some of the camps men were wounded in their tents.

No. 38, Vienna, Virginia, April 3, 1863 (Note: this is his birthday)

My Own Dear Wife,

This evening finds me well and trying to converse with the choice of my youth. I am happy to hear that you are getting better, but am sorry to hear Emma is sick. I hope you are all better now. Yours of the 26th got here tonite, so I have got 2 letters from you this week. And Al wrote some in your letter, and I think the picture very nice.

I have no news to write except that the regiments are here yet and we are in the wood business yet. Probably will be for some time. If the boys don't stay at home this summer, I guess we had better try and get one of Uncle George Cook's boys to come and do the work on the farm this summer, hadn't we? Hire him by the month and keep him all the time. What do you say? Let Al have the pin if he wants it.

I sent a letter to you this week with $4.00 in it. I hope we will get some pay before long, perhaps next week. If we don't, I will send you $2.00 in my next, for I have most $4 left and I will divide again.

Mother is with you I suppose. You and Mother must find something else to talk about besides political matters. She is entitled to her opinion, and she is the eldest, so let er rip as you say. I hope this will find you all in good health. You said in your other letter that Mercy had gone to the oyster supper with John. Did you mean Hat or Mother? Mother cannot think that my coming to war was what you said, for she knows better than that. If she means it, I will talk to her.

Those verses were very nice. I am sorry that A. Moore died last Saturday. Thus those two little ones are left without father or mother. It is hard to see them fall thus, but God knows best. We have no chance for meetings, but we have a chance to pray, thank the Lord. Russell Cook was here tonite and the Doctor is here vaxinating (sic). So I will have my arm pricked and see if it will be sore.

Well, the Doc has pricked my arm and I have resumed my writing. We don't get our mail near so regular as we did before we got so far from Washington. But if we get it 2 a week, it is better than nothing I tell you.

I have heard from Philadelphia since I wrote to you before. It was from a letter I sent since I sent for your jewelry. But he don't write, so I don't hear anything about the letter I sent concerning your jewelry. He merely puts the certificates and a handbill in an envelope and sends it to me. In this last draw, some of us drawed a vest chain valued at $15.00, but I drew a blank. I suppose it was a mistake, but I will do well enough. I hope you will get your prize yet. I will write to Dean again next week.

Give my respects to somebody that thinks enough of me to inquire after me. I will write soon again and write to Al. I was pleased to hear from him once more.

It is time to go to bed and I must close. Your short letter was thankfully received and here is one in return, for I want to send this in the morning.

Dear Wife,

B. A. Cook

No. 39, Vienna, Virginia, April 5, 1863

Dear Wife, I thought I would write to you again today, as I have time. Last nite was a very windy, stormy nite and the snow is a foot deep this morning. But we are in the depot yet. I suppose we shall move from here this week towards Falls Church to get a large quantity of wood that is cut there. Steve has sent Kate a map of 150 miles around Richmond that has every little place on it. You would be pleased to look at it, for you can see where we are all the time. I hope she will get it.

Well, this is great for the sunny south. If you have as much snow as we do here, accordingly you must be snowed under by this time. But I hope you will thaw out by the first of May. There are 3 regiments here. They have been digging rifle pits to stand in if the rebs should ever come this way. I suppose the letter I wrote on my birthday, the 3rd, has not gone to Washington yet, for I hear that our mail did not go yesterday. I hope this will find you all in good health and in good spirits.

Thad Sterling's father was here yesterday. He is going to take the body home with him. He said the people in Philadelphia think the war won't last long. I hope the boys are with you this stormy weather to do the chores and cut the wood. You won't have fodder enough to last 6 weeks will you? I think hay will be very scarce. How does your meat, potatoes, and grain hold out? If you have any bran or grain, give the sheep some every day. If you have not got it, get some if you can and not let them get as poor as they were last spring. For the sheep will be the main thing for your clothing next year. You will shear $30.00 worth of wool next summer, for wool will be worth twelve shillings per pound and maybe 2 dollars.

Now my gal, it is difficult writing here for there is all sorts of noise and if one don't get run over he is lucky. But it is nothing after one gets used to it. Well, to come right down to it, I would like to be by your side today. This you do not doubt. But if we were together today, we would be happy perhaps but for the thoughts that

116

I would soon have to leave you again. I hope to get home one of these days and not have to come back again. I often think of the many happy days of our past lives and often dream of thee. Last nite I dreamed Hatty Mercy was dead, but I soon awakened and rejoiced that it was a dream. But when we dream good dreams, how natural it is for us to wish them real. Thus we see what selfish creatures we are.

I guess you think I write often, but you are sick at home and I am bound you shall hear from me often. I suppose you will find no fault if I write every day, will you Wife? There has been a little fighting 12 or 15 miles from us with the cavalry. No important movement has been made yet, but as soon as the roads get settled, there will be something done. The people of this place say they never saw so backward a spring here before. I don't know but we shall stay in the wood business as long as the war lasts if it don't last too long.

It takes a soldier from 3 to 6 months to get his discharge. That is if he is bound to get one. He has to lay around in the hospital and feign himself sick and thus get his discharge. They say that some robust men get their discharge this way, and some that ought to have their discharge don't get it. But I don't want a discharge yet. I come down here to do something for Uncle Sam.

Yours in love Wife,

Bishop A. Cook

This letter is dated Apr. 63 (?) (The first page is faded to the point of illegibility typing begins on page 2)

to me I must answer them soon. I see in the paper that they are fighting in Vicksburg and Charleston and I hope they will be successful. The papers also state that the Rebel Congress is at work to have peace that was 3,000 women armed themselves with clubs and stones and went into the State house in Richmond and helped themselves. The militia was called out to stop them but they could not do it until Old Jeff came out and told them they could have what they wanted. You see it is hard for men to fight women. The regiment is at Vienna yet, you spoke about the 143 helping us get wood there is wood for us all to work at and government needs all we can get and have got to have somebody to get it all the time. Steve and the Goulds & I tent together yet there is no other 4 in Camp that hang together as we do.

Friday Morning 10th. John B. Cole our second Lieutenant that deserted had his trial and sentenced to be shot but Uncle Abe has saved his life but I suppose he will be finished in some shape. I must go to work now.

Friday noon. It is a very fine day and I hear that the probability is that Charleston is attacked but no particulars but it is hoped that our forces are successful. I suppose you have milk by this time and maple molasses, as to my getting home to do the haying it is uncertain but if things goes rite I think most of the fighting will be done in a short time. I can't think the war will last long if it does last until my 3 years have expired one 4th of my time will soon be out for 8 months is gone the 13th of this month. You say you want to see me you have so much to tell me why don't you write it now. I have wrote everything I can think of but I would say that one of our Company went to the Hospital today but we have had pretty good health since we left the Regt. E. W.g(?) is in the hospital and Aaron Travis. I don't think they will be of much service to Government but I guess if they were at home they would soon be all strait.

Saturday 11th. I find myself 15 miles from where I was yesterday at this time we are at Cloud's Mills 3 miles from Alexandria. We were relieved yesterday by Co. B and we have joined our Regt, but the wood Superintendent is up in (illegible) because we had to leave and went to Washington last night to see about it and said he would have us back in the wood business. Two men were here today to see the Capt. and have gone to Washington to try to get us ordered back in the wood. The Co. that relieved us did not like to leave the Regt. at all, we shall know in a day or two whether we go back or not. Our regt. marched the 15 miles yesterday after 2 o'clock and today I am on guard. I feel a little sore after carrying my house, bed and implements of war on my back yesterday--to be continued.

B. A. Cook

No. 42, Alexandria, Friday April 23, 1853

I seat myself to write to you and let you know we are well and aboard of the boat bound for Fortress Monroe or some other place. Our Regt went day before yesterday and I was left behind guarding the ambulance wagons but my knapsack and haversack went with them so it left me without anything to eat or anything to sleep under but when nite came I found a plenty to eat with (illegible) cook and a good place to sleep and yesterday we came on board the Boat and 5 of us found a place to sleep so we rested good.   I suppose we shall be on our way for Norfolk in an hour or so, it has been stormy for the last 2 days but I guess the storm is done. I am writing with a gold pen and silver holder that Dean sent me for my commission. It is a nice present. I hope you will get along and have hay enough for the cattle, I got Uncle Orlo's letter and have answered it, receive my hearty thanks for your good long letters. I would write more if I had time I want to send this before I start, from your dearest

B. A. Cook

Saturday 18th. I could not send this yesterday so I can write more. It is very pleasant today and we expect to reach Norfolk at 5 o'clock this afternoon. We passed Mount Vernon yesterday and Hampton Roads and Aquia Creek Thurs. We are passing down the Bay getting farther from home and those we love. The water is green and salt but smooth and nice, we are in site of Virginia yet but on the other side there is no land to be seen and the clouds come down to the water. Sergeant John Whitaker is with me he has been home on furlough and came down the river he said he saw Almus. He has money and is very kind to me he bought some bread and cheese and butter and I eat with him and I borrowed 50 cts. of him to buy tobacco and paper. I hope I shall find my knapsack for I had about 2 dollars worth of paper envelops and tobacco as well as my house bed and everything except what I have on you and all. But what Government furnishes me I will not have to loose anyway for I was left on duty and it was no fault of mine but my private property I shall have to loose if lost, I had our (your) likenesses and the hairs of your heads in my jacket and my gold pen so they are safe.

Rus. is on the boat and we have good times he is a clever boy that is so. Soldiers care for each other and must stand by each other, whether Steve has gone down the River or behind I don't know he was left on guard at the camp when we left and is there yet for what I know but the 2 Goulds went with the Regt. They were on the Boat when I was taken off for guard. They went on a steam boat but I am on what they call a barge and it has no sails but is towed by a little steam tug we are moving at the rate of about 8 miles an hour. How does the Pox get along in Danville I hope it does not spread if it does it will be worse than war. I suppose we shall see some fighting before many days but I may be disappointed and not see any fight at all. I am not over anxious to get in battle but if I do I don't expect to get kilt. Tell Nate I wish she had her pocket full of candy and when I come home she shall have some candy. Tell Hattie that I don't expect to winter down here next winter. If England sets in I think the war will soon end and I see by the papers that there is some prospect of it at present. I hear from a soldier that has lately visited the City of New York that if they go to drafting there it will be resisted to the last and to arms and it is doubtful whether we can whip the rebs with what men we have now in the field. I will cease writing for the present for I can't send this until I am on shore.

Sunday Morning. We are at Norfolk and will soon take the cars for some other place. I hope I can send this today. I will write again as soon as I get a chance.

Bishop A. Cook

No. 42 (double number 42) **Suffolk, Virginia, April 23, 1863**

Dearly beloved wife,

As it is raining this morning I have time to write a little to you and tell you I am well and living in hopes you are the same for I have not heard from you in several days as there has no mail come to us since we left Clouds Mills. We are encamped near the village of Suffolk near the bank of the Nansemond River and we have dug rifle pits as much as 2 or 3 miles. This place is well fortified there is forts and plenty of artillery and we have gunboats in the river. Our force is said to be 60 or 70 thousand strong. The rebs are on the opposite side of the river they are fortifying but our gunboats and field pieces distribute a few shells among them occasionally which keep them back a proper distance.

Our company was on picket yesterday at the rifle pits near the river bank and I saw a reb come from his hiding place and shoot twice. I could see the smoke from his gun but he was more than a mile off so he was not likely to do much hurt. However there was a 12 pound shell sent that way from a field piece that stood close by me and as the shell exploded I saw three men run like men running for their lives. The rebs do not bring any big guns to bear on us as yet, for if they have them it is difficult for them to plant them in site of here for as soon as they make their appearance in any shape there is a shell presented to them.

One nite this week 7 or 8 hundred of our men went over the river and took a fort without any fight. The rebs had just got their cannon fixed to prevent our gunboats from running up and down the river when our gunboat was firing at them and attracted their attention. When our boys came up in their rear and took them by surprise. There was 125 men and 6 cannon and 10 tons of ammunition all told and nite before last they got 8 or 9 more reb prisoners. I did not go to town to see the prisoners but some of our company saw them.

Well it continues to rain, the fruit trees are in bloom and everything is lovely here. They say it is only 17 miles from here into North Carolina. I think Virginia is a very large and wealthy state. Norfolk is 23 miles from here and is quite a large place. Suffolk is a smart little town. I suppose the rebs are after these 2 places and they are worth fighting for.

Norfolk is situated on the Elizabeth River and there is a good chance to defend the place by water as the river is navigable at that place. But we expect the rebs will have to do without these places yet a while.

Oh, I am anxious to get a letter from my old wife but I know it is not your fault for you have write often without doubt. But I don't expect we can hear from one another as often as we have heretofore.

But I hope we can get the mail once in a while or we can't stand it can we. Well I suppose the snow is nearly gone up there and Spring has got there and I guess you will be glad to see warm weather once more, won't you.

I suppose you are anxious to know when I am coming home, well when the war ends I expect to come home or if I get wounded I shall try and get a furlough.

I suppose we are likely to be in a fite any day but I guess we shant do much at fighting very soon for I think the rebs wont attack us here. But probably we will cross the river and hunt them.

But I heart the rebs give us until 8 o'clock this morning to surrender this place but it is noon now and the place is all rite and I guess it will be for all their takeing it very soon.

There is lots of water around our tents and a few drops come in through the tent occasionally without any invitation. The soldiers here with a few exceptions are as happy and cheerful as tho they were agoing home next week. To see us and hear us here you would not think we ever thought of danger. I guess it is going to clear off this afternoon the robins are singing sweetly and the rain has ceased to fall.

Give all the good folks my respects.

> I think often of thee Dearest L
> And I hope this war will soon cease
> So I can come home my story to tell
> And live with those I love in peace.

B. A. Cook

Written on the side of the letter--Harriet M. Cook be a good girl, E.M. do. Mate, do.

No. 43, Camp near Suffolk, Monday April 27th 1862(?) 63

Dear wife

It is with pleasure that I write you a few lines to inform you that I have received your letters No. 43 & 44. I was almost certain you were sick when I was on the way here for it seemed so to me our mail had got regulated so it comes every day. It came last Saturday for the first. I have been in great suspense the last 2 days concerning you for Kate wrote to Steve that you were sick. But I am greatly relieved this afternoon to get another letter from you. I am happy to hear that you are better. Oh, how I wish I could of been there to help and console you in your sufferings. But thank the good Lord he is able to bring us through all our trials. Knowing this let us trust in Him.

I have not felt very well yesterday and today. I have eat but little except a few crackers and some of the dried berries you sent me last winter. Now hear me you must not work so hard. Keep out of the Sugar Bush for you have enough to do without going there to carry sap and cut wood to boil it.

The paymaster is here and we expect some pay this week so in my next letter I will send you something to get Sugar with and help you through the Spring. I am glad you have a new milch cow and hope you will have good luck in raising a team.

It is quite warm today and pleasant. We have good water here and it is a fine country for nature has done much here. And yet it is not what it ought to be it is not like our free States for there when one travels by water or by rail they will see fine villages every few miles. But here the Villages are 20 and 30 miles apart and then there is not the neatness there is at the North.

The other day we were in line of battle but did not leave our camp. There was 8 thousand of our men went out to feel of the rebs a little at one point about 3 miles from here. And drove them from their entrenchments into the woods and then retreated back to their own lines of breastworks. There was a few killed on both sides. We were called out in line of battle every morning at 4 o'clock gest to please some officer. The rebs may attack us anytime and they may fall back to some other place and not fite here at all. But time will tell.

You must not have so much trouble about me for through the help of the Lord I am coming home if it is his will. What a blessing it is to have a hope of meeting in a better world if we are not permitted to meet on earth. But I hope to see your face in a few months. We are to be mustered again the 30th f this month.

I have no particular news to write so I will tell you about the negro town here. There is in site of here about 800 colored persons that have gained their freedom and assembled here. And they have built them nice little houses so they have a nice little village. Them that are able to work work at digging entrenchments. One old fellow told me that he and his family draw rations that is so much meal and so much meat and they had plenty to eat. They have built a school house they have over 100 scholars. They have male and female teachers. There you see they have a chance for education, they say that 6 sheets of note paper like this is worth 10 cts here but I bought a quire for 25 cts and brought it here knowing it would be higher here.

I feel pretty well this evening it is a very calm nice evening. And soldiers feel as happy as so many frogs in the spring. I hope dear wife this will find you well but I fear it will be several days before you will recover entirely. I hope you will be careful of your health for my sake and for the sake of those dear children for what would they be without their mother.

Love

Bishop A. Cook

Tuesday morning 28. I will write a few lines this morning to let you know that I feel pretty well and hope you do. There was considerable firing last night and yesterday afternoon among the pickets, I hear that Stonewall Jackson has come with 30,000 reinforcements so maybe they will attack us soon. But we have a large force here and they will find it out if they attack us. There is all kinds of stories afloat here and one can hardly tell what to believe. Yes it is hard for us to be parted thus but let us trust in God who is able to keep us and protect us. I hope and pray that we may be spared to enjoy each others society many days to come. But life is short at longest in this world but let us try to live so we may be happy in the world to come where life will never end. Wife I will write often to you if I can't write long letters for I know that a letter is prized highly by you and you are anxious to know something about my welfare. I know how you feel when you don't get a letter from me after you think it is time you should get one. The time is very long but one thing remember that is when I am on the move. I have no chance to get a letter mailed. Now wife I will close as breakfast is ready and I have other duties to perform. I have written all I know.

Yours ever, Dear L.

Bishop A. Cook

125

No. 44, April 29, 1863, No of Allotment 3254

Dear Wife

I could not send my letter yesterday as I expected so I will write a few words and enclose this 40 dollar check and a five dollar bill for I received 4 months pay, 52 dollars, I will keep 7. I dont know but we shall have to move from here before tomorrow morning. You will lay this money out to good advantage for I may not get any more in 6 months. But i hope you can collect some this spring to pay our debts. You must write often and I will do the same. I hope you will get both of these letters in about 4 days and I hope they will find you recovered from your sickness.

> From your soldier boy
> Bishop A. Cook

No date but following No. 44 in the stitched portion

Dear Mother

A few words to you. I am very glad it was you could be with Louisa when she was sick for then is the time when one needs friends by their side. I hope you will stay there as long as you can. I am needed at home but I am here and expect to live through and come home. The time passes away much faster than I expected it would. I would like to hear from you again.

> In God is my trust
> Our cause it is just
> And conquer we must
> Though many lay in dust

> B. A. Cook

MAY 1863

May 1st, Port Gibson, Miss.
May 1st to 4th, Chancellorsville, Va.
On Steamer *Spaulding,* May 5th to May 7th
West Point, Va., May 7th to June 1st.

History summarization pages 90 to 105

In the afternoon of May 1st the brigade was called out to cover the return on General Corcoran's Brigade. He had made a dash against the enemy's works, carrying an outer line, but was repulsed on reaching their strongly fortified main line. Eight men killed in this action were buried in a graveyard near our camp on the next day. On May 3rd a reconnaissance in force was ordered, the troops crossing to the west side of Nansimond by means of a temporary bridge made by using the gunboat *Smith Briggs* as the center pier. Soon a piece of woods was reached in which the Confederates made a stand having some buildings to shelter them. After a short skirmish the enemy gave way. By noon they had been driven within their main line and met our advance with a hail of shot and shell.

Prisoners taken described their works as being very strong and indicated that it would involve a heavy battle with great loss should we attempt to assault them. The 144th was in reserve division and did not take part in the active fighting of the day. On the 5th of May the Regiment had directions to provide itself with three days rations in haversacks and on the same day went by rail to Norfolk, where it was embarked on the ocean steamer *Spaulding* which proceeded at once to West Point, Va., reaching there a little after noon of the seventh. On the 23rd the Rebels made known their presence in our vicinity by firing on the mail boat *Swan*. They had posted a section of artillery on the bank of the York River, about two miles from West Point and opened on the steamer when within range; but the plucky Captain brought his vessel in with flying colors and with but little harm done to it.

Col. Hughston bade the 144th farewell on the 27th and left for Delaware County, having resigned his position as Colonel of the Regiment. On the 29th, Col. H. J. Kilpatrick, 2nd N.Y. Cavalry, afterward Maj.-Gen. Kilpatrick reached White House Landing with his brave troopers, four hundred strong, with whom he had made his successful raid around Richmond, passing within a mile of the city and inside the fortified lines.

On the same day that Col. Kilpatrick reached our lines, Generals Dix, Keyes, and Peck came to West Point to attend a council of war. The conclusion of the council was that the troops should be withdrawn from West Point at once. Transports however, did not appear until the 31st, when troops and material were moved to Yorktown.

No. 45, Monday morn, Suffolk, Va., May 4, 1863

My Dearest Wife

It is with extreme pleasure that I take this old pencil and answer your letters No. 44 and 45. The latter I received yesterday while on the field of battle. We have had considerable of a time the last 3 or 4 days and nites. Last nite was the first nite I had a chance to lay down and sleep all nite in sometime. For we have been called out at all times a nite. Sunday morn at 3 we were called out and went over to town and was held in reserve while some 6 Regt. went over the River to skirmish with the enemy but about 11 o'clock the ambulances came in occasionally with wounded men. At 12 we were marched across the river accompanied by 2 other Regiments. After crossing the river we were ordered to rest which we did by sitting on our blankets until 6 p.m, when we were ordered to advance to guard a battery which was throwing shell at the rebs at a furious rate.

And they the rebs sent some unwelcome thing over our way but they done very little hurt. It was not long however before we could not hear any thing of the rebels. So as it was getting near dark and the field was ours and no enemy to fite the artillery returned and then we followed it to the river. Which after they crossed with their cannon and horses we crossed and came to our camp where I am now writing. This is the second skirmish that has been near here and we have had no chance to fire on the rebs yet. But I am satisfied if I never get close enough to shoot at them. The 89 N.Y.S.V., the 103 N.Y.S.V., and one of the Rhode Island Regts. were engaged skirmishing. They drove the rebs from the field into the woods then the rebs got up into trees. The 89 took a double quick and fired at them there.

They came tumbling and jumping out of the trees and skedadelled. I should think by the ambulance wagons I saw there was over 50 wounded on our side and several killed, among whom was the Col. of the 103rd N.Y.S.V., well I have wrote enough about this.

11 o'clock. I have been out drilling, it is pretty warm it is good weather for farming and I see by your letter you wish me to say something about your farming. Well your best way is to get some one to draw manure onto the ground we planted last year and plow it and that is as much as will be profitable to plant. It is not worth while to try to sow any thing as you would have to hire it all done and help will be scarce. I guess you will have money to buy oats for Jenny cheaper next fall than you can raise them. If you have hay enough this year you will have enough next year if you can manage to mow the same amount of ground over. Which you will do if you run the fence as you mentioned. That is from the colts pasture up to Steves line.

For the oat and spring wheat ground will be to now this summer in place of that back of the colt pasture. You need not fear having too much pasture for we never had half enough. But try and get it fenced so as to give the stock part of it at a time while the rest is growing and they will have enough to eat and be peaceable. Now if you can make any improvement in this plan you are at liberty to do so. If the weather is favorable it will be time was up and time to plant (illegible) and make garden, when you get this.

I hope you have received the letters I sent from here. One contained a 40 dollar check and a 5 dollar green back and I think I will enclose another 5 in this for I have got over nine dollars. For I have got some that I had lent months ago. If I do it will make you an even 50 dollars for this time, and it will help farm it some. Some in our company have spent 14 or 15 dollars since payday but I have hardly spent as many cents. It is but little use to pay out money here for one cant get the worth of it if he does everything is so high. But I have to buy paper and envelopes, stamps and tobacco but I have enough on hand to last 3 or 4 weeks. So you see I am all rite.

I have got a certificate that I will send to the boys if they want them. I will enclose them in this letter so they can send and get the things if they like. As to the sewing machines, I think if you and Charley go into it you can make some thing. You need a sewing machine very much and perhaps you had better get 6 of them and see how they will go. I think Chas could do pretty well selling them. We are having a nice shower to lay the dust.

Now wife I am highly pleased to know you are so punctual; in writing to your old boy and I will try and comply with your request as far as writing often is concerned. For I know it does you good to hear from the one you love. If it was not for your kind letters I should be quite disheartened at times. But when I hear from you often I feel all rite, there is some talk that we are going back to Norfolk soon. For I suppose the rebs are leaving this place and have given up taking it at present. I think they are wise to do that, we have good news of late our armies are too much for the rebs at all points.

Yesterday was the day Charleston was to be attacked. I hope our forces will succeed in taking that and hold it for that is equal to Richmond as it is the stronghold of the rebs.

I suppose Hat makes you think of me every time she moves or speaks. So if you cant see me you can see my acts through her so there is nothing wrong about that. I would give a good deal to see my little girls, you better believe. But I think this was will soon play out so I can come home to see you all and then we will have grand times wont we. Does Meate grow and she is going to school this summer. Things are quiet here today more so than they have been before since we have been here.

The weather is very fine the lilac are in bloom and summer is here and so am I and I suppose it is rite I should be here. But is is hard to be a soldier especially when one has a loving family at home. If I had no one that loved me I dont know but I had as leave be here as any where, that is so.

I have jest eat my dinner, I had bread and boiled fresh beef for dinner. I have gest bought some Maple Sugar 2 little cakes about 2 mouthfuls apiece and gave 10 cts for them. It tastes quite natural.

I hear that the rebs have retreated and one white man and 7 Negroes come over and gave themselves up. They say our artillery last nite made great work among the rebs. It put them all in a fluster and they had much the hardest of the battle. It is so warm today that a fellow sweats sitting still. It is as warm as any June day I ever saw.

There was two of our ablest men said they were sick yesterday. They got over the river and expected to have to go fiting. So they fell out and staid behind. But I dont see but they are well enough today. Perhaps seeing the wounded made them feel rather stronger. It is not a very pleasing site to see so many wounded soldiers. Some shot in one place and some another. The slightest would I saw was one fellow had the skin jest grazed on the cheek so it bled a little. Some ware shot through the heel, some in the arm. Well I guess you are tired of reading so I will close this hoping you can read it and receive the contents cordially. This 5 will buy you a sewing machine if you and Charley go in to that business and have some left to buy thread with. I remain the same

B. A. C. to L. M. C.

written up the side of the last page When I want money I will send for it

No. 46, Suffolk Va., May 5, 1863

Dear Wife it was yesterday I sent a letter to you with 5 dollars in and I hope you have received the check and money I sent you last week. We pulled up stakes this morning and came here to town and are waiting for cars to take us to Norfolk. We shall probably go to fortress Monroe from there to some other place.

The rebs have left here they got badly whippet Sunday. There has been hundreds of em picked up and brought in here yesterday. Some come in of their own accord one officer came and give himself up and offers to fite on our side. Many of their soldiers are bare footed and some of them are good lusty looking men but they are pinched for rations. They don't draw only about half as much as we do and salt is very scarce with the rebs.

I thought I would write on this letter and send it to you, as it is a good letter, and has the details of the engagement which I want you to have. I got this letter last nite accompanied by yours wrote in Kates room. Mr. Brandt sent me 4 stamps in this so I will have to write to home again. I cant agree with Mrs. D. any better than you can as to her sentiments. I hope you will be careful of your health and try to doctor your throat if you have a cough maybe you could get some Balsom that would help it. I hope you will have good success in getting help to farm it. No more now

Norfolk, Wednesday Morning 6th May 1863

Dear L this morning finds me well after being out in the rain all nite. We are to leave here today on the Steamer *R. S. Spaulding.* I will write soon as I can again. I hope this will find you well.

Ever yours, B. A. Cook

No. 47, West Point, Va., May 10, 1863

Dear Wife,

I am happy to tell you I am well after being exposed to the storms of the last week and sleeping on the ground 2 nites. I don't mind sleeping on the ground when it is dry but when it is so wet and rainy it don't go so good. There is several of our Company sick. I hope you have got the letters I sent you in the past 2 weeks, 4 in number. No. 44 had the check and $5.00 I sent No. 43 at the same time on the 4th of this month I sent No. 45 with $5.00 in it the above letters I have had no answers to. But I hope you have got them ere this. Steve got a letter from Kate this morning it was wrote one week ago. I guess I shall get one from you the next mail. The weather is very nice today. This morning 8 or ten of us went down to the forks of the river and went out into the river and got some Oysters. So I have had all I wanted to eat. We came from Norfolk to Fortress Monroe from thence up the York River to the forks. Then we debarked and marched about a mile and a half where we are encamped.

We are 5 or 6 M strong. Beside we have some cavalry and artillery. We have all been at work building breastworks and digging rifle pits. It is surprising to see what a few thousand men can do in

133

a short time. This can be made a very strong place for the river is so the gunboats can come up each side of us as we are situated on the point. There was a railroad from here to Richmond but the rebs have taken the rails to Richmond. We are near 40 miles from Richmond.

Hooker has been engaged with the enemy but we hear various stories as to his success. But we are waiting to get the official report which I hope to get soon. If he is successful he is to get his supplies from here and we are here to hold this point and repair the railroad and guard the stores. We may stay here all Summer and things may work our so we will leave here this week. But I hope we wont have to March much this hot weather. When folks find you have got money I hope you can get enough to put up the fences and other work you want done.

I hope your health has improved since I heard from you last. Oh how I would like to be at home today with my little family. But I am thankful I am as well off as I am. I have been favored with health thus far and hope shall be for the future.

Dear Wife the months are long and dreary while we are separated but I hope you will enjoy yourself as well as you can and I hope you will not be deprived of my company as long as you have. For I hope this war will end in a few months. I can imagine how everything looks at home, so I have not forgot how home looks yet. Neither have I lost the desire to be with those I love best.

If I live to get home I think I will know how to prize a poor mans home better than I did when I left it. I have seen many nites that I would of been very glad to get into our barn and lay down on the floor to sleep. But a soldier gets used to such hard fare by degrees and I don't know but he can stand as much as a beast.

Our Cavalry have taken some few prisoners here. There was a few around here when we came. I see one pretty decent fellow that was taken, he was a teamster he had 4 mules and a wagon loaded with corn, he had got of some of the rebs here. The team and wagon and corn come very acceptable and the man said he wished the leaders of this was on both sides ware obliged to come out alone and face each other and fite it out alone. He thought they would soon compromise, he said we never could take Richmond with any force we could bring against it unless we cut off their supplies. I guess I will wait and see if I can't get a letter from you.

Monday, May 11. This day is very nice and we have the most of the day to ourselves. So I have done some washing this forenoon and have been reading the *Tribune* of the 9th to see how Hooker came out.

I think the rebs got the worst of it without doubt you will see the news before this reaches you so I will not write concerning it. But I must say I think the rebs have all they can tend to about this time for the Yanks are getting their army pretty close around them. To close for the rebs comfort. I suppose we shall have to go and dig some tonite while it is cool. As I told you we come up the York River you can see it on Kates map, we are encamped between the 2 Rivers, Mattapony and Pamunky. They are large enough so gunboats run up some piece. I hope I shall get a letter from you tonite.

I believe I will finish this and send it this afternoon and when I get one from you answer it. We are called up every morning as soon as it is lite but one don't want to sleep as much on the ground or on rails as they would on a good bed.

I have no more to write now this is three I have wrote wince I received one yours ever

B. A. Cook

(In large letters on the bottom of the last page is written) **Where is Mother?**

No. 48, West Point, May 15, 1863

Dear Wife,

I will answer your letter No. 48 which I received the 13th. I ought to of answered it yesterday but we had to go digging at 6 in the morning and come in at 6 at nite so I had no time. We have to go at 6 this morning but I will try and finish it today some way. I am very glad that our mail goes and comes so prompt. Your money will help you through the spring pretty well and I hope some body will pay you what they owe you so you will have lots of money. You say mother has gone to the river to live. Does she rent her place or does Charley intend to work it? You say C. is going to help you, I am sure glad he can live with you this summer. I shall be very thankful I guess everything will work rite don't you?

Now as to where you plant corn and potatoes, plant them just as it is convenient. There is not much difference in the ground. It will raise a nice lot of stuff for it is better than it was last year for I put a little manure on it and the manure this year will make it good enough for anything. E. Wily has not joined us yet and I think he don't intend to.

Capt. Plaskett has not resigned but I rather think he will, time will tell. You need not fear for me I don't know but I am as safe here as any where. I dreamed last nite that you and I was at Doc. Theems on a kind of a visit. I thought that I had just got back from the war and you stuck close to me and we took lots of comfort. We are now out at the digging we dig one hour and rest one hour so you see I have a chance to write to my love. You say to me keep up good courage that is good and I think I do for I am well and have as good courage as I did months ago. And the kind lines I receive from you make me happy. But I still am anxious for the welfare of my little family and wish to be with them. I am also anxious for the welfare of my country and hope to God that the was will soon end and we be able (illegible) to live together again. And I have faith to believe that our wishes will be granted. It is as good as any way to buy flour and meal to live on this summer.

Steve was telling a dream last nite he said he dreamed that he was somewhere and saw Kate to a party and she hardly noticed him. But he saw here and a fellow hug each other and kiss. I asked him if he supposed it was so he said he knew better, she want that kind of a woman. I said no more but I could not help thinking of the Sugar Party.

I suppose the fences are all down and everything is out of repair. But the worse of all is your health failing on account of my absence. Well I suppose your getting married was the best thing you could do for your health don't you? Well I would like to be there to drive stakes and one thing or other. So as to have everything rite but there is to many miles between us at present. How does the cows get along has the other one come in yet and what about the calve? How is Jenny? Mate is quite a soldier she thinks pa will be home when he gets the rebs all killed, bully for her.

There has been another bloody battle at Fredericksburg. The rebs claim a victory and we claim one to. Hooker fell back across the river but he got a fine lot of prisoners and some guns and the rebel loss was greater than our loss. I suppose you will see the news in the paper before you get this. We are in Gordons Division at present. I have seen letters from those that were in the late fite as Fredericksburg. Some Regiments lost but very few men, others lost a good many. W. Early is all rite yet he has stood it pretty good this week.

4 boys of our company went over the river and got 2 wenches and brought them over and what they done to them I don't know. But in the course of the day they thought that it would be cunning to take them to the general and deliver them as counterbands. So they proceeded accordingly but the general arrested the boys and has them in confinement. And I hope they will be punished severely for they are the worst boys in our company. They were Hancock boys. The general has forbid any burning of buildings or meddling with anything. But if they confiscate anything they must bring it to Headquarters and tell how and where taken. Yesterday there was 18 head of cattle and a flock of sheep drove in that were confis-

cated, bully for that. It is my opinion that the rebs will hear from Hooker soon again. I suppose you know the rebs have lost there best general Stonewall Jackson got shot in the arm it was amputated he has since died from the effects and the old fellow is buried and I hope he wont dig out again.

I had $4.50 this morning and I gave $1.50 for a pound of tobacco. So I have $3 left. That will last me a good while. I have now $2.00 worth of tobacco on hand and I have paper, envelops and stamps on hand so I am all rite. I have got used to soldiers living so I live first rate. We have pork and beef, beans, potatoes occasionally and coffee and sugar and some times soft bread but hard tack most of the time. If you would like to see one of them I will buy a paper and send to you with one in it. If you want me to. Steve is not well at present he has been off duty 2 days but he is at work today.

I don't know but I have wrote enough but I will keep at it if the lice don't bite to bad. They are very numerous in our Regiment, for the past week. I have found 5 or 6 on me. They are body lice I never saw one until lately, if you can put up some scotch snuff in a letter I think I can fix them. What I fitcht with me is most gone. If I had a lot of snuff I could fix a lot of it and if it kills the lice I can sell it at a high price. I want a little Camphor gum to scent it with. Then I am all rite for every body will want it. I can get grease here and mix it and sell it for 10 cts per ounce for every body is lousy and they will eat us up if we don't fite them. Thus you see we are forced to fite, we call them gray backs, and if we have no other foe to fite we must fite the lice.

It is most noon I have wrote all the time I could get since sunrise and I guess I will get quite a letter wrote if I keep writing. I suppose you know I like to hear from you often. It was 9 days before I got the last letter, after a week passes I begin to look for a letter with both eyes until I get one.

Well we have eat my dinner and we have this afternoon to fix up around our tents but I will finish writing. We have nice weather, the forest is all leaved out. The peach trees have got peaches on as big as beans. The corn is planted here some time ago and it will be time your corn was planted by the time you get this or it will be planted by the first of June. But I suppose you have got the potatoes planted by this time or nearly ready to plant them. You can plant the most of your tates in the garden and then you will have room for turnips, beans, and other things. I will close knowing that your taste and judgment is as good as mine. I remain as usual ever yours.

B. A. Cook

N.B. Direct to Bishop A. Cook as there is an Alfred B. Cook in the company.

No. 49, West Point, Sunday, May 17th, 1863

Dear Wife

Your letter of last Sunday is before me so you see I received it in due time. I was pleased to hear from the ones I love best and hear you was all well. I received a letter from Mother at the same time. They were both mailed the 12th and I must answer it today.

I wrote to Brandt yesterday and Aunt Hattiet, we had to attend roll call at 4 this morning. At nine we went out on inspection and have just returned so I will improve my time in writing. The weather is very fine and I would like to be by your side. I think it would be very gratifying to us. But we should be very thankful that we can hear from each other in this way.

Yes I remember 9 years ago of carrying little Hatty in my arms and gazing upon her little form with fatherly love. And I remember the morning after that when you went out to take the morning air. How feeble you was but you got stronger day by day until you could walk alone. How pleased I was to see your health improving with my little girl by your side. As you say little did I then think that I had got to take up arms in defense of our country. But thus it is but it won't always be so for I expect to come home and take comfort with my little family.

Benjamin Reynolds is here in our tent to see us today.

I am glad you have done something at farming. I hope C. will stay. Mother said he was going to help you this summer and I hope you and he can do well with the machines if you go into it. If George's pigs are decent they are worth 14 shillings a piece and I suppose you need a pig. As to the heifer I think you had better keep her if Mother won't take her away. If you can get a fair price for your old cow by and by let her go but save the youngest and best unless you can get a big price. Bet has no calf this spring and if she don't give much milk dry her off and she will get fleshy and low will give a good price for her. I don't know as she will ever have another calf without cutting her, after she is served to make her hold it as grandfather told me to. I done it year before last and she stuck but last year I neglected to do it so she is farrow. I didn't know as it had to be done every year, I didn't know but once was enough. I am glad the calves has fell.

I hope you can get the girls and self some new dresses. But if you send for the sewing machines that will take some money. But never mind that if there is a chance to get it back in a few weeks and more with it. Fir I hope you can collect enough this summer to buy what you need. And I hope to send you some more money in 3 or 4 months. If you get 6 machines it seems as tho C. could sell them in the course of the summer without spending too much time. Maybe some of your neighbors would like one and pay half down when they get the machine and 5 dollars in 2 or 3 months. Well I have no news to rite only every thing is quiet here and I see no signs of our leaving here very soon. Oh how cheering it is to get a letter from the one we love. I believe I have answered your letter so I will close hoping to hear from my little girls to. Charley wrote in Mothers letter and I have got to answer them today, from your soldier boy.

B. A. Cook

No 50, West Point, Virginia, May 20, 1863

Dear Wife,

I am happy to tell you that No. 50 found me well and it found me on guard duty on the evening of the 17th.

Well, we have got our tents arranged and fixed up very nice. In front of our tents we have poles stuck in the ground and bowed over and brush woven in so that it is very nice shade. We generally think that we will move soon. It is a pretty good sign when we are ordered to fix up our tents. But we may stay here for some time. It depends on how things move at Richmond and Fredericksburg. The rebs are considerably troubled of late for they see they are getting in close quarters, and Gears cavalry raid in Mississippi destroyed $8 million in property and stores that they needed very much.

I do not doubt but you feel that I am your best friend, but I am inclined to think you were fearful that I would not write often enough to you. You rather thought I would forget you after I got down in Dixie, but I know who loves me and who I love in return. I am your guiding star, yes very true, and I could have guided you astray. But no one but a coward and traitor would do that. It would be rendering evil for good and hatred for love. I won your affection and wherein I have not appreciated it, then I ask pardon for I never intended to underrate your good qualities. I reassure you that I have never had to regret marrying you and I hope you have not. Although you have suffered much and born many trails, I hope the remembrance of past joys and the hope of future comfort will help you to bear the present trial.

I have been sweeping the campground but I will try and finish this so it will go tomorrow. Yes, it makes one feel streaked to go up and face the foe and hear the booming of artillery that scatters the iron hail. It was Charles Cole that showed himself the one that came after Steve and me to go to Hancock to swear in. I learned after that he claimed he could not find his gun.

141

I am glad the fruit trees are doing so well and I am glad you are going to have some grapes growing. I have got to go to sweeping again.

Well, our sweeping is done and dress parade is done for tonight. Tomorrow we are to go on fatigue duty.

I hope you had good luck at Deposit. I am glad Mary is doing well and I suppose the big girls need me to look after them once in a while. I think it best to lay down the butter and sell it all at once because that way you will get something.

The papers bring pretty good news tonight. I think the rebs will get all the fight they want before long.

I hope this will find you well. Tell Charles that I will write to him this evening if I have time. I have had three letters from you in 5 or 6 days. I am running short of stamps with only 3 or 4 left. If I can't get some here, you will have to send some from home. I haven't seen any for sale here.

I have written often to you, but I can't get the start of you. What a blessing it is that we can hear from each other often. If we could not hear from one another, there would be no relief for our anxiety. As it is we hear often from those we love and we will trust God.

Generals Grant and Rosencrans are troubling the rebs of late. Hooker is reinforced and he will hit them so they will feel it before long.

There is a Negro living here close to our camp. He planted some corn and it is up.

The bugle blows for roll call, so I must close and wish you good night.

B. A. Cook

The following note to his brother-in-law Charles Alexander was included with this letter.

Dear Brother Charles,

I have eaten three hard crackers and drunk a cup of coffee for my supper and have lit a candle to write a few words to you.

This is nice country here for it is level, but it has been cursed by slavery. I was settled as one of the first states, but it lacks the nice villages such as we have in the north. It is a very common thing to see large fields grown up with bush. Last winter we drew hundreds of cords of wood off land that had once been cultivated. This country has been going down hill for a number of years, but if you and I had a farm here and the war was over we could make money like dirt as the old saying goes.

B. A. Cook

No. 51, West Point, Virginia, Sunday, May 24, 1863

Dear Wife,

I received the above No. 51 from your hand last nite and it found me well. I was happy to learn that you were all well.

I have no important news to write except that there was some cannonading yesterday down on the river a short distance below the point. I heard the rebs had a battery and fired at one of our boats, but they were soon put to flight by our gunboats. You will probably see it in the paper. The rebs are teased to think we are here and they may try to rant us when they get time. But they will probably consider well before they try to take this place for we have protection against artillery and cavalry. In fact, we are pretty well fortified.

The weather has been pretty warm the past week and the roads are getting very dusty. One of our company died last Friday. His name was Wm. Steinrod. He died of fever after being sick only a few days. He was a fine young man and one that attended our prayer meetings last winter. I trust he has gone where trouble and war is not known. I helped dig his grave. There are 6 or 7 of our company sick, but not dangerously.

I hope the blisters on your toes have gotten well. What makes you so poor? Are you sick or are you so anxious about me, or are you trying to kill yourself at work? I have told you often to try and take care of your health. Now do it for the sake of those who love you. I don't know how much I weigh. I guess 155 lb..

You must write how much you weigh for I have forgotten what your weight was last June. I think it is too bad that old cow never will be worth anything, will she. But your fruit trees are doing bully well. I took care in setting them and manured them. If I was there now, I would dig the grass away from them and leave the ground loose and put a little manure around them, and see that no worms built nests in them.

Sunday eve. Good news. Gen. Dix just got a dispatch from Gen. Grant that he has taken the first line of works and 57 guns and has the rebel Gen. Pemberton with his force surrounded. So if all works well, that wonderful place Vicksburg is in our hands.

I am glad you have gotten something in the ground. Where was Charlie that he only helped plant part of the potatoes or was he doing something else? I am glad you have got a yoke of oxen. I hope you will have good luck with them.

We have been in line of march in front of the Colonel's tent where he read the dispatch, and we gave three cheers for Gen. Grant.

I was out last nite to support a battery. We stood one hour each, but I lay on the ground and did not sleep much. My head aches a little tonite, but I guess some sleep will relieve it. Oh, if I could sleep with you tonite. Wouldn't we be happy. I think so. I am ordered to blow the lite out.

Monday morning. It is cool and looks like rain. We are called up every morning at daylite. This morning I have to clean the street, so I can write no more.

From your old boy,

B. A. C.

No. 52, West Point, Virginia, Sunday, May 31, 1863

Dear old gal,

I seat myself on the ground by the side of a pine tree to tell you I am well and to answer your kind letter No. 52. I received it Friday nite last accompanied by one from Aunt Harriet and Mother Dickerson.

The reason I did not answer your letter yesterday was because we had to pack up everything to be off at short notice. So we packed up and were expecting to move every hour. But the last evening we were told to take our blankets and lay down. So we did so and at 11 o'clock I heard the Colonel's orderly inquiring for the Colonel's hostler. I knew something was up. Well, directly the Lieutenant came and ordered us to fall in with gun, equipment and canteen.

We marched down to the river and tore down some earthworks we had put up, fearing they might be of some use to the rebs after we are gone. It is not likely we shall stay here 24 hours for we shall leave as soon as the boats come take us. I would like to tell you where we are going, but that can't be. Even the officers of the regiment don't know where they are going. We may land at Washington and we may land on the banks of the Mississippi. But let me go where I will, you are not forgotten and you shall hear from me often if it is the Lord's will.

Did Uncle B say anything about writing to me? I am glad he stopped to see you and helped you a little. That miserable old cow never will be good for anything. We have had to winter her for

145

nothing. If Jerry had taken her away last fall, it would have been better for him and us too. He said at Delhi last fall that if we had a mind to keep her and if she had had luck again and died, she would die his. But we were all in hopes she would have better lick next time.

Folks need not talk about you paying for her until they know something about the bargain. I hope he will get recruited up so he can take her and sell her. How do the heifers get along? Won't they both give as much milk as Jerry after the feed gets good?

I am sorry that Charles had to leave, but it may all be for the best. Is the manure all drawn out and the fences up? Who did the plowing? Have you settled with B. Evans for what he did last fall? He paid that note so punctual he deserves praise. Are you likely to get any money this spring? Tomorrow will be the first day of June and I suppose the money will begin to circulate and shell out of the hands of the lumbermen.

Did you get the letter I sent you from Brandt stating how much we owed him? About $53 I think up to the first of this month.

I hope to banish the gray backs with what you sent me. I am much pleased with the way you compounded it. I will send you a hard tack before many days. I guess you had good luck getting grape vines. There is a snake before me six feet long which one of the boys has just captured. I suppose you planted corn last week. I hope you will have good luck with your vegetable production this summer and I hope I can come home and eat some of them.

I am very glad your health has improved, but be careful and don't overdo. When you get tired, rest. And don't try to do too much in a day, but get up early and go to bed early. I am up every morning before the stars are out of sight, but I can't go to bed till after toll call at 8 o'clock. Then a feller is on guard or on picket or someplace two nites a week, so he don't sleep to hurt himself.

I don't write long letters, but I trust you will make some allowance and receive them with all the love I send you. Aunt Harriet's letter is in this. I will write again as soon as I get anything worthy of note. Every yours LMC,

B.A.C.

Sunday afternoon. I will write a little more as I have time. Very likely you are writing to me today. This writing is a great comfort, but I will be a happy fellow when I get close enough to talk to you and do away with this writing.

This is a lovely Sabbath and how I would like to be at home and walk out into the fields with you, and see the fruit trees and look in the garden. And then come to the house and sit down in a chair and eat a decent meal when suppertime comes, then do the chores, and then come in and play with the children a while.

And when bedtime comes, get into a good bed with a good woman that loves me, then get away trouble. I would be happy if I know myself. Home, home, I hardly dare think of home more than ten minutes at a time for fear of being homesick. I expected when I left home that I would be homesick down in Virginia, but I have not been troubled that way yet. But if I couldn't hear often from you, I could not stand it a month.

Give my respects to all inquiring friends, and any that wish to hear from me can by writing to me. I want to send this now, so I will close. Kiss the girls for me.

B. A. Cook

JUNE 1863

Yorktown, Va., June 1st to June 91h
> **June 6th to 8th, Milikan's Bend, La.**
> **June 9th, Beverly Ford, Va.**

Williamsburg, Va., June 9th to June 11th

Twelve Mile Ordinary, Va., June 11th to June 15th
> **June 13th to 15th, Winchester, Va.**

Barhamsville, Va., June 15th to 25th
> **June 25th to 30th, Rosencran's Campaign,**
> **Murfreesboro to Tullahoma, Tenn.**

Camp two miles north of Barhamsville, Va., June 25th

Camp four miles south of White House, Va., June 26th to
27th

White House, Va., June 27th to July 8th

History summarization pages 105 to 108

Transports however did not appear until the 31st, when
troops and material were moved to Yorktown. Here we debarked and went into camp on the old grounds occupied by
McClellan when he laid siege to the place and on grounds occupied by Washington when he had Cornwallis shut up in
Yorktown. While in camp at Yorktown we were joined by
our newly commissioned Major, Calvin A. Rice. He had been
promoted to this position from Captain in the 77th N.Y. Vol.
Another movement toward Richmond by the way of the Peninsula was begun June 9th, called the "Blackberry raid" by the
soldiers, because of the quantity of this fruit which the sol-

149

diers found growing wild in the fields and by the roadside of territory traversed. The first day's march brought us to Fort Magruder within the fortifications of Williamsburg and on the ground which marked the battle of Williamsburg in McClellan's campaign. A reconnaissance was made from Williamsburg while an advance was made to Twelve Mile Ordinary and the force encamped there. On the 15th, the 144th with several companies of cavalry were detached for a special movement to Barhams, nine miles away. It proved to be a sort of picnic for the several companies that were sent out to do picket duty among the farmers. One company drove the cows up regularly night and morning and attended to the milking. The owner tried to circumvent them by placing calves with the herd but these soon disappeared, while in camp some very toothsome veal appeared. On the 26th the line of march up the Peninsula was resumed and on the 28th we reached White House Landing. We found a large body of troops gathered here and others constantly arriving.

No. 53, Yorktown, Virginia, Monday, June 1, 1863

Dear Wife,

We left our camp at 9 o'clock last evening and came down to the dock, but we could not get on the boat until 5 o'clock this morning. We were steaming down the York River at 11 o'clock. We found old Yorktown to be a very good stronghold. The rebs evacuated this place last year. They thought the gunboats on the river and a large land force would be too much for them, so they dug out.

I don't expect to stay here long. We have not had much rest the past two nites. Yesterday I slept some and wrote to you, and this morning I took a nap on the boat. Last nite and the nite before I lay on the ground with my head on my knapsack and slept some. We are like the cattle--lay on the ground and take no cold. If I don't get a fever this summer I think I will make a bully soldier. We have got our tents up to keep the sun off and there is a good breeze, so it is comfortable.

Tuesday morning. I think there is some prospect of our staying here for some time, but cannot tell. Another young man from our Company is to be buried today. He had been sick for some time. His name was Fletcher.

Arthur Tompkins is here in a battery. He came to our camp yesterday and was pleased to see me. He got his discharge from the 56th Pennsylvania Vol. and went home sick a year ago last winter. But he got well and enlisted in the 8th N.Y. Battery where he now is. He has been here over a year. He doesn't have to move very often.

This is the place where Cornwallis surrendered to Washington. It is a very old place, but not much of a place. There are a few nice buildings and that is all.

We have nice weather and the wind blows a little. Steve and I have just been doing up 2 papers and 2 hardtacks to send to you. They will go with this letter tomorrow. Will write more later.

Tuesday after dinner. I have been to the burying of our comrade. He was buried in the Union Cemetery within a few rods of where Cornwallis delivered his sword to Washington.

The roses are in full bloom and peaches are more than half grown. If we stay here I think I will get my teeth into some of them next month. I look a little for a letter from you tonight. I was in town today. There are three or four nice buildings and the rest are regular Negro houses.

There is no great news, particularly in the papers today, but out army is still at Vicksburg and I hope they will take it before long. I am anxious to hear of its fall.

We have no drilling to do nowadays. There is some talk that we are going to Williamsburg about 12 miles from here. But we don't know anything, only as we are ordered.

There is not anything planted in this region. I guess you will raise as much as some of the southern planters this year.

Mother writes that she is in her old home. Charles writes about those clothes. Let him have them and make your own bargains. I am glad he can help you some. I was very glad to hear you are all well.

That old cow is a great trouble--it is too bad to be bothered so. Mother says Hat is with her. She thinks she will have lots of fruit for herself and you too. I am in hopes of getting home to eat some of it, but this war is a big thing and it moves slowly. When it will come to a focus no one on earth knows.

I am thankful to you for your frequent letters. I had a good dream last nite that I was with you and had a good time. I awakened and I was here and you were at home. I hope it won't always be a dream and I think God will spare us to meet again.

Wednesday, June 3rd. I have eaten my breakfast of hardtack and coffee and it is raining. But I am happy to tell you that I am well. I thought I would write these few words this morning for it will be one day later news from me when you get it. I will write soon again.

Ever Yours,

B. A. Cook

No. 54, Camp near Yorktown, Va., Sunday, June 7, 1863

Dear Wife,

I will improve the present hour by answering your No. 54 which I received yesterday. I have no important news to communicate only that Grant is still at work at Vicksburg with a determination to take it, and Banks is at Port Hudson bound to take it. This is the news I get from the *NY Herald* of yesterday.

I am pleased to hear your corn and things are up. I think you are a bully farmer, but I'm sorry you have to work so hard. We know when we hire anything done, it ain't half done, but we can't do everything ourselves. I won't scold not didn't intend to, but I don't want you to overdo yourself.

Cases like the fence falling down are extreme cases, but it is provoking to find so many cattle in mischief and so much fence down. I am sorry one of the sheep is missing, but maybe she will come out with another one with her. I hope so at least. It is time to shear sheep, but it is better to wait until they lamb for it is dangerous to handle them with lamb. I don't know where you get milk to make the spotted pig, the hog, and 2 calves grow much. But you can buy meal.

Yes, get yourself some things and go to quarterly meeting. How much have you got yet? I have $2.50 yet. You see I don't spend much down here, but if I was at home I would spend a pile, wouldn't I? HA. HA.

I am writing in a hurry. Please excuse my brevity in writing. I am happy to know that I have a true and loving wife and that I can hear from her so often. Our letters are worth everything to us while so far from each other. I have good courage and hope you have. I think the fighting will soon be over if our forces are successful this month. But if the rebs are able to resist us, then we have got to fight on. Time will tell.

It has been quite sickly, but few deaths in our regiment. If I was sick I should try to doctor myself instead of going to the doctor. I think this is a healthy place and it looks like we're staying here for some time.

The Conroe women have joined the regiment again. I suppose they have been to Washington ever since we left Alexandria. They arrived here yesterday. They had plenty of beans in the afternoon and evening.

Steve and I enjoy ourselves first rate. I got 3 eggs yesterday morning for 10 cents and fried them for my breakfast. In the afternoon, we (Steve and I) were detailed to go to the slaughter house to load some beef. We bought a liver for 40 cents. When we got to camp everyone wanted a slice, so we sold 50 cents worth and had enough left for our supper. This is the way we get most of our spending money.

I have 2 stamps besides the one you sent to mail this. We get our mail every day.

What do you hear about E.W.G. He has been ordered to his regiment and has not come. Some say he is in the convalescent camp but if he doesn't show himself before long he will be marked a deserter.

Oh, I must tell you, Col. Hughston has resigned and gone home and left us. Ain't that great. Capt. Plaskett is with us yet. He has been sick and hasn't had command of the Company in a month.

Monday morning, June 8th. All is quiet. It was very cool last night. I should think you had a frost up at your house, but I hope not to hurt anything.

There is a great talk about some regiments going home. Some say we are, but I don't see it. There is some talk that we are going into a fort here, but we can't tell. I wish it may be so.

Are you raising chickens this summer? Have you got your calves out to pasture yet? Are the beans planted? Have you one or two hives of bees at home? One died, but I have forgotten whether we had 2 or 3. I have asked enough.

The bugle sounds for drill, so I must go. So good day Love.

Bishop A. Cook

No. 55, Camp near Williamsburg, Va., June 10, 1863

Dear Wife,

I seat myself on the green grass to write a few lines to my own gal. It is only a day or two since I sent you a letter, but I will tell you of our move. The afternoon of the 8th we got orders to be ready to march at 10 a.m. on the 9th with 3 days rations in our haversacks and all our traps. So we started at that time and reached here in about 7 hours, making it 5 o'clock when we reached here. I suppose we marched about 14 miles in 7 hours. It was the first march we have had in a long time. The men fell out along the road and one or two died on the road. A great many threw away their knapsacks and the overcoats. Clothing of all kinds lay along the road. Very few of our regiment fell out or threw away their clothes. The 127th and 143rd were ahead of us and they fell our by the hundreds.

I succeeded in bringing everything with me and kept up to time/ My shoulders are pretty sore today, otherwise I am all right. We crossed the old battlefield last nite. You will recollect that Steve Leonard fell here at the battle of Williamsburg and many others, but we hold the ground. How long we are to stay here no one knows. Whether we shall get a fight here or move on we cannot say, but I don't expect to stay here long. We are on the same track that McCllean was on last year when he was on his way to Richmond. So I say onward to Richmond. I suppose we shall go up the peninsula.

We have pretty encouraging news from Vicksburg. I got a line from Charles A. with some stamps. I washed a shirt and a pair of socks this forenoon. I have to wash something in a mudhole without soap. I expect when I get home I can cook and wash and make a bed on the ground or on the floor, and you can do all kinds of farming and raise cattle. We have put up our tents to sleep under tonite. We were too tired to put them up last nite.

Wednesday eve. Latest news from the front is that all is quiet on the peninsula. The bugle blows for roll call. No signs of our leaving here tonite, but if we lay down we don't know but what we will be called up in an hour.

George Wheeler you know ran away last winter and went into the cavalry. They say he was taken prisoner and taken to Richmond. Then he was paroled and has come back to Alexandria in the paroled prisoner camp. I guess he will live to see this was end if anybody does.   E.W.G. is detached in the Invalid Corps so we shall see no more of him in this regiment.

My gold pen is spoiled. One of the points is off so I sold the holder for one dollar. I have got 16 stamps and 3 dollars in cash. The news now is that we are to march at 5 in the morning so good evening Dear Wife.

B. A. Cook

Thursday morning 4-1/2 o'clock. We are up and almost ready to start. We don't take knapsacks, but 3 days rations. We leave our tents. I suppose we are going on a kind of raid. I have no more time to rite. I will try and take care of myself.

Yours Ever,

B. A. Cook

No. 56, Near Williamsburg, Virginia, Friday, June 12, 1863

Dear Wife,

All is quiet in front. I was stationed on picket last nite. We retreated 3-1/2 miles and at 4 p.m. we stacked arms and lay down by them. About 11 o'clock several guns were heard in the direction of our pickets. The Colonel straddled his horse and we were up and ready to clench our guns in 3 minutes. The order was given directly to lay down again, which order we obeyed without hesitation. The firing was done probably by a party after fresh meat.

Sunday, June 14th. On Saturday morning I went and got some black cherries like on that tree that stands near the corner of the house. We rested all day Saturday. All nite we went on picket and I am now there. Someone came to the post near us and there were 4 balls sent after him. He got out. It was very dark, but we could hear him walking. We saw his footprints this morning.

It is cloudy today. I expect to hear from you when the mail comes. I have had no letter since I left Yorktown.

This is great paper to write on, but I left my paper and things in my knapsack at Williamsburg. But I am bound to rite to my old wife.

Every white man has gone into the Army that is fit for it, and the women and some darkies are left to farm. There is considerable growing here. In 2 weeks, if we are around here, we can have new potatoes. We have fresh meat when we are amind to go and kill it.

Our brigade has taken several prisoners and had one man killed and one wounded. That is all. We may go back without a fight, but time will tell.

When the Sutler comes I will get some paper and write to you. I know when you get a letter I wrote at Williamsburg you will be answering so as to hear soon from me again. This will let you know that I am safe and well and that is worth the 3 cents to know, ain't it?

The mail has come and none for me, but one for Steve and he is reading it now. There is one Union woman in this Company. The rebs took her horses and Negroes from her. She is a widow. They took her and her children to Richmond and kept them in prison 8 months. She is well off. She said she was put in prison on her brother's account for he was a Congressman in our Congress and opposed the rebellion. They couldn't get him, so they showed their spite on her and her children.

Well I must close for this time hoping this will find you and the children well. I will rite as soon as I get one from you.

From your
B. A. C.

Note written on the inside of an envelope addressed to Bishop A. Cook, 144 Regt. Co. F., N.Y.S.V., Washington, D. C.

On picket 10 miles from Williamsburg, June 15th. Yours No. 55 is at hand this morning I am happy to hear from my good wife and hear you are all well you must be very lonesome when the children are at school. I am glad you are getting some lamb, never mind loosing one sheep when we are 50 years older we wont know the difference. Make any terms with them that will suit Brandt so he will give a receipt that the judgement is satisfactory and after you get the receipt you will have to give it to the justice and he will send it to Honesdale where it will be recorded then it will be all right. We may stay here all summer on the peninsula it is a nice country here. I have 15 stamps now so I won't need more very soon.

I know you love me L. M. C.

So I love you B. A. C.

No. 57, 18 miles from Williamsburg, Va., June 16, 1863

Dear Wife,

I am happy to hear from you so soon again. I have just received the letter with the snuff and 2 stamps.

I was glad to learn you had the luck to find the lost sheep with a lamb. I am sorry you are afflicted with the headache so much.

Well, yesterday morning I told you we were on picket. We were called in and drew two days rations and started on a march at 12 o'clock towards Richmond. It was very dusty. The sand and dirt is 2 to 4 inches deep in the road. It was a dusty old time you better believe. We marched about 8 miles and stacked arms and got our coffee. After dark we lay on the ground with our blankets. I had a good nite's rest, the best I have had in some time. But we had not been here 10 minutes before a part of our Regiment went out on picket. That is the first thing done when we stop so that it the enemy is near they can't surprise us. I suppose we are here to attract the enemy's attention and draw them away from Richmond and Fredericksburg so our forces can do something there. I don't know what else we are here for.

We have killed pigs and cattle and chickens, so we don't lack for fresh meat. The boys are not backward about confiscating what we want. There were two pigs killed in one day to my knowledge. They were about 6 weeks old.

I hope you can make that turn to pay Brandt without much trouble.

I don't know whether we are to go ahead or go back. I guess we shall go back before night. My knapsack and things are at Williamsburg. The likenesses and everything is there. I hope they will bring them to us or take us back, for I want the contents of mine very much. But I've got some paper and envelopes so I can write with a pencil. They can't fool me out of writing to my old gal.

We are going out on a scout pretty soon so I must hurry up. Yes, that will be a happy day when we can live together again. I long for the glad day to come. I asked a citizen the other day when he thought the war would end. He said when Congress sat again. He thought the fighting would be all done this summer. I think so too. I want to get home to keep you warm next winter. I will write soon again. Ever yours,

B.A. Cook

No. 58, Camp Near Barhamsville, James City County, Virginia, June 18, 1863

Ever Dear Wife,

I must talk to you a little now. I have just been reading your letters No, 55 and 56. It is quite a task to be man and woman both, but I expect to be home to relieve you one of these days. You ask if I keep up good courage. My answer is yes. I expect to come home again, of course. I don't think I came down here to get killed.

In my last letter I told you we were going out on a scout. Well, we went about 3 miles. Only our Company went. We deployed skirmishes. That is we strung out in line on each side of the road 5 paces apart, and went ahead scouring the woods to see if there were any rebs in there. But we found none. We went to a house where there were some females, but no male to be seen. Those that haven't gone to war run and hide in fear. Well we passed the house I saluted one lady in military form and she made a very nice bow in return.

We went a short distance and came to the picket lines of one of our brigades. So after a short rest we filed onto the road and came down opposite the house above mentioned. The Lieutenant ordered us to stack arms and rest. After the arms were stacked, I and 3 others started for the house which was 30 rods from the road (all of the houses in this country are farther from the road than ours). The Lieutenant said that we must not take anything. Then he said he would go with us. The ladies were sitting in the doorway. We asked them where the spring was and they pointed to the path that led to the spring. But I had water in my canteen so I stayed and looked at the shade trees in the yard. One of the ladies asked me if we were going back to camp. I said yes. She then asked how long we were going to stay up here. I told her I could not tell, for we didn't know one hour where we would be the next. She said that was the case with soldiers she supposed. While I was admiring the shade trees I happened to spy a large cheery tree full of black cherries just like the our tree near the corner of the house. I asked her if it would be any harm if I should get some cherries to eat. She said no, help yourself. So I went up in the tree and filled myself and the rest did the same. In the meantime the rest of our Company were on the other side of the road in another tree filling themselves. So we thought we were paid for our journey here. We returned to camp well.

Yesterday morning quite early one of our company, William Fish, captured a reb near here. He was the owner of the plantation we are now on. He has been one of those confounded guerrillas or bushwackers as we call them. By what I could learn from one of his darkies yesterday, he has been at it ever since the war commenced. Last fall he received a wound in his right arm, so he has been at home since then. His arm is not well yet. His darkie said he told him he had better stay at home and some of his friends too. But he said he would kill some of the Yankees and they wouldn't catch him. But the darkie said that he hadn't killed any yet, but that he had shot at them a good many times. He said his boss is now catched. I am glad of it.

The prisoner is about 36 years of age. He has a wife and several children. When he found that we were coming, he put into the woods to keep out of sight. But yesterday morning he got out to the edge of the woods to see if he could not see some of the children or darkies to get some communication with his family. He had no gun but Fish had his gun and saw him first. He did not dare to run for fear of getting shot. So he is a prisoner in his own house with 4 men well armed to guard him.

Think of this secesh woman. Her husband a prisoner in his own home, soon to be torn from her embrace, not knowing what his sentence will be. Then to see the Yanks come into her garden, take all of her garden trash and milk her cows (as I did yesterday). Some of the boys dressed out a good 3-year-old cow and, after 3 shots, brought another hog down this morning. We are living nowadays--yesterday for supper we had fresh beef, fresh pork, eggs and milk in our coffee.

We are on picket. We came out last nite. We are in sight of the camp as we call it, but we have no camp here, no tents and no second shirt. I took my shirt off yesterday and washed it and hung it on a fence a while and then put it on. You see, our knapsacks are still at Williamsburg. I have 19 stamps and $3.50 in cash and some tobacco. But I have enough to last me a month in my knapsack if I ever get it.

The paymaster was here after supper. He paid our Company 2 months pay. I have got my check and will send it in this letter. I will send you some money when I find that the mail goes straight thru from here, for I don't want but 2 or 3 dollars at a time.

I received yours of the 12th this forenoon when I was writing. I was glad to hear from you again. I think we are writing pretty often, but we must write if we can't talk to each other. I am glad you have some money left. You will need some to do your haying with and get some hoeing done. Everything is so high that anyone who does work for a living has to have big wages. So you will have to pay pretty high for what you get done. And it takes money to keep you and the children in food and clothing. But if you are all well, we need not complain of hard times.

We learn from the papers that Lee is in motion and our state Pennsylvania is in danger. But Governor Curtis is not asleep and will soon have men enrolled for the defense of the state. On the whole, I think Lee's movement will turn out a good thing for us because I think if he gets into the free states it will stir up thousands to the cause of the Union that would otherwise sit still and suck their paws. Grant is drawing the bands tighter around Vicksburg. I tell you the month to come will be a great page in history. I hope the back of the rebellion will be broken in less than 2 weeks.

Rest assured dear Wife, I am better satisfied with soldering than I expected to be--although we have coarse fair and see hard times and lay on the ground. But it seems to agree with me, so what reason have I to complain.

You have said nothing of that old cow lately, so I suppose she is still alive. I am glad you got the sheep sheared and are getting along so well. Don't be afraid of my finding fault with the way you spend your money for I send it to you to spend. Get yourself some things if you want them. It is well to keep an account of everything you spend for then you will know what it costs to live per year. It is so dark I must stop now till morning.

Morning of the 19th. We had a nice shower last nite. We needed it to lay the dust and cool the air for it was very hot yesterday. There is some prospect of our moving ahead before long. I dreamed last nite that I was on a horse where we used to live. I rode down the hill towards the creek and met you. You asked me where I kept myself. I thought we weren't married, but expected to be. No more so good morning Wife.

B. A. Cook

No. 59, James City County, Virginia, June 23, 1863

Dear Wife,

We are still here near Barhamsville. We do picket duty 24 hours and then off duty for 24 hours, so I have time to write. I received yours of the 14th in due time. I was glad to hear from you so soon again. I'm sorry your bees didn't stay hived and the lamb died, but them that have must lose. If we never lost anything we would get rich too quick. We need not look for constant prosperity and no adversity.

So Jenny is fat as a bee. Well, I don't want to part with her unless we get what she is worth. And more that that, she is just what we want on the place when I get home. But if I don't get home to take care of her next winter we must try and let someone have her to work or keep through the winter. You can't take care of her another winter. I think there is a prospect of getting home next winter. You are going into the cabbage business. I am obliged to you for the invitation to come and eat taters and cabbage. I hope to be able to comply with your request. I am so far from anyplace, it would be difficult getting anything you might send. So I think you had better not send anything for it may not find me.

The minister had bad luck in breaking his wagon. I am glad you can go to meeting often. I can't. Yes, the thoughts of meeting and living together again are worth everything to us, that is so. We will have a wedding supper when I get home, won't we? I wish I could see my sweet little girls. It seems to me I would be the happiest man in the world if I was home now and this war settled.

I got a letter from Al last week. I answered it and sent him a dollar. So I have 5 dollars left of my 2 months' pay for you. I hope you have for your check for $20 before this time.

I have got a letter written to send to Aunt Harriet. We expect our knapsacks here today. I don't know but we shall stay here all summer. There is not much danger of getting a fight very soon here. We are enjoying ourselves well. The weather is cooler than it was since the recent shower.

Starvation is staring the inhabitants here in the face. They can get no coffee or sugar. Flour is worth $45 per barrel and corn $8 per bushel. Their main subsistence is cornmeal. There are scores of colored men, women, and children falling in the rear of our lines. Thus they gain their freedom. I have no more to write this time. Your is love.

Bishop A. Cook

No. 60, 20 miles from Richmond, Va., June 28, 1863

Dear Wife,

We are at White House Landing. I am happy to tell you dear Wife that I am well and got your No. 59 this morning. I was glad to hear from my lovely old gal. You say you are lonesome. No doubt you see many lonely houses, but I think you would be far lonelier if it were not for the children. But consider or compare your case with some of the poor women of this state and think how much better you are situated than they are here. But dear Louisa I hope we can live together many long years yet. I hope the time of our separation will not be as long as it has been.

We have a heavy force here and will probably march on Richmond this week. We are under General Keyes. We got here yesterday and are here to get rations and get troops concentrated. We have had rather nasty weather during our march. It has rained a little every day and night. It has been rather muddy and we are laying on the ground, but we stand it first rate.

There is great excitement in Maryland and Pennsylvania for Lee is out there. But he had better be at Richmond to take care of it. I hope Hooker will handle Lee pretty rough. I hope Lee won't scare more people to death than he kills. Our cavalry did a nice thing yesterday--they captured 140 men, 300 mules, 600 horses, a train of baggage wagons and a train of cars. They are tearing up the railroad track 8 miles from Richmond. I guess the 21st of June will be celebrated this year. I would like to hold the 4th in Richmond. It is not impossible, but I don't much expect it.

I suppose you have got your check. Well, I have got more money than I want, so I guess I will send you this $5. You can send me a few stamps occasionally.

I was on guard last nite, so I must clean my gun for inspection. So I will stop for a time. Well, I have got my gun cleaned and sit down again. So the lost sheep returned with a lamb--bully for that good luck. The lamb is worth $10. I'm glad to hear about that nice swarm of bees. I hope they will stay and work well. I hope you had a good quarterly meeting. I guess it is pictures that you are going to send. I shan't see my knapsack back this summer I guess. It teases me because our likenesses are in it. But I guess I will get it this fall if I don't before.

Quite likely we shall move from here before morning. You must not look for long letters from me at this busy time. But I will write often to my Dearest. It is pretty hard getting things here, but the Sutlers make out to supply us with some good things at high prices. But they don't get much of my money. I manage to make what money I spend of late by buying and selling. I made nearly 2 dollars in the past week. I sent Al one and spent the other. I still have $3.70 after sending you this $5. Ain't that pretty good? I send home all my pay including the dollar I sent to Al, and I have 70 cents more than I did when I was paid.

Well, I suppose you have some hoeing to do by this time. Who helps you do the hoeing? How does C.S. (her brother Charles S. Dickinson) make it go at home? I must write to him rite off. I hope this will find you all well as it leaves me to L. M. Cook. From

B. A. Cook

Sunday nite. We are here yet and more troops coming in. It has rained a little today. We shall probably move forward tomorrow.

I have no news to write except that I have eaten 24 cents worth of cheese for supper. We had fresh beef for dinner. One of my friends, Thomas Beavan, bought a box of tobacco for $2.50 and it will bring $3.50 if we have good luck. Steve sent his best respects to you. I guess you will hear from me again before I get to Richmond. There is a great flat here containing about 300 acres that belongs to General Lee. There are gunboats in the river here. The river is not navigable farther up than here. There was a railroad, but it is torn up now. But I understand that it is to be put in order to run our supplies up as we advance.

If I have time, I will write more in the morning.

B. A. Cook

Monday morning, the 29th. It is cloudy this morning and no rain last nite. I had a good nite's rest and feel well this morning. I suppose or mistrust that Richmond is to be besieged. Therefore, there is a very heavy force collecting here. Some say that on the James River and here there are 150,000. I don't think we will try to take it by storm, but take time as Grant is doing at Vicksburg.

Well, the mail will go this morning. I don't know whether we shall move today or not. I must get my coffee boiled, so good morning love.

B. A. C

JULY 1863

White House, Va., June 27th to July 8th
   July 1st to 3rd, Gettysburg, Pa.
   July 1st to 26th, Morgan's Raid
Camp near Barhamsville, Va., July 8th to 9th
On Steamer *United States* from Yorktown to Washington, D.C., July 9th to 10th
Washington, D.C., July 10th to 11th
On cars to Frederick, Md., July 11th to 13th
Frederick, Md., July 13th to 14th
Camp near Boonsboro, Pa., (Md.) July 14th to 15th
Berlin, Md. (Brunswick) July 15th to 19th
Camp near Leesburg, Va., July 19th to 20th
Goose Creek, Va., July 20th to 23rd
New Baltimore, Va., July 25th to August 1st

History Summarization pages 110-116

On the 5th of July news of Meade's victory at Gettysburg reached us and the troops were called into line at eleven o'clock at night to give three cheers, emphasizing our appreciation of the good news. A few days later the good word reached our camp that Gen. Grant's siege of Vicksburg had resulted in the capitulation of the city on July 4th. The railroad tracks were torn up and telegraph lines taken down on the 7th and on the 8th we began the march down the Peninsula. Gordon's Division leading, followed by Getty's and Foster's. We moved out at six o'clock in the morning taking the roads to New Kent Court House. It rained hard all day making the roads very muddy but the men pressed steadily forward in spite of the rain and encamped at night near Twelve Mile Ordinary. At the time, it was not known to the soldiers why such a rapid march was made, but later it was known to be an effort to transfer the division from the Peninsula to the Army of the Potomac as quickly as possible. The 144th was on board the steamer *United States* which brought us safely to Washington, reaching there at 6 p.m. of the 11th. Gen. Gordon was directed to secure transportation for his division direct to the army of Gen. Meade, going by way of Frederick, Md.

Accordingly, on the 12th the troops went aboard cars and by seven in the afternoon were en route for Frederick, distance by rail about seventy miles. For the first and last time in the history of the Regiment, we found ourselves under the control of Gen. Barleycorn. While the Regiment was in line, waiting orders to take the cars, a number of men in each company left the line with a string of canteens intent on the apparently laudable effort to secure a supply of water; but just behind the line, or near at hand, were a number of women ready to prey upon the soldiers. The women were supplied with canteens filled with whiskey and very soon the empty canteens of many of the soldiers took the place of the full canteens of whiskey. It was not long after the cars were under way before the full effect of this new water supply became apparent and in most of the cars pandemonium reigned until the excesses of the drinking men ended in sleep or a drunken stupor. There was another unlooked for result of Gen. Barleycorn's rule. The men in their hilarious condition, were disposed to share the contents of their canteens with the train men, this is the generally accepted explanation of results which followed. When we had reached Monocacy Junction our train stopped to take water. Owing to the muddled condition of the train men, they did not flag the train running behind, having on board the 142th N.Y. and 40th Mass., and the result was that it ran into the rear of our train, telescoping several cars and injuring some sixteen soldiers so severely as to compel their going to the hospital. Owing to this accident the line was blocked for a time delaying the movement of troops over it. Our own train did not reach Frederick until the next morning, when without the accident the run should have been made in two or three hours, and our entire Division been reported for duty at Frederick before ten o'clock p.m. Four thousand fresh men within striking distance of the enemy might have given a different conclusion as to attacking the enemy on the 13th and a very different result than the humiliating one reported on the 14th, that the enemy had escaped across the Potomac into Virginia. The Historian does not say that but for this accident caused by Gen. Barleycorn's leadership that our Division would have prevented Lee's escape. He only suggests it as among the probable "might-have-beens."

Early Tuesday morning the Division, marching toward Gettysburg, was under way. The conditions seen in Maryland were in marked contrast to what we had been accustomed to view in Virginia. The farmers with harvesting machines were hard at work gathering in their crops. All this seemed to be entirely out of keeping with moving bodies of troops and the accompaniments of war. In Virginia there was but little of these evidences of thrift and industry in the sections in which we had been and the surroundings seemed to be more in keeping with conditions of war. In the afternoon after passing Boonsboro orders reached us which turned us to the right-about and a little later we took a road leading direct to Williamsport. After proceeding several miles toward Williamsport, orders reached us directing another right-about. We marched back to near Boonsboro and encamped for the night. The next day's march took us over the battlefield of Antietam. Nightfall found us at Berlin (Brunswick) on the Potomac, toward which place the Army of the Potomac was concentrating and where as Col. Lewis has suggested it "joined us." While the troops were concentrating at Berlin the engineers were hard ar work constructing a pontoon bridge over the Potomac. It was completed on the 19th and on that date the army moved into Virginia and down the valley of the Shenandoah in an effort to overtake Lee's retreating army. The first day's march brought us to Leesburg and the next to Goose Creek where an early halt was made. When we left Goose Creek, Thomas Beavan of Co. F., who from some cause had fallen behind was captured by the enemy and held a prisoner until Sept. '63, when he was paroled. The march of July 23rd was one of the hardest of the campaign. It reached away into the night and brought us to New Baltimore. One of the compensations of campaigning in Virginia at this time was the quanity of luscious blackberries on the bushes by the roadside, and proved a great comfort to the soldiers. Our Division was moved to Warrenton Junction and on Aug. 1st to Greenwich.

No. 61, White House Landing, Virginia, July 1, 1863

My own Dear Wife,

I received No. 60 yesterday. I am a thousand times obliged to you for a sight at my little girls. How they grow. How fleshy Mate is. Oh how sweet they look. Accept all praise for your good management of things at home. I hope God will give you health and faith too. The poetry is very good and quite appropriate.

You are having pretty good luck with the bees if they all stay. I hope you will do well with the sewing machines. Mr. Mapes has only one note against me and that I think was $32 and some cents. The account is small. It was for the flannel, cap, belt, etc. for my home guard suit. The interest on the note is quite a sum and if you have the other note for 20 dollars, he may have some interest charged on that too. The debt looks rather large but by seeing Mr. Mapes I guess he will explain it to you satisfactorily.

As to Mr. Squire, I do not consider him any more responsible than G. Thomas. Let George pay it when he can. I did not expect Brandt would release us and take any man's note. They are able to wait and willing, so let the thing rest and give yourself no trouble about it for the present.

I hope you have got your check before this time. I sent a five dollar bill in a letter 2 or 3 days ago which was the last of my 2 months pay. But I have 3 dollars yet after sending away all of 6 months pay except 2 dollars.

The troops are leaving here but their destination I don't know. There are all sorts of stories about Lee. Some say he has captured Harrisburg. Some say our letters are not permitted to go through to our friends for fear of conveying some information concerning movements. We have no news. It is all rumor and not worth mentioning.

We had a heavy rain yesterday and laying on the wet ground I feel pretty old. I think you are doing about as well with things at home as I could, but it is a great task for you. I am not discouraged about the war for it must end by and by. I hope soon, but we can't tell when neither can anyone else on earth.

The morning of July 2nd. All quiet and some say that we are to stay here to do the guarding of this landing. The mail is soon to go, so I must close. Ever yours Dear Louisa,

B. A. Cook

The eve of the 2nd. I was too late to send this this morning so I will write a little more and try and send it in the morning. It has been very warm here today. We had one drill in the forenoon and one in the afternoon and dress parade at nite. We got a loaf of bread tonite for the first in a long time.

The cannon are booming some 6 or 8 miles above us. I think we shall move before long but don't pretend to know. I feel pretty well tonite although my head aches a little. I hope old Lee will never get out of Pennsylvania without losing his army. If we can get Vicksburg and Lee's army, then the war is over. But if Lee should get back and have his own way, and if we fail to get Vicksburg, then the rebs are as good as we are for fighting a while.

Fears are entertained that Russ Cook and another ambulance driver are captured for they started to go out to the 142nd Regiment yesterday noon and have not been heard of since. They say there are no more prisoners to be paroled on either side.

It is too dark to write. I shall expect to hear about the check tomorrow.

B. A. Cook

Unnumbered Letter, White House Landing, Virginia, July 5, 1863

Dear Brother,

As it is some time since I have written to you, I will improve a few minutes this Sabbath morning in writing to you. This morning finds me well. We had no drill yesterday, but the flags waved over our camp and on gunboats on the river. At noon our battery of 6 guns was in line and fired a few rounds.

We have good news from General Meade. He is doing a nice thing with Lee's army and I hope Meade will meet with continued success.

The weather is quite warm and the river is lined with soldiers in bathing every day. One of our Regiment drowned on the 3rd. His buddy (sic) was found this morning. I don't know but you are under arms now for the defense of Pennsylvania.

Well Charles, I have just come from inspection which we have every Sunday. It is very warm here so I stick up some poles and lay a blanket on them for shade.

We have been here over a week and there has nothing of interest taken place yet. If you read the *N.Y. Herald* you will read about General Dix or Keyes on the peninsula. That means us. We are less than 25 miles from Richmond and some of our cavalry has been very near Richmond the past week. But sir, what we want now is to destroy Lee's army and I hope, if there is not sufficient force already at him, we may get a poke at him.

I must go and see a soldier at the hospital. He is having fits. Well I have returned to my writing. It is a hard sight to see a man lay on the ground with his body and limbs all in a tremor for a few moments, then come to, and then go into another fit again. Whether he lives through or not I will tell you if I can before I close. One of the boys says he is dead. He belonged to the 4th Delaware Regiment.

I want to hear from you and hear whether you are ready for haying or whether you are off in defense of the State. I expect a letter from Al every day, for I wrote to him last. It is some time since I have heard from you Brother.

Remember me in prayer.

B. A. Cook

A few words to Mother,

I am enjoying myself as well as circumstances will permit. I hope that I can get home to winter for soldering wears on a man. Even if he is robust, he can't lay on the ground week after week without feeling the effects of it. But you know I have stood it beyond our expectations thus far, and I hope God will give me health in the future.

There have been some skirmishes with the rebs a few miles from here. Along our picket lines there have been several killed or wounded on our side, and 9 on the other side killed and a large number wounded.

I look for a letter from (?) (illeg.). I like to hear from my friends. You must excuse me this time for I have no convenience. I have to carry my paper and writing utensils in my pocket. So you see I can't carry everything in my pocket.

Soldiers generally have enough to carry.

B. A. Cook

No. 62, White House Landing, Virginia, July 6, 1863

Dear Louisa,

I received yours of last Sunday nite and one from Aunt Harriet. She wrote a very good letter to me. She told me of your being there with the children and how glad she was to see them. I am happy to tell you I am well.

I must tell you of last nite. About midnight we had a shower. All the shelter we have is a blanket put up on some sticks. Well, the rain came into my face and woke me. So I got into the position of a sleeping dog as near as nature would permit. I was bound to lay still. but the wind blew our blanket almost entirely off us. Fortunately, the rain soon ceased, so we shook ourselves and lay down again till morning.

Two men drowned last week in the river. One of them belonged to our Regiment. Another died of fits yesterday--he belonged to the 4th Delaware Regiment.

I sent Charles a letter this morning. Have you heard about our attack on Richmond? I haven't and don't expect to very soon. The fighting seems to be going on in Pennsylvania lately. The news we get here is good for Lee is being driven and whipped.

I am glad your garden is doing well and I hope you can get help to hoe the corn. I hope your sewing machines have come and will work well. If you can get someone to work in haying for one of them, it will be as good as cash. How much did you say 6 of them cost? I forget exactly how much.

You are being visited to death. Who are they that are so friendly nowadays? Maybe you feed them too well. If you want to get rid of them, feed them soldier's fare and they won't come so thick. But you know we generally had plenty of company this time of year. I dare say that those that visit you most now would have least to give you if you were in want.

No, I can't remember to number from the letter that went with Kate's, but this is No. 3 (*Louisa changed the number to 62*). and when you get some of these that are numbered, which I keep a record of, you can tell me what their number ought to be. Then I can correct the number.

I am glad you got the check and hope you received the $5. I would like to send Mother a picture but I can't get any taken until I get to some town.

As to letting Jenny go, we know it is death to a horse to have everyone running with them. She is young and liable to be injured in many ways. In the first place, by driving her until warm and thirsty and then letting her drink and stand still. Or by giving her grain when she is warm. In fact, there ain't half the folks that are to be trusted with a good or poor horse for they don't know how one ain't to be treated. You should be very particular who has her if she goes at all. These 4th of July trips would be rather dangerous for a horse because some would get a little drunk and drive a horse half to death. It would have to be some steady fellow, and responsible, if I let her go to the 4th. Now you must act on your own judgment about letting her go and who to. If some decent body wants her a day and will work a day in return, it will be making her help do the work.

Evening of July 7th. You see I did not send this this morning for at daylight we were called up to go in fatigue duty, so I had no time to mail it. Our regiment has torn up the rails of the railroad leading to Richmond. They took the rails to the dock and put them on steamboats to run them down the river.

I have had all the apples I have wanted for 5 cents. And I picked all the blackberries I could eat too. Ain't that doing pretty well? I expect we shall leave here in less than 2 days. I sent a dollar off to Philadelphia for some jewelry and spent 25 cents today and have about $2.50 left. I think I hold my own pretty well. Now it is dark, so I will close hoping to send this in the morning. Good nite Louisa M. Cook.

Morning of the 8th. I think often of you old gal. Oh how I would like to see you. But be patient. I will get around that way in the course of a year if the Lord is willing. I have no news to rite, but you may send me a few stamps for they beg them away from me at 5 cents apiece.

Be careful and not overdo yourself my own dear wife. From your boy,

B. A. C.

No. 63, Williamsburg, Virginia, July 9, 1863

Dear Wife,

As I have a little time I will write to you and let you know that I am well, but pretty tired out--we have had but little rest of late. If you got my last letter, I told you that we were tearing up the railroad tracks. Well, the next morning we were called up at 2 o'clock. We fooled around until daylight and then were on the march with wet blankets. I rained a good deal during the day so the mud and water were over the shoes in many places. The mud here is slippery as ice and I saw several fellows fall flat into the mud. It was the worst day I ever experienced for the mud and water got into our shoes and ground our feet well in this condition.

We marched 17 miles and then stopped for supper. We washed our feet and then marched 8 miles further. It was 10 o'clock. They ordered us to make coffee but no one did because we were too tired. We lay down on the ground in our wet blankets and slept the best we could.

Well, this morning we started in good season and reached here about 1 o'clock after marching about 12 miles. Very few men fell out yesterday, but today their feet were so sore that more than half of the regiments fell out. Some companies hadn't 10 men when they got here. I got a little ride in an ambulance myself because I had a touch of the rheumatism in my leg. It doesn't bother me much now. We are to stay here till morning and then we will start for Yorktown.

I think you are doing well in the berry line. I hope you can get a good amount of dried fruit for winter for it is a great thing to have. I have got here in my knapsack enough for one mess of the blackberries you sent me last winter. Oh, I must tell you what I had yesterday for dinner. I bought a head of cabbage and cut it up. I put salt, pepper and vinegar on it an it was good. I also had 2 nice cucumbers and they tasted natural.

I have written often, but I have felt a little fearful the letters didn't go thru. But I have received your letters regularly and thank you for writing so often. I don't care for postage stamps when I can get them, but you must send me some the first opportunity for I have only 3. I will use two of them on these letters--one to Aunt Harriet and this one to you Wife. I will write more by and by.

B. A. C.

No. 63-A, On the steamer at Yorktown, Va., July 10, 1863, 6 o'clock p.m.

Dear Wife,

We left Williamsburg about sunrise this morning and got here at 11 o'clock. Here we found our knapsacks all safe, mine in particular. I have looked at the old likenesses and I have got all our pictures.

Well, I am on my way home. I don't know but that I shall get as far as Washington, but we may go somewhere else. Maybe we are going to help Meade finish Lee's army. The news is good.

Well, I got your letters No. 62 and 63 today. Glad to hear from you again. I wish you could get some help to do your haying. I should think Kate would feel ashamed of herself. Well, if they act you out they won't come so much. All you have got to do when such cases come is to tell them how much you are behind with your outdoor work and go out at it. They can't blame you for tending to your own business.

Al has not paid any of that note I gave him for Mapes nor anything for wintering the heifer I suppose. And C.S. (*probably her brother, Charles S. Alexander*) wants the watch. Well, I suppose you are aware that the watch is worth nearly as much as the heifer was last fall when you took her. Well, if your grass is good, you can trade if you like for you need another cow. Now it is almost dark, so I must stop for tonight.

July 11th. I had a good rest last nite and feel well this morning. We are out of the bay and are running up the Potomac. I heard the officers talking that we are going to Washington so I can carry this letter part way. I would like to fetch it to you. I don't know as you can read this for the boat don't run steady. It is on the jiggle all the time. It is warm and pleasant today.

I guess you had better trade with Charlie and get the cow for if she comes in this summer she will be worth 20 dollars at least. And if Beth ain't never coming in again, I would suppose you want to get rid of her. Have you taken or sent any of the cows to bull yet? If I was there to use the knife to Beth after she was serviced it would make her stick. How is the red cow--is she good for anything?

How is your pasture? Is it good and does the stock look well? Yes. it would be very pleasing to you and me if I could come and look at your nice crops and your nice home. I do think we have as nice a home as most anyone. At least it suits me and I long to be there to enjoy it with you.

Have patience Wife. Time is passing away fast and I hope soon to greet you one of these days. You ask how many days it ought to take to do the haying. Well, if Steve was there with me, us two could do it in just 8 days. That would be 16 days work, but I don't believe you can get it done short of 20 days work. But hire someone if you can that will do it good and save the hay good even if you have to pay big wages. It is almost time to begin now and if Al comes to help C. they can do their haying and yours too in a month if it is good weather. It will cost considerable to do your haying for the board will amount to considerable.

Well, I sent you all the money I could and will send more as soon as I get it. We are almost up to Alexandria so I must finish up to give this to the Domany(?) so it will go. I think we will get to Washington in good time and likely we shall have to march from there to someplace. I will write again soon my dear Gal.

B. A. Cook

No. 64, In Maryland near Harpers Ferry, July 16, 1863

Dear Wife,

I find time to write to you today and let you know that I am well although we have seen pretty hard times since we left Washington. We left Washington on cars for Frederick, Md. We were all nite and all day getting there. I think the distance is about 90 miles. We got there Sunday nite and encamped until Tuesday morning. Then we left our knapsacks and started after the enemy. But after marching one day, we learned they had crossed the river. So we turned our course and got here last nite pretty well tired out. But we rested today.

We are right with the Army of the Potomac. I have seen E. W. Early, Squire Layne and several other of our friends. Wallace was in the late battle at Gettysburg. He was hit by a spent ball on the knee, but it didn't break the hide. He was hit by one once before, so he has been pretty lucky. William Serryne was within 2 feet of him when the cannon ball killed him. Wallace says that Hugh McCreda was killed at Gettysburg, so that report you heard last winter was false. Wallace had seen him lots of times and went to his Company to see him since the battle and was told that he was killed. Nelson Early was wounded in the leg.

They say Lee lost about 33,000 in killed, wounded and prisoners. Also Port Hudson has fallen with 18,000 prisoners, and Sherman and Rosencrans are giving the rebs fits. On the whole, I think the thing is working pretty well. I could rite more but I suppose you get the news in the papers.

I forgot to tell you that we had a train run into our train when we were some 15 miles out of Washington. It injured several men. One Lieutenant in Company A had his leg broken.

We have had no mail since we left Yorktown, but I guess we will get some before long. I got into a cherry tree today and filled myself. Also got a cup of milk that was good. The part of this state that we have come through is a very fine country. There is lots of wheat and corn here. In fact, it is just as nice a place as any one can ask for. But old Virginia looks desolate. I have lived pretty well since we have been here for we can but bread, butter, milk and pie. The inhabitants had things baked to sell to the soldiers.

Well, I have all my pictures in my pocket and I shan't leave them behind unless I lose my coat. I suppose you haven't got anything done at haying yet, but I hope you will have good luck in getting it done. I've got to go and get my rations, so no more at present.

Friday morning, July 17th. It is raining this morning. We shall not move today I guess, so we will get a good rest and some letters I hope. I have not heard of you getting a letter from me in some time, but I hope they have been received. Wife, if we were at home together we would be happy. God grant that we may live together again. I tell you, it takes a good man to stand it three years in the service even if he is never shot at at all. The hardships of a soldier's life are wearing on a man. But Wallace looks just as though he was at home.

Well, I think this was will end in a few months, Dear Wife.

Bishop A. Cook

No. 65, Loudoun County, Virginia, July 21, 1863

Dearest Wife,

This morning finds me well and in good spirits, but I am lost without any mail. I have had none in several days but I guess we shall get it soon.

We are in the 1st Brigade, 1st Division and 11th Army Corps. We left Maryland Sunday morning, crossed the Potomac on a pontoon bridge and traveled about 15 miles before noon. We took dinner, rested a few minutes and started out again. But it was very warm and some were sun struck. I never came as near it myself. We only marched 8 miles in the afternoon. There were a great many fell out by the way and came in after we stopped. Yesterday we only came about 12 miles, so there were but few fell out. I don't know what minute the bugle will sound for us to get ready and start, but we may leave here today.

But I am in good marching order after eating a good breakfast of fried mutton. In a field close by here we found a fine flock of sheep. Most any of us can dress one, so it was not long till 6 of the sheep were down and how many more I don't know. Steve and I have fried 3 or 4 pans full and have put it in our haversacks to eat on the road. We stopped at 4 o'clock last nite and I picked a quart of blackberries. I stewed them and put sugar on them, so you see I had a fine dish for supper. Nite before last I was tired but I went some piece after we stopped for the nite and dug some potatoes for my breakfast. I boiled them in a little quart pail I carry for making coffee in. Then I put them in my frying pan with a little gravy and fried them--and don't say they weren't good. We have to do all our own cooking. We have had no soft bread in several days. They get us up before daylight generally, but this morning we weren't called up until sunrise.

This country is as hilly as it is where we live. There is a lot of grass not cut yet, but the wheat is cut and in the fields. The soldiers use acres of it to lay on and feed horses. You see we don't spare things in Virginia. The report here is that Charleston is burned, but I don't credit it.

How are you getting along with your farming? I want to hear from you but it is not your fault for I know there are letters on the way. I believe our mail carrier is too lazy to go and get our mail, but it will come after a while.

I think we shall see no fighting very soon. General Howard is our General and we are now in the Army of the Potomac under Meade. Where Lee is I don't know for I don't get any papers. We begin to know something about soldiering and the hardships they are subject to. But I supposed when I enlisted we were coming into it sooner than we have.

I tell you it looks hard to march men under their load until they fall down in the road helpless. But it is done, for I have seen it with my own eyes. But I haven't had to fall out yet. I keep in my place and can as long as I am well. But this soldering wears on a man and some it wears out, and some are killed. But I trust in God that I shall be spared to enjoy the society of my little family, for I know my presence would make glad the hearts of the dear ones at home.

I stick to it that this summer's campaign will finish the fighting. Our armies have had good success this summer. I guess the old women's saying will come true--In 1861 the war begun, in 1862 we had all we could do, and in 1863 all would be free. I hope I shall be free before this year is our and at home, for there is no place like home. I hope this will find you all in good health. Tell my girls I look at their pictures often. They look so lovely, but I long to see the original. Wife, kiss them for me and children kiss Ma for me.

Yours ever,

B. A. Cook

No. 66, Warrington Junction, Virginia, 41 miles from Alexandria, July 27, 1863

Ever dear Yf,

It is with pleasure I seat myself on the ground to talk to the one I love and let you know I am pretty well and am glad to inform you that we have got our mail. It brought three letters from my love and a locket from Dean with a glass in each side. I don't know what to do with it. If I could get my likeness taken for one side I would send it to Mother and get yours on the other side. But I will keep it a spell and see. Maybe I will sell it to someone.

I am glad you have got your haying commenced. I hope the boys help you and you can pay them the money.

I have received your letters all rite and 6 stamps. You better believe I was glad to get word from home again. I am pleased to hear our daughters are learning so fast. Did you pay the whole of our tax? If you did, it is no higher than usual. Mt dear, you have a hard row to hoe, but it is nothing compared with soldering. Tell the boys (*he is referring to her brothers, Almus and Charles Alexander*) they may thank God they are not soldiers now.

I will give you a little history of the past week. When I wrote to you last we were in Loudoun County. Well, we went on a scout some 8 miles Wednesday afternoon and took supper at Aldie. Then we were marched back and got to our camp about 11 o'clock at nite. The next day at 10 o'clock we started out again and marched 20 miles before we stopped to get anything to eat. We took supper near the Bull Run battleground. Then we marched on until 12 o'clock at nite. One of my shoes gave out early the first day, so I threw it away and went with one bare foot. It was tough work getting over the rough road in the dark. My foot was very sore and swelled. We layed over one day here at a place called New Baltimore. The next morning at one o'clock we were called up, drew rations, got breakfast and at the first peep of day we were moving. We kept moving, wading creeks and mud holes, and before noon we were encamped here 16 miles from our starting point.

Yesterday was Sunday and I was on guard. Today it is raining a little. My foot is not very sore now, but I don't think they will march me much more unless they furnish me with shoes. It makes me mad to see men marched to death by their officers. I have some thoughts of getting out of this as soon as time can bring it about. They are bound to kill a feller unless he is tougher than an Indian and I didn't come down here to be killed by out own commanders. That is so. I was thinking the other nite that if I had the leaves of poison ivy to put on my legs and poison them, the doctors wouldn't know what it was. I couldn't march so they would send me to the hospital and then I wouldn't have to march nite and day. I haven't seen any ivy here, but I saw some on the peninsula. This is private so you can burn it if you like. If you see fit to send some leaves in a letter you can do so. They may be of use.

I asked Steve what he wrote to Kate. He said that he told her that I said that she had been there every day that week. I told him that when he asked me if my letter said anything about his folks. So I told him yes, Kate had been there every day that week. I didn't think anything of that and Steve says he didn't. But he says Kate took it wrong. So I guess if you have had any trouble about this matter you and Kate must not charge it to Steve and me for we haven't seen any trouble about it and are sorry to think you have.

Steve and I are just going to eat dinner. We drew beans this morning for the first time in a good while. We boiled them with some pork until done. Then put them in the frying pan and cooked them dry. So I expect they will be good. We will have these for dinner with some hardtack and a good cup of coffee. If you were here you could have some of the pork and beans.

Russ (*I believe this is his cousin, Russell Cook, son of his uncle, George W. Cook*) has come back to his company. Our Regiment has turned in all ambulances except two, so the drivers have to come back to their Companies.

I am glad George paid you some money. You didn't say anything about getting $5.00 from me that I sent near the 1st of this month. I hope you got it for I'd hate to lose it. If we stay here long I expect we shall get some more pay. I would like to get enough to do the haying, buy your provisions and pay Brandt too. But get your work done it you can get anyone to work. Don't neglect your farming. Have you traded your watch for the heifer? Maybe C.S. (*Her brother Chas. S. Alexander*) would like to trade and take your calves and watch. Or don't you want to let your steers go? You must get them altered, if you have not, when it gets a little cooler weather. If you let them run till spring it will make them look staggy. I am glad your sheep and lambs are doing well and you have your wool picked. Granny Turrell is very clever to help you pick wool. The old gal thinks a good deal of me and you must respect her.

I expect our Regiment will be filled up with new drafted men. Some 20 officers and men have gone from our Regiment to Elmira to get men to fill up the regiment. I hear that some of the Vincents are drafted. They are going to fill up the old Regiment with these men, so they will soon become soldiers. We will soon have 300,000 more men in the field, so I think we can annihilate the rebs. I should think that one more battle against them would discourage them. Some of the citizens tell me they think there will be one more big battle and only one--and that will be fought at Manassas.

Steve is going to send a line in this. I have 25 cents and everything I want. I guess there is rest for the weary up yonder, but not here.

I am sorry Clarry has lost her lover, but many have fallen. Thurstin Dickinson (*probably Louisa's cousin*) was killed so Charles Smith told me. He was shot through. I want to go and see W. Early this afternoon if I can. There is some prospect of our staying near here for some time for it is a very convenient place for getting supplies and for getting men that are drafted. There is a railroad from here to Alexandria and Washington. The distance is 41 miles.

Accept my thanks for your faithfulness in writing to me so often. those verses are lovely and I will send them home again after a little. I will send you some of my hair if I can get it cut off.

This makes 6 letters this month that I have written to you. I don't think that is very bad, do you? If we lay here long I shall write long letters to you. But when we are on a march, you can't expect long letters--only to hear from me.

I believe I have written enough and all I can think of for now. Ask Almus (*her brother*) if he got an answer to his letter that he sent me in June. Give all of the good folks my respects.

Yours ever Dear Wife,

B. A. C.

No. 67, Warrington Junction, Virginia, July 29, 1863

Dear L.

As I have plenty of time, I will talk to you a little today. We are getting a good rest but have poor water and have to go half a mile after the most of it at that. They are diggin all over for water and some are successful while others are not. Our company is digging but I don't see much sign of water.

Yesterday we drew the first ration of whiskey in our Regiment. The doctors dealt it on account of our having bad water.

188

Russ and I had quite a visit last nite. Today I got his razor and shaved for my face had gotten pretty rough looking. I feel much better than I did 2 days ago when I rote to you concerning the ivy. But I may see the time yet that I would use it if I had it. It grows near the house along near the lane that went to the pasture.

I wrote a letter to Aunt Harriet yesterday. I sold my locket the same day for $2.50 to Bill Garlow and will have to wait till payday for the money. Well, I forgot to put my hair in the other letter till after I had sealed it. I will try and put it in this.

The snuff keeps the lice pretty thin on me. I am fearful you have poor haying weather nowadays. But I guess August will be better. Is the grass good or thin? Have you got your sewing machines yet? Don't be discouraged with them, but keep them until you can trade them off for the full value or sell them. If you should trade them off for grain, meat or anything this fall, you could allow a good price for what you get for a machine. If you can't sell them, it won't cost anything to keep them--only the interest on the money. I suppose you have 3 of them and I hope one of them will save you much time in doing your sewing. I expect to get some shoes in a day or two.

The papers state that they are trying to take Charleston, but it is a stronghold and will take some time to get. If General Gillmore hangs with it as Grant did at Vicksburg, he will gain the day. These places cannot be taken in a day or a week. Pemberton's army that was at Vicksburg is entirely disbanded and scattered. He has no control over them and the reb soldiers in general are tired of fighting. But they are forced into the ranks and when a battle is to come off they get whiskey and powder in their canteens so they become wild and fearless. Many of our soldiers have told me that when these rebs are killed for a short time they turn black in consequence of drinking powder and whiskey.

Steve is on guard today. Our Company went on drill this forenoon, but some of us with bare feet couldn't see the point of going on drill. The Captain asked me what was the matter with me. I told him I didn't like to go in the ranks to get my toes stepped on. He

189

looked at my feet and said no more. There are 2 or 3 others bare-foot.

July 30th. This morning finds me feeling pretty well. Steve and I had some fresh beef so we put it in the kettle and boiled it and put in some hardtack. It made quite a breakfast. After breakfast I went to the creek which is about a mile off and washed myself and my shirt. I got a new pair of shoes last night.

There are no visible signs of our moving soon, but we may go before nite after all. I hear that Grant is moving on Richmond in the rear, but do not put much dependence on what I hear. We had a hard shower last nite and today the air is very reviving and cool.

You wrote that the cherry trees had blossomed but there is no fruit on them or the new apple trees. Oh how I would like to be there and take a walk with you and look at things. I dreamed nite before last of being at home kneeling by a chair--and you were on your knees by the same chair. I was praying. When I awoke I could but praise God that I had the privilege of attending family worship even if in my sleep. I also prayed that it would be real in a few months.

Most of our soldiers feel encouraged much by the late victories. The Confederates are becoming discouraged. This you see gives us a decided advantage in fighting.

I am glad your cows have all been away and I hope you will have good luck with them next spring if I don't get home. But I have some hopes if the war stops they will let those who want to go home go. They can get enough to volunteer to stay that have no families and would just as soon be in the army as anywhere. You planted quite a lot of corn, but do you have potatoes enough?

We have just been ordered to move, so I must stop writing.

Well, we have moved half a mile for a better camp. Steve and I have got our shelter up and some leaves on the ground to lay on, so we are at liberty to write. I hardly know what to write, but I expect a letter from you tonite if the mail comes.

I think Mr. Reynolds must be some help to you if he will take a cow away for you. You must try and pay him for his good deeds. Does you head trouble you as bad this summer, and are you regular or as you was last summer? I found a ring in camp the other day and I will put it in this letter for you.

They call E.W.G. *(I believe this is Elias Garlow)* a coward and everything. He is in the invalid corps but the Captain says he is as able a man as he has. Will Dan has said all the time that we would serve our 3 years before the war would end, but he begins to shorten the time of late. I stick to it that the fighting will be done before winter.

Well I believe I will stop for dinner. I can't send this till morning, so there is no hurry. Well, I sit down again to my writing. I have just bought a map like Kate's with a lot of cards and fancy envelopes like I had last winter. But I sole the paper and envelopes to one and another and finally sold the map. So all I have left is the pen and holder I am writing with. I gave 45 cents for the thing and sold it for 75 cents, so I made 30 cents in 20 minutes. The 45 cents was all I had. His price was 50 cents, but he took 45 and said not a word. The $5.00 I sent home worries me some for I haven't heard from you about it yet and I know I have received answers to letters written since that went. Yet I am in hopes you got it all right. If you haven't, I shall wish I had kept it, won't you?

We have a nice campground here in a field and the air circulates freely today.

Friday morning, July 31st. I was on guard last night and today. I've got to stand again in a few minutes. I got your good letter last night, postage stamps and all. I think it came quickly--mailed on the 28th and I got it on the 30th. I will write more soon. I want this to go this morning. I will try and get a lock of hair to put in here. I think Lib Dimmic has done it.

Ever Yours, B. A. C.

P.S.--My hair is short.

AUGUST 1863

Greenwich, Va., August 1st to 3rd
Warrington Junction, Va., August 3rd to 6th
Alexandria, Va., August 6th to 7th
On steamer *John W. Warren,* August 7th to 8th
Newport News, Va., August 8th to 9th
On steamer *John Rice,* August 9th to 12th
Folly Island, S. C., August 12th to 17th
Morris Island, S. C., August 17th to 29th
August 21st, Quantrell's Sack of Lawrence, Kansas
Folly Island, S. C., August 29th to February 23rd 1864

History Summarization pages 117-138

Our Division moved to Warrington Junction and on August
1st to Greenwich. The surroundings of this place seemed to
indicate a more prosperous condition of affairs than we had
found in any other place in Virginia. The explanation was
found in the fact that the owners were English and had
claimed and received from both Union and Confederate forces
immunity from foraging. At Greenwich the Regiment was
called to take part in the execution of the extreme penalty
visited by military law upon soldiers who desert. At a court
martial held some time before, six men had been tried for desertion, found guilty and condemned to death, five of those
condemned had been pardoned. The sixth one, Bradford

Butler of the 157th N.Y.V. who had been the ringleader in inducing the others to desert and this added to the fact that this was his second offense, it was felt that he should suffer the extreme penalty of law. The several Regiments of the Division were marched past the dead body and back to their respective camps. The next day is marked in the diary as a "quiet day" it was the Sabbath and the next day we marched back to Warrington Junction. The Paymaster, Maj. Austin also gladdened the hearts of the soldiers by coming to us here and disbursing arrears of pay, due. The 144th found itself at the water front in Alexandria on a beautiful sunlit morning, going on board the *John W. Warner* for a trip to Newport News, where ocean transportation awaited us. At Newport News we were transferred to the ocean steamer *John Rice*. At Charleston Gen. Ames who had preceded us on the *S. R. Spaulding* came alongside and gave us orders directing us to report to Folly Island. We landed at Pawnee Landing on the west side of Folly Island. Later we marched to the middle of Folly Island where we established our camp close beside the ocean.

The 144th was on guard, that is, doing duty in the advance trenches on the night of the 25th, but powerless to assist in the movement of the navy or to give aid in the disaster which overtook it. one of the 200 pound Parrot guns blew out its breech, one of the fragments hitting William P. Fish, of company F., inflicting a mortal wound of which he died the next day. On the 29th of August the 144th returned to its camp on Folly Island. A new camp was laid out a little south of the old one and tents were set up. It was at this camp that we fought the hardest battle and suffered the greatest losses during the siege of Charleston and indeed, during its entire service. The long marches and blowing sand and no way to properly cook brought on "camp disease." Every day and sometimes several times a day the muffled roll of drum would announce the sad fact of diminished numbers.

No. 68, Camp in Virginia, August 2, 1863

Dear Wife,

This morning I seat myself to write to you and tell you it is very hot weather and that we marched 10 miles yesterday. We suffered fearfully from the heat of the sun.

In the afternoon our Brigade went out into a field to witness the execution or the shooting of a deserter. He was a private in the 157th N.Y.S.V. There were 16 men detailed to shoot him. Some of the guns were loaded with blanks and some with ball. His breast was pierced by 3 balls. They sat that some of the men that were ordered to fire did not discharge their guns and they are to be punished for it. He was blindfolded and was kneeling by his rough box praying earnestly when the fatal balls struck him. He fell over on his back and died without a struggle as near as I could see.

We are in camp near Greenwich Church. The Major says we may stay here several days. I hope we will for it is too hot to march. There were several men sunstruck and fainted yesterday. I fell out of the ranks myself for I won't march until I fall down. I saw 3 men carried into the shade helpless when we were standing in the field yesterday while they were preparing to shoot the deserter. I hear that he went into the rebel lines and supposedly told them how much force we had and how they were situated. But it happened that he was talking to our cavalry instead of the rebs, so they arrested him. His name was Bradford Butler and they say he came from Madison County, N.Y. Some say that he confessed the murder of his brother or brother-in-law before he came to war, and he fired at our cavalrymen when they undertook to arrest him. So he was a hard case I think.

We are to have inspection this morning as it is Sunday. We have a good deal of style in the army about some things and some not so much.

Monday eve, August 3rd. We didn't stay long where we were for last night we were informed that we would have to get up at 1 o'clock. So we were called up and got our breakfast and started at 3 o'clock. We marched back to within 2 miles of the station at Warrington Junction. It was extremely hot in the middle of the day. I saw several that were partially sunstruck. We do not have good water--it is warm, muddy water. I have seen men drink out of more than one mud hole. It is so muddy it gives us the shits and it makes a great many very weak.

The paymaster is here and we may get our 2 month's pay this week. Then I can send you a $20.00 check. Steve got a letter from Kate last nite. It brought bad news of Br. Lake (*someone from their church*). Poor man, I had hoped he would recover. I got a letter from C.S. (*her brother, Charles S. Alexander*) last nite. He is trying to make hay but has had bad weather. He is anxious to get done so as to try and do your haying. He says you have nice corn and garden and grass.

I don't know as we shall get into a fight very soon and yet we may get in one before a week. I stood the march pretty well. We got almost to our journey's end by 8 o'clock. We only came about 8 miles. It is too hot to march in the middle of the day--if we move, we have got to do it in the middle of the night.

I guess you will have haying weather this month, but you won't get it done before the 15th or 20th of September.

Will Dan (*a neighbor from home*) is sick so he could not march to-day--he came in an ambulance. It is dark and I can't see to write Dear Lousia.

Tuesday morning, the 4th. I feel pretty well this morning and will try and finish this letter. You are very good in writing to me so often. I will kiss you for every letter when I get to you. Will that do? If it won't, I will do something else.

How much milk do you get to a mess? Has the heifer come in yet? I hope we can have 4 cows next summer. How are the bee hives? Are there as many apples on the trees as there were last year? Does the tree I got from Mother do well?

Well, my arm is a little sore--it begins to itch some and look pretty red. Oh, I guess my arm got against some leaves Sunday and poisoned it.

I just went and bought a pound of maple sugar in 4 cakes. I gave 50 cents for it and when I got here in the alley the boys almost got it all away from me. One gave me 15 cents for a cake another gave 20 cents and one I sold for a shilling. So the cake I ate cost me 3 or 4 cents and it was all I wanted to eat. So all right, go ahead driver.

The boys think they are going to get their greenbacks today. If we do, your check will come in the next letter. Steve has gone to get a dollar's worth of sugar from the Sutler. If he gets it he will probably make 25 cents on it.

How do your calves do and where do you keep them? Are they alike? And have you got the pig we had when I left home and how does it look? Is it as good as her mother was when Sol Travis wanted her for ten dollars? I want to wash my shirt this afternoon.

I saw a Deposit *(Deposit, NY)* paper with the names of the drafted in Sanford. I see Jacob Gardinier is in, but I suppose Nick will pay the $300 and keep him at home. Tell C.S. to stay away from here for he cannot stand the soldier's fare. Many of our best men are giving out. We had 6 Coles in our company--one sold out at Delhi, one deserted, one is at Yorktown in the hospital and the other 3 are here, but only one is fit for duty. And there were three Cooks, 2 of us are here fit for duty and one in the hospital.

The children are going to school I suppose and you are doing the best you can. You said you did not get much done in drying berries. Well, you can't expect to do everything now, but when it comes time to dry apples you will have a little more time.

The Sutler has sealed cans with a pound of honey in, which he sells for 50 cents and a pint can of strawberries for 15 cents. If you have any honey to spare this fall, it would pay to strain and can it and send it down here. It would bring almost any price. I shall want another box this fall if I have to stay down here. These good things we get from home are worth all the United States to a soldier. I will write no more till after dinner. We will be paid this afternoon.

Well, I have been to dinner and will finish writing. I will ask some more questions and probably you have answered them already. Have you sold C.S. the clothes we were talking about and how are the sewing machines going? And how much money have you left? You see I am very inquisitive, don't you. But I like to know something besides the military style. Will is better than he was yesterday. I have written all I know. Be a good girl. Yours,

B.A.C.

No. 69, Camp in Virginia, Thursday, August 6, 1863

Dear Wife,

We got our pay yesterday and are on the move this morning. We are near the station waiting for the cars to get in shape to take us someplace. I hear we are to go to Alexanderia. Someone said we were going to New York to drill the drafted men, but I can't swallow that.

I will send the check in this hoping it will reach you in due time. But the $6.00 I will keep and see what I can do with it here for I don't know where we shall go.

I feel pretty well, but my left arm is swelled pretty bad. If it keeps on I shan't be fit for duty in a day or two. I haven't shown it to the doctor yet. I will not write more now but wait and see what takes place next.

Well, at 12 noon we got on the cars and at half past 2 we started towards Alexandria. It is now 6 o'clock and one more hour will bring us to Alexandria or Washington. Now the cars are in motion and this is crooked writing, but I want to finish this so I can send it from alexandria or some other place.

Today is the day Lincoln appointed for prayer and thanksgiving.

One of our lieutenants says we are going to New York to drill conscripts and some say we are going into Delaware County to enforce the draft because they are bound to resist it. But all of this I don't believe. Where we are going I can tell you better after we stop. We may go down and take Charleston or go up the peninsula and take Richmond. But one thing I think is sure, we shan't fight much till the hot weather is over. Now I will wait till I get to someplace.

Friday morning. We are in Alexandria. This morning the little gals and boys are bringing pie and cake of all kinds, and all kinds of fruit--even watermelons and milk. I got some milk and a new loaf of bread, so I had a good breakfast. Now we can get everything we want and the money flies. But you will find that my money don't go without getting something in return.

We shall probably leave here today for someplace. You shall hear from me again soon. I expect a letter from you soon. From your soldier,

B. A. Cook

No. 70, Newport News, Sunday, August 9, 1863

Dear Wife,

I am happy to inform you that I am safe and sound and hope this will find you the same. We got into the boat Friday the 7th about noon. We had a very nice boat to ride in but the weather is very hot. I never sweat so in my life. Set still in the shade and the sweat runs off in great drops. Where we shall go from here remains to be told. We have good water here. I have been down and bathed in the river this morning. The water in the river here is salt so it is good for a fellow. We got some mail last nite but I got none but there is 2 days mail back and I hope it will come tonight. If it does I shall get a letter then I can finish this.

I tell you I have lived pretty well the 2 days that are past for I have had pie and cake and cheese and milk and lemonade and peaches, pears, apples and watermelon. And here we can get fresh fish, I got some last nite for supper and we have got a head of cabbage for dinner. Steve bought some warm biscuits for breakfast so you see we live bully, but it takes cash.

Well you know I was about to run short for money some time ago but I kept along and bought my tobacco. And I had money all the time, you know that all I have kept of the 6 months pay previous to the last 2 months was 2 dollars. For I sent you a 40 check and 10 cash, next I sent 20 check and after 5 cash which I haven't heard from. The other dollar I sent Abel that I haven't heard from. This time I kept the 6 dollars and sent the check. You may think that my money is low but my 6 dollars is good yet. I have got a dollars worth of tobacco on hand and 2 lb.. of sugar and $6.25 cts. So you see I am living on the interest of my money.

Well I suppose you are in the midst of haying and if it is as hot as it is here you can make hay without much trouble after it is cut down. There goes a button off my pants, I had to borrow a needle and thread yesterday and sew two on. Send me a needle and 3 or 4 needles full of thread in your next and by and by you can send the like again. For if I try to carry needles in my pocket I sweat so that they will rust all to pieces. I have to wrap tinfoil around my post stamps to keep them from sticking and spoiling.

There has been a good deal of talk of our going to Charleston and I should not wonder if we did take a ride on the big water before long. I will wait and see if I don't get some mail for I shan't send this until tomorrow.

Tuesday, August 11. We are on the old Atlantic. I have not seen any land since last nite but the weather is very fine and I hope we shall have a good time and get to journeys end tomorrow. You see I commenced this Sunday and Sunday nite we got no mail. But we were up all nite to get on the boat, we got on about midnight and lay down but we didn't start until the lite and we have kept going ever since. It was Monday p.m. before we left Newport News. I bought a box of cigars containing 200 cigars for 2 dollars and have just sold the last of them. And I now have $8.75 cts besides I have spent over a dollar on this boat. But I got the cigars very cheap and sold them without any trouble. Well I guess we are bound for Charleston and I will get this ready to send back by boat *(the rest of this letter is illegible)*.

No. 71(?), Folly Island, August 15, 1863

Dear Louisa,

I finished a letter for you on the morning of the 13th and sent it. We landed here on the 12th. On the 13th, we moved about 3 miles for encampment, so I am now able to tell you something about this island. It is not more than one mile wide, but several miles long. The side that our encampment is on is washed by the waves of the Atlantic. The other is bounded by the same water as near as I can learn, but it looks like a river. Vessels run up and down it at high tide.

There are five of us on picket today over on the river side of the island. We have fine times for we can get all the oysters we are amind to pick up. I have just been eating fried oysters and oyster soup for supper. I would like to make some soup for you and you could put a lump of butter in it. Then it would be gooder, but a soldier thinks it is good without butter.

I went bathing this morning just at break of day. The waves rolled two feet high. The beach slopes about 4 inches to the rod so you see we can wade out a good ways from the edge of the water.

Fort Sumter was in sight before we came here or before we moved down the island. We could see it plain 10 or 12 miles away with the naked eye. We don't get any news of her attack. I haven't seen a letter or paper since I came here--except old ones. They are booming away every day more or less on Morris Island.

There has been another steamboat load of soldiers gone by while I am writing. I suppose they have landed on this island. The men that have been here 4 or 5 weeks say they have had as good health here as anywhere. But the water doesn't taste good. The boys often say they would give a dollar for a canteen full of water from a good cold spring in Delaware County.

I am afflicted with a cough, but don't seem to have any cold. I slept but little last night and have coughed considerably today. I have a little boil on my arm, but I feel pretty well. After all, if I could get the mail I should feel better. I don't know what to write because I don't hear anything to write about.

The Lieutenant told me that they were building a bakery on the island and in the course of a week we would get bread. By the looks of the old camps, there have been soldiers on this island all winter I should think. But they have left and we have taken their places. How long we shall stay here no one knows.

Well, it is too dark to write, so good night and give me a kiss.

Sunday the 16th. This is a fine morning and how happy I would be if I was at home as I dreamed last night. I thought I was at home talking with you and holding Mary on my lap. I wish it could be so, While I was looking at all of out likeness yesterday, I thought what a happy family if we were together. But the absence of one makes all gloomy, especially you. I don't know as the children miss me so much, but I guess Hat and Em have not forgotten how they felt when I left to go to Delhi. If they have, I have not. Neither have I forgotten the last time I left my home and all that was dear.

I asked myself then shall I ever see this dear spot again. And that is the question yet. But, Louisa, I think that everything will come out right for you know the Lord has always been on our side, and if He is for us who shall be against us. Therefore, let us trust in Him and all will be well.

B. A. Cook

This is marked 71 continued (no date)

There is much to be learned by being a soldier. I have seen a great deal of territory and have mingled with thousands of men. I've seen lots of officers, some that were gentlemen and others that were not worthy to be called men. And there are some privates that are gentlemen, and others are lower than the beast.

I said there was much to learn. Yes, and many learn these things, *viz.* to swear the wickedest of oaths, and play cards for money and win or lose a month's wages in a few hours. Not only this, but they would be complete drunkards if they could get licor *(sic.)*. I saw one of our company pay $2.00 for a pint of whiskey and then go and sit down with 2 or 3 others and play cards. He played all afternoon (it was on the boat). The next morning he was looking for his pocketbook and did not find it. He said there was over $15.00 in it, so he is without a cent. He hasn't sent any home. It is all gone. I lent him 95 cts. for he is a clever good fellow, but he gives away to bad habits.

Well, we are on picket yet. I stood on the post from 10 to 12 last nite and could see the flash of cannon and bursting shells all the time. I could hardly hear the report, for it is so far. It was up about Charleston somewhere. I had so much coughing to do, I didn't sleep such. Well, it is now my turn to stand 2 hours, so I go.

Now I am in camp after rations. They say the mail goes tonite, so I will leave this to go. Our whole brigade went up to Morse Island yesterday. So you see I was one of the lucky ones to be detailed here on picket and not have to march 6 or 7 miles. It may be that some of the reb shells will come near some of our boys. We expect them in tonite, but we shant be relieved before tomorrow or the next day. I don't care if it ain't in 3 weeks, for I'd rather be on picket than in camp or on a march.

Oh, I ache so to get a letter from you. Why don't the mail come? Well, I have wrote all I know. I wish to be remembered to all the good folks and give my respects to all who inquire after me, if there be any such.

B. A. Cook

No. 72, (written on letterhead Camp on Morris Island, 1214 Reg't Co., F., U.S.A.) Aug. 22, 1863

Dear Wife

I seat myself on a Sunday nite to rite a few lines to the one I love best to let her know I am above ground and enjoying myself as well as can be under existing circumstances. We come from Folly Island onto this island Monday nite. We have had no tents this week but lay down on the ground under blankets in the sand and nothing over us. When the wind blows the sand drifts here just as snow does up in our country in winter. And it is impossible to cook anything without it get full of sand. We have to eat sand, drink sand, and sleep in the sand. But I hope we shall get away from here before many weeks.

There has been continuous firing here all this week with the big guns. Forts Wagner Craig and Johnson Creesh(?) forts on the Is..(?) are in our way but we have forts here too and they throw shell at each other. But our guns have directed their mostly at Fort Sumter whose walls look pretty ragged. The old ironsides has put a good many shots into Fort Sumter. Sumter has done no firing of any account. They say the guns are taken out and put in position in other places.

We have laid in intrenchments every nite until last nite. The shells are quite numerous but there has been no one of our Regiment killed as yet. Thare (has) been several accidents happen with our guns. One went off prematurely yesterday and killed 4 of the men and one of our 300 pound guns had a shell burst before it cleared the gun and bursted it at the muzzle. But they sawed it off so it will work yet, it hurt no one.

The bombardment goes on night and day but there is but few killed to what one would suppose to hear the firing. I suppose you get the news in the paper so I will write about something else. We have had no mail yet.

I tell you the time seems twice as long when I can't hear from you. I hope we shall get our mail in a day or two. I hope you have got your check. I have $9.00 now so you see my pile don't get any smaller.

I hope you are getting along with your haying. Well if you have had as good weather as we have it has been good. There is no use of talking I want to hear from home, don't you think I do. Is the school most out and how are the girls enjoying themselves?

I did not like the idea of coming down here in the hottest of weather but as yet I haven't felt the heat as I did in Virginia. For here we get a breeze from the ocean all the time. But the sun pours down on this sand very hot and if it was not for the ocean breeze we could not live.

There are many in our Regiment unwell and no place to put them to make them comfortable.

My cough is better so it don't trouble me much. I hope your health is good. I would like to hear from you and all the rest of the good folks. I don't know as I shall write again till I get a letter, yours ever

B. A. Cook

No. 73, Folly Island, S. C., Aug. 31, 1863

Ever faithful companion it is with extreme pleasure that I attempt to address you this first day of another year with you as yesterday was your birthday. I hope you can take more comfort this year than you have the most of the past year. May the good Lord give you health. I am sorry to hear the children are dying so up there it seems hard don't it to see those flowers cut off. I pray it may not enter our garden for what would we do if we should loose our little sweet girls. Oh how I long to see them and the old girl too. But have patience I think all will work well, if things don't go to suit us we must be or try to be resigned to the will of the One who rules all things.

We buried 2 out of our Co. while we were on Morris Is. George A. Mudge and Wm. P. Fish. Mudge died of fever and Fish was killed by the bursting of a 200 lb. gun. The breech blew out and struck in the pile of Sand Bags which he set behind and threw them with such force against him that it broke his left arm and bruised his body so he only lived a few hours. The breech of this gun weighed not less than a ton. It passed by him and went to the next Sand Bank and stopped. If the breech had struck him it would have ground him all to pieces. Not more than 5 minutes before I was by his side, but I left while the gunners were loading the gun. For there had 2 or 3 guns burst within a week and killed and mangled men. We were there to support these guns lest the rebs should come and take them. There has been nearly as many of our men hurt by our own cannon as by the enemy.

The last nite we were up in the pits just at dark when we were to be relieved the rebs began to throw shell like fun. They bursted and struck all about us but no one hurt. When our relief came we had to leave the bomb proofs and let them in. So each Co. went out in single file or any way they had a mind to until we got out of reach of the shell and whistling bullets. So we all got to camp safe.

We left the Is last Saturday and got here in the evening and yesterday I went to Brigade headquarters to put up some tents. I see the mail come for the Brigade, there was 53 bushel sacks full and another almost full. I suppose I got my share for I have got 5 from you and one from mother beside the line come in Steve's letter.

I am glad you have got done haying in good time and got it all payed for. The barn is full of hay of course but it will settle quite a bit. They changed their mind about the heifer have they. Well let them take her away or do as they see fit, if they should see fit to pay something for keeping her a year all rite if not all rite, you will keep track of all of these things of course.

Has Al ever said anything about the note you got of Mapes last winter? You know he was agoing to help pay that if I let him have it. But I suppose he will soon get rich when he gets educated and make us all rich. I expected it would cost about 40 dollars or over to do the haying, board and all. You said you was at Deposit to get the money on the check. Did you refer to the one I sent in June or the one I sent in August for I don't think the last one had hardly reached you.

I was glad to hear you got the $5, I got the 50 cents and every thing all strait. Only you and Kate must not get so close together as the change men for I got one from her saying Dear Husband and you put the wrong letter in the rite envelope but it all come out rite.

(No Signature)

SEPTEMBER 1863

Folly Island, SC, August 29th to February 23, 1864
September 8, Commander Stevens' night attack on Fort Sumter
September 19th and 20th, Chickamauga, Ga.

History summarization pages 131-144

On the 29th of August, the 144th returned to its camp on Folly Island. A new camp was laid out a little south of the old one and tents set up on it and more comfortable, and all the surroundings made as comfortable and healthful as circumstances would admit. it was at this camp that the 144th fought its hardest battle and suffered its greatest losses during the Siege of Charleston and indeed, during its entire service. The hard marches during the summer and now the poor water and the drifting sand that found its way into all our food, and added to all this issue of a flour ration with no means to properly cook it, had brought that great scourge of the soldier, "camp disease." A good illustration of the effect of mind conditions as affecting the health is found in s letter written by Lieut., Frank Heimer of company C. "While on Folly Island in September, 1863, you will remember that very near every man in the Regiment got sick: the cause being in my opinion that everlasting marching in Virginia in the hot summer and then being transplanted to a sandy island in South Carolina with bad and unhealthy water to drink. Well, for about three days I was the only officer for duty, the others reporting sick, and the common saying was, 'You can never kill a Dutchman unless you hang him and he will get used to that.' But soon some of the officers got better and I too came on the sick list and got worse and worse every week. Surgeon Leal's opium pills did not do me any good: only just put me to sleep and being asleep saw lots of little men dancing and laughing with all their might around me. One week passed and no better: another passed and still worse, and another week commenced finding me worse. Now things began to get serious. You will remember also that we buried our dead over and beyond a sand knoll marching by the dispensary tent."

So much sickness prevailed that an examining board of surgeons was appointed to examine applicants for furloughs. So many men came before the board and were granted furloughs that Gen. Gillmore determined to establish a convalescent camp to which those granted furloughs on account of disability should be sent. This convalescent camp was established at St. Augustine, Fla., and in pursuance of the order establishing the camp the hospital boat Cosmopolitan included this among its trips.

While disease and death were making such sad inroads on our numbers the Siege of Charleston was being pressed vigorously. After the commencement of the fifth parallel it was pushed steadily until it reached the moat of Wagner. By the 5th of September the work had progressed so far that it was determined to attempt capture by assault. Accordingly on the 6th the fort was subjected to another bombardment from land batteries and war vessels, with intent to prepare for an assault ordered to be made at nine a.m. of the 7th. The enemy did not wait for this but evacuated Wagner and Gregg on the night of the 6th. So silently and efficiently were the plans of evacuation carried out that the movement was not discovered until after midnight when nearly all had left the island. Only seventy men were captured.

September 27th marked the anniversary of our "muster-in". The year of service make marked changes in the regiment, both among officers and men. Lieut. Penet alone remains of Co. E' officers and Capt. Plaskett of Company F. Of the men fifty-five had died, one hundred and six had been discharged, and a number deserted.

No. 73, Camp on Folly Island, September 1, 1863

Dear L.

This morning finds me well as usual and trying to talk to you. I was home on a furlow last nite and enjoyed myself first rate. Well you asked some questions which I will try to answer. As to the cow if you can get a fair price for her and get your winter wood cut before winter it would be a nice thing. It is just what you want and you had better get your wood before winter. And if Brandt takes the cow if Bill Taylor will take the coat and vest and cut wood let him do it. As to hiring money of Kate if you can't collect and raise enough to pay Brandt. If Kate will let you have money at 6 per cent interest get it. If not let it go until George pays for it will take all I can send home to keep you agoing. I don't know what Bet is worth but do the best you can with her and if you can get one or two yearlings do so. I believe you are doing gest as well at calculating as I could do and the more you do business the better you will understand it. I suppose our stock has had some help to eat the pasture. Does the new fallow afford much feed or did it not seed good, Buckwheat is bad to seed after. The orderly says bring in the mail so I must wind up short. I will rite soon again, you must excuse me for not writing in over a week for we have been moving and yesterday we were mustered again for 2 months pay and I hope we shall get it in 2 or 3 weeks.

Ever Yours,
B. A. Cook

No. 74, Folly Island, September 3, 1863

Dear Wife;

This morning finds me feeling pretty well for a soldier and we or I live pretty well now days for I bought onions for 20 cts a doz and some butter for 50 cts and cheese for 40 cts and we drew some flour yesterday. So we have minute pudding and pancakes. I have no particular war news to rite and you can hear what is going on here by the paper. And we get news here very often there has been heavy firing on the front.

This week especially nite before last the gunboats were at work. Charleston has got to come under after a while. I see by your letter that about the time I got down here your mind was rather troubled about me. Well it was rather ticklish coming down here in August. But I have seen no very hot weather yet here but the air feels like fall just as much as it does at home this time of the year.

Well I can't blame you for feeling troubled about my welfare but after all I don't know but I am as safe here as anywhere for God is here and everywhere. But I feel for you and your burden is greater than mine and I hope to get home to relieve you in a few months. I think very favorably we shan't see a fite this year but time will tell.

Mother says Louisa stands it bravely for you haven't been to see her but once since she went to house keeping and she hasn't been to see you but meant to go soon.

Well Louisa you must be of good cheer there is better days coming and I trust we shall see many happy days together. Yet I think we have been favored the year that is past for many have lost children and friends while our family is unbroken.

I have got no letter since the one you was at Deposit, no the latest is 72 Sunday 16th but when the mail comes I shall get one.

I want some explanation about that 12 year old boy and I want some more snuff for I lost what I had when we moved. You must send a little at a time then I can treat the gray backs once in a while. You think if we are permitted to lice together again we will know how to take comfort.

I think so to, you Dear Wife have been an affectionate companion and a kind Mother. You have been to me all I could desire and all I ask is to get a chance to enjoy your society again with out little ones. So Dear I have got to go on drill.

Thursday Afternoon. I will tell you what I had for dinner. Some wheat pancakes and pork gravy and boiled beans and we drew some pickled cabbage just as good a dinner as I could wish for here. Now I would like a pocket full of apples to eat this afternoon.

The news has come here that the Stars and Stripes float over Fort Wagoner and Gregg and Fort Sumter is a perfect wreck deserted by the enemy and I hope it is all true. But it is too good to believe all at once. We have to go on drill twice a day and attend roll call 5 times a day. We drill from 9 a.m. to 10 a.m. and from 4 p.m. to 6 p.m.

Every day makes one less, it will be 1 year the 7th of this month since we were mustered into the United States service. So we have only 2 years to serve at the longest and I hope 2 months will finish the war and it would if it wasn't for the miserable officers that want a long job. They think as long as they can lounge around and draw big pay it is all rite. But it ain't so with the private they want to fite their way through and get home about their business and not stay down here and die of old age.

Ben Raynolds is here he comes to see us quite often. There is about one half the regiment goes to the doctors every morning so the word goes. There is a good many sick in the regt. but we have got a new Quarter Master and he will get us something to eat so we will feel better. No more ar present.
(written in the top margin).

Friday morning. Everything is quiet the mail goes out this morning. So I must send this as it is. I expect a letter tomorrow from you. I will answer it more directly (last two words questionable).

B. A. C.

No. 75, Folly Island, S.C., September 7, 1863

Dear Wife,

Love prompts me to write a few lines to thee and let you know how I get along. I haven't done any duty in 3 or 4 days. The doctor excuses me from duty for I have had your headache, I guess and a little touch of the diarrhea, but I have plenty of money and I get what I want to eat and make something besides. For I have about 9 dollars now I want to send you 5 before long.

I got your good long letter No. 73 the 5th of this month. I am sorry to hear you are afflicted with the headache so much for it is not a very fine thing to have and I hope you can get something to help it. As to the farm I expect the brush will get the start but I guess I will get home next year to tend to them and fix the fence. I suppose it is very difficult getting help and you have to pay a high price for what you get done but don't get discouraged for you are doing pretty well at farming.

The cows do fat out pretty well that it so and if you can get rid of them and not winter them I would do it at some price and get something that will come in next spring. For 2 good cows are worth mote than 4 poor ones and it is not worth while to winter anything that will be of no use next summer unless it is young stock. Unless Mother has got something she wants kept let them have their way about that cow and keep cool and I will and see what they will do with her.

I think your dream a courious one and I can't interpret it but as to your lover being untrue that will not be while he is alive and I am satisfied as to your virtue. I have no fears of your proving false. No never for those vows are just as binding if we are thousands of miles apart as though we were together and we feel for each others welfare just as such as though we were together. But we cannot comfort each other and do for each other as we could if we were together. I think Nel's wife is in big business and I have no reason to disbelieve he truth of the story and Nel is just as mean as she is I guess so let them rip. I wont write any more till after dinner.

Well I have eat my dinner. I had beans and hardtack with worms in but I buy cakes to eat most of the time in the place of hardtack and I had some Maple Sugar for dinner. I got 5 little cakes for 25 cts. They are very small about 2 mouths full apiece but it tastes good. I am going down to the sutler to see if I can't but something to sell again so it will pay.

Tuesday the 8th. I will rite a few lines again. I have been on drill this forenoon but it makes my head ache come. I bought a box of figs last nite and sold them out and made 25 cts. this morning. I bought 5 mackerel for 10 cts a piece and sold them for 15 cts a piece trust for you see money is getting scarce here. Some of the boys have spent their 26 dollars in a month well they have nothing else to do with their money. But I am glad I can let my money go where it will do somebody some good ain't you? If I had felt well the week that is past I could of saved 3 dollars more than I have but when a fellow don't feel well he wants something all the while and the Sutler have most everything to sell. Now I have lent and trusted 3 dollars more and have got $8.50 in my pocket.

Steve is off duty to he ain't very well and a good many of the Regt. I will stop writing for the present.

Tuesday evening. Well I have made up my mind to finish this and send it for you will think I am a good while answering your letter. We have quite flattering news today. They say that Fort Wagner and the whole Island is in our hands. Also that the magazine in fort Moultry is blown up. I hope you will get glorious news in the paper before long. If you have not got it before this time.

It is reported that there was 200 dead in Wagner when our men went into it and in one place there was 4 dead bodies tied together and they thought there was a trap there so they went carefully and tied a long rope and got off a proper distance and pulled the rope and off went a torpedo. So you see the rebs are up to all manner of deviltry to kill the Yanks.

Wednesday Morning. Well I am most out of money for I bought a nice little pistol for $2.00 and this morning Gould and I bought a barrel of ginger cookies for $11.00 which we intend to sell today and tomorrow. I will tell you in my next how I get along and I bought a bottle of lemon Syrup for one dollar and put a spoon full in a cup of water and sell it at 5 cts a drink and make something on it for it makes a good drink for the water is poor here.

The captain of Co. C died last nite he is to be sent home. I believe the health of our Company is improving a little. I think at least we have more men for duty. Some say the mail won't go until the last of the week so I shan't send this today.

The news concerning those forts is confirmed this morning. they say they took some prisoners but how many I don't know. but likely before you get this you will get the particulars in the papers.

The morning of the 10th. Before sunrise. I thought I would write a little this morning and tell you that I am well only I have the Shits a little. Just as quick as the roll is called I must go to selling cakes for breakfast. Our barrel is two thirds gone and we want to finish them this morning.

Well I must get ready for roll call. After breakfast I am on guard duty today and our company are going on *(illegible)* parties down at the dock and I will send this letter this morning anyhow. Hoping you will forgive me for not writing sooner for I have been busy you see.

> From your old Soldier
> B. A. Cook

No. 76, Folly Island, South Carolina, Friday, September 11, 1863

Ever loved Wife,

I am happy to tell you that I received your letters today. They were written from the 23rd of August up. One was mailed at Hale Eddy on the 30th and the other at Underwood on the 31st.

I am glad you are in such good spirits and have plenty of berries and sauce to last you all winter. I hope you will have health to enjoy it. I have some little hope of getting home before you get it eaten up.

You need not borrow much trouble about me for I think I will come out all rite. I got the leaves but haven't seen fit to use them yet. The letter with the thread and needles came all right.

I hope you have good luck buying at the sale and I hope that the minister will take Jenny to winter--then you will be all rite for the winter. I guess those men you heard were someone a cooning. But I think someone wanted to do something when they took the bars out and opened the doors.

I think it would be best to keep your rolls until you can manufacture them to your notion. I would write often but I suppose the mail leaves here only once a week. If that be the case, you would get them only so often anyway. But the mail leaves here tomorrow, so I hasten to get this ready to go in the morning. Likely it will overtake the one I sent this week. I don't get many letters except from you, but you are faithful in writing. I think we shall get nearer home before long so it won't take 10 days to get a letter.

It is no use for me to tell you the war news for you will get it a week sooner than I can send it to you. Our barrel of cakes are sold and we got our money back and had a good many cakes to eat. There is but little money in the Regiment so it's no use trying to buy and sell anymore till after payday. I have quite a notion to send you

$5 in this for I have $7.00 and about 20 postage stamps. If I send it I will say more about it.

I hope Emmy did not get sick with sore throat for the children are dying with it all around there.

I suppose it is cold up there. But not here. Last nite I was on guard and lay on the ground with nothing over me. So you see it ain't frosty here.

I will write a few words in the morning if I conclude to send the $5. I don't know but it would be best to trade my pistol for a watch if I can make a trade to suit.

Saturday morning the 12th. It is a very nice morning and I would like to take breakfast with you and the children. I dreamed of being at home last nite. Good morning L.M.C.

B. A. C.

No. 77, Folly Island, South Carolina, September 15, 1863

I will rite to you a little today, but don't suppose it will go till the last of the week. But I must tell you that last nite I got a letter from my old true Wife--No. 76 mailed Sept. 3rd. I am glad you are sociable for you are almost the only one up there that thinks me worth talking to. But you are faithful in writing to your old true heart.

The suction came out as I expected for I supposed the things would bring all they were worth. As to Jenny, the main thing is to let someone have her that will take care of her and use her well. If the minister don't take her and if Deroy wants to buy her at a fair price, let him have her. Or if he wants to take her and keep her through the winter or as long as you can spare her, I think it will be all right. I think he would use her well. If he takes her and don't injure her, but keeps her well, no charge for service. That is, he takes her as his own until called for. I will rite to him immediately. No I won't, for the minister may take her yet. But if he don't, you can send Deroy word for that will do just as well and perhaps better than my letter as you know all about the matter more than I do. I think it will be a great relief to you and to the haymow if someone takes her through the winter. So charge nothing for service, but if they should overdrive or injure her, then we would expect them to pay for it.

I am sorry Em has got the summer complaint, for I have had it a good deal this summer. But I hope she is better. I suppose you are getting lots of blackberries dried and I hope I can get home to help eat them. If I don't, you can send some of them to me this winter. I am very glad you have got sauce enough to last through the winter even if I come. But I tell you, I could eat a good pile of vegetables. But I don't eat much here--I am getting poor. And I am bound to get poor for they have marched me around about all they will for nothing. That is so, now remember.

Tell Mate that I say she must mind and be a good girl or Pa won't like her when he gets home. I have got some nice seashells that I want to send the girls, but some say we are not allowed to send any such things from here.

Steve and I are both marked "quarters" by the doctor. We haven't done but little duty in several days. I stood guard once, but I need not if I had went to the doctor. But I feel pretty well, so I went and stood guard. I feel pretty well this morning. The doctor put me on "quarters" so I have no duty to do, not even to attend roll call. I am weak and it will probably be some time before I get strength to do much duty.

I think you made Bowl Thomas a bully answer--I would like to hug you for that.

I would give 50 cents for what johnnycake and butter I could eat this morning. I suppose you would let me have it for nothing if I would come after it. Well, I guess I will be after some one of these days. I dream of being home with you most every nite. I wish I could awake some morning and find myself at home for good, don't you? Well, I will rite no more now. But I guess I will finish this for there is some talk that mail goes in the morning. I will enclose five dollars in this hoping it will reach you safely. I have 50 cents left and 3 dollars coming to me in the Company which I guess I will get when they get their money from home. And we ought to be paid off in about 3 weeks. Excuse this short letter Dear One. I will rite soon again, so good nite Wife. I sleep alone tonite for my tent mates are on picket.

B. A. Cook

Continued on Sept. 17th. This stormy day finds me all rite, only I am weak and thin in flesh. I have just been looking at our pictures. I don't look as fleshy as I did then or as I did at Vienna last winter, for I had a hard summer's work and hard fare. And I suppose you look as poor as I do with all of your care and labor. I have kept the six pictures, including Al's, as nice as can be in my pocket.

I could not send the letter as I supposed. You see, I can send only once a week. Now I will grumble a little for our Regiment has little nasty shelter tents--no shelter at all. And all of the other regiments have good tents. And that is the way it goes.

Leroy Thompkins of Company A has got his discharge. Chas. Stiles of Company A has started for home this morning on a 30 day furlough. There have been 3 or 4 buried out of our Regiment this week, and more are on the same road. One of our sergeants, John Whittaker, is very poorly--his papers have been sent in for a discharge. When I get poor enough, I will send for mine.

Last nite after the first shower, the whole Brigade was called out and went to the other sister island and came back this morning. Of course, those not fit for duty didn't go. So I stayed in camp with the biggest half of the Company. There are only about 20 in our Company fit for duty.

Now Wife, I believe you are working too hard and I beg you not to do it. If you never pay a debt and if you have to sell a cow to get wood, do it rather than kill yourself cutting it. For people as young as we are better off without a home and having health than we would be with a home and no health. Now this is my view on the matter, so do the best you can and I will do the same. And God willing, I will meet you in a few months at the longest. No more at present.

Friday afternoon, the 18th. I am feeling pretty well today, but I ain't on duty. I have been writing to Lib Cook *(probably an uncle)* today to see if I can't hear from them once more. You ought to go there before Jenny goes.

I expect a letter from you in a day or two. I can't send one as often as I want to, but I will do the best I can. Time passes away pretty fast and I am coming home one of these days. So keep up good courage.

How do your calves look? Are they worth wintering and will you have much of a hog to kill this fall? And how many chickens will you winter? Did you ever get anything from the potatoes I planted over at Lee's? Can't you buy some buckwheat from someone? If you could get 6 or 8 dollars worth it would be a fine thing. How much is flour worth per sack?

You will miss Jenny for running around getting your things. But you had better pay ten dollars getting your things fetched to you than winter her. And I guess Turrell's folks will do your teaming and let you go with them when they go.

Well, this is full, so I must stop Dear One.

From the same old boy,

B. A. C.

No. 78, Folly Island, South Carolina, September 22, 1863

Dearly beloved Wife,

I seat myself to write a few words to let you know that I am well but am not doing duty yet. I feel too weak, you see. We don't get much to eat except hardtack that has bugs and worms in it. So we or I don't eat much of them (for fear they will make me too strong).

We got 7 new A tents for our Company the other day. The sick were ordered to put them up and go into them. So there are 4 in each tent which makes 28 sick or on the sick list.

Since the 18th it has been very cool at nite. So most of us have suffered for want of covering having no blankets over us. They are getting blankets and things and expect some more tents in a few days. We are so far from home it takes a good while to supply all our wants.

I got the letter you finished on the 8th some 2 days ago. I would have answered it immediately, but the mail would not go out so it's no use rushing. I was very glad to hear from you and to think you and Kate can take some comfort together. Steve and I are doing well together. I would like to have been down to Grandma's with you and gotten some good apples to eat.

I suppose it is pretty cool and frosty up there nowadays for it feels like fall down here. Did you get your corn cut before the frost killed it? And are you likely to get any help to gather your corn and potatoes? And do you have to cut your wood yet? I am anxious to hear that you have got a good lot of wood on hand and that you have got the stock fixed to suit. If Brother Hewet takes Jenny and you can get rid of Bet, you will have hay enough to winter 2 or 3 head of young cattle or cows if you could get them. If not, then you will have hay to spare which will come into play next winter no doubt.

As you said, (shit what a pen!) Mother is anxious to get these pictures. Well, you might have them taken without me for if Almus and Charles get married, then there would be no place for the rest of the children. So you see it will be all rite if she gets you three and the rest separate. But you must do as you like. I will come as soon as I can and have mine taken for her because I don't see that I can ever get it taken in this country.

Tuesday Afternoon. They say the mail will go out in the morning, so I will finish my letter. I have got some new pens, but they ain't much better than the old one. But if I can't write with a pen, I will take a pencil for I will rite to my old true lonely wife. I know that the time seems long to you and it looks hard to see other men get their discharge and your man not come to you. But be of good cheer Wife and trust in God and I think all will work rite. You man be sure that I long for your presence and the comforts of our little home made cheerful by the presence of our dear children. I hope to be there to help you farm it next year.

I think that if I were at home a month or two I would recoup so as to be as good as new. I have that nasty headache today as usual, and I shan't do duty until it gets better.

I suppose Mrs. Dimmick feels ugly at everybody that looks at Strickland, but it can't be helped. I think Cornelia has split herself anyway, but no one ought to find fault if she is satisfied.

I suppose Gremmy Turrel *(neighbor near farm)* has gotten back by this time and I hope alive. If Issac is drafted there will be a good many 300 dollars paid out. I would like to know who was drafted in Scott.

Well, I have signed up for a new overcoat, blanket and pants. My old ones have not come, and I hope they never will now for I don't want 2 overcoats.

Dear One, I expect a letter from you when the mail comes for you are faithful in writing. I have written all I can think of, so I will close.

Yours ever Dearest Louisa,

B. A. Cook

N.B. I want you to acknowledge the reception of things when you get them. Did you get the ing I sent from Warrington Junction? And did you get the $5.00 I sent in No. 76?

Wednesday, the 23rd. It looks like rain and the air is quite cool. I hope you are comfortable and well. There is not much firing in front of late. I have no news to rite, but wish I had some good news. It is sickly in the Regiment yet and they have buried several. As the weather gets cooler it will be healthier I hope.

B. A. C.

No. 79, Folly Island, South Carolina, September 29, 1863

Dear Old Wife,

I will write to you again as the mail is to go tomorrow. I feel about as I did when I wrote before only my head don't ache much more. So I feel pretty well, but don't do duty today.

We are expecting soft bread tomorrow--we have had none in 6 months. We have had two mails the past week and each brought me a letter from my love. The last, No. 79, I got two days ago. Are you not foolish to think I don't write to you? I did not think so when I got no mail from you. I send one every mail. I thought when I wrote that I would not write again until I got one from you that I ought not have said that, for you would look at that pretty sharp. I wish you could hear from me more often, but I can't do any better than send one every mail.

I am very sorry you would have any thoughts that I could distrust your virtue and stability. But you cannot help feeling bad when you don't hear from me often and I know it. I wish I was with you so we would not have to depend on the mail to hear from one another.

I am glad you got a good, warm coat for winter and I want you to get all you can for your and the children's comfort. And don't talk about my scolding for I don't feel like scolding when you are doing so well.

Evening of the 29th. It is just a month since we returned to this island from Morris Island. I am a thousand times obliged to you for writing so often and when I get a chance I will pay it back.

The health of our Regiment doesn't improve much. In the year that is past there have been over 100 men discharged besides 23 commissioned officers.

And some 56 men died of disease and three killed. Three officers died--2 of them the past month. One was buried today--Lieutenant Dewit Mayo--he died of dysentery. Our Regiment numbers a great deal less because many were left behind in hospitals one place and another. And some few have deserted.

Well, I don't hear that you have traded and gotten yourself heifers yet. If they both come in in the spring it will do. If they are small, you are giving him a pretty good bargain if you pay 6 or 8 boot--unless they are nicer than I think they are. If one of them should fail to come in, then you would not be bound to pay the boot. But if you have got or do get them, try and keep them growing all winter if you can so they will be something in the spring. If he doesn't take Bet you can sell her for the cash and buy the mule from George or buy a good cow from someone by looking around a little.

I think it may be that Uncle Orlow or Brainard *(his uncles Francis Orlow Cook and David Brainard Cook)* have got cows they would sell or trade for one to beef.

I must stop for tonite. I wish I was as close to you as this sheet is to me.

Good evening dearest Wife,

B. A. C.

OCTOBER 1863

Folly Island, S.C. August 29th to February 23, 1864
October 14th, Bristoe Station, Va.

History Summarization pages 144 to 145

Among the men who succumbed to the camp scourge was
James M. Way of Co, D, who died at Folly Island, October
7th. In his death science lost as well as arms. His profession
before entering the army was that of stone mason. In his profession the brain was active as well as hands, and made to
read the secrets stored up in rocks. In doing this he discovered at Franklin, N.Y., in the Catskill strata of rock, fish bone
and fish scales, a fact that had escaped the observation of
other geologists in that section. Mr. Way continued his stu-
dious habits in the army, always on the lookout for something
new in geological surroundings. Because of these habits he
was known among his comrades as "The Professor."

October 24th, Col. Gregory resigned his command and immediately left the island. Lieut. Col. Lewis assumed the
command and by his vigorous and judicious methods brought
the Regiment up to a good standing among the various commands and so commended himself to his commanding and
associate officers that they all joined in a request to the ex-
ecutive of the state of New York, Gov. Seymour asking that
he he commissioned a Colonel. Other influences prevailed
and Wm. J. Slidell was appointed Colonel.

Judicious sanitary methods and precautions were instituted
and insisted upon resulting in material improvement in the

health of the Regiment. The October 1863 report of a sanitary inspector, sent to examine as to the health conditions on Folly Island, showed the sick rate of the 144th as 41.1 per cent, the highest on the island, the average sick rate at the same time being 17.2, but the following months of the year, November and December showed a very great improvement.

No. 80, Folly Island, South Carolina, October 4, 1863

Dear Wife,

As it is Sunday, I will rite a few lines and tell you that last Friday I got 2 letters from you. I see you are getting the start of me in riting. Oh, I wish our mail went twice a week--this mail won't go till Friday. So you see, you can't hear from me as often as you would wish. But it does me good to hear from you often.

I am sorry you have to work so hard. Those nasty sheep cut a great caper. I think it is too bad. Well, I hope you have gotten something from George that will give milk next summer. If she does well, she will be worth more than Bet to you.

Well, make a husking and get your corn husked for it will be quite a help.

Monday morning, the 5th. I feel pretty well this morning, but will not do duty yet. Steve is off duty too. We get a loaf of good bread every day and potatoes and onions once in a while--fresh beef once a week. So we are living pretty well lately. But we didn't get paid off yet and I am our of money just like the rest of the boys. I can get along a while if I don't have money.

I think you had better try and buy another cow between now and spring so as to have 4 cows. Is there no hope of the red heifer coming in in the spring? If there ain't, don't winter her if you can trade her off and get anything towards another cow. If you get a good cow, she will pay 25 dollars in butter next summer. The heifer will be worth nothing if she don't come in, but I am in hopes she will come in. If she ain't coming in, she ain't worth more than a yearling that is coming in.

I think those verses are very nice. They are nice books you got the girls I guess. I suppose they will learn some of the verses. I am very glad to get the snuff. I don't blame you for not lending money for once lent it would be hard getting it back again I assure you. I hope you had a good camp meeting.

Monday nite. Well, Willie Dan has his discharge and will probably come home sooner than this mail will reach you. I will finish this and send it with some shells for the girls. I will also send my little pistol and a few cartridges. It cost me $2.00. If you find anyone that wants it, you can sell it. It costs $5.00 at Delhi. There is a spring on the underside with a screw to bear onto. Then you can swing the barrel to one side and put the cartridge in and swing it back.

I hope you can get the briers cut in the new lot. I got some new clothes today and if they would take me home I would think a great deal of them. But as it is I don't prize them very highly.

I have considerable pain in my legs when I stir around. So I believe I will keep kind of still. Will Dan is pretty bad off, so I am glad he can go home. By and by you will see me at home.

Rosecrans has had a fight and I suppose we will have to stay down here till Charleston has surrendered. I hope that won't be more than 6 months for I mean to be home in the spring if the Lord is willing. Yes, our trust is in God and he will protect. We have no frost here, but the air is chilly at nite. But I have a good blanket to cover me tonight. So good nite Dear Louisa.

B. A. Cook

NOVEMBER 1863

Folly Island, S.C., August 29th to February 23, 1864
November 7, Rappahanock Station, Va.
November 14th to December 4th, Siege of
Knoxville, Tenn.
November 24th to 25th, Chattanooga, Lookout
Mountain, Orchard Knob and Mississippi
Ridge, Ga.

History Summarization pages 145 and 146

On November 13th, the 144th with the 40th Massachusetts were detailed for temporary service with Gen. Schimmelfenning's brigade and went with it on a reconnaissance to Seabrook Island. It proved to be a hard, heavy march through sand, mud and water. The expedition returned on the 17th without having accomplished anything except some hard marching.

On the 29th, the Regiment went out on a tour of seven days fatigue duty to Kiowah Island where fortifications were being constructed. Details for picket duty were sent out from time to time on Cole's Island. On this island very amicable relations were established between Union and Confederate pickets. A "neutral zone" was recognized on a bridge which separated the lines and here there were exchanges of coffee for tobacco and other small trade with occasional exchanges of newspapers and quite a large exchange of "chinning" and "chaffing" with some "pumping". Frequently a Confederate soldier, tired of the conditions of soldier service in Dixie would come into our lines and give themselves up.

No Number, (Continued) Saturday Eve the 11th   (This letter may be out of sequence)

No salutation

Wife I will scribble a little this eve as I do not have to go on guard again until 11 o'clock. I must tell you that I received your good long letter No. 41 today, it was mailed the 9th, it came quick. I was glad you received your 2 dollars and hope you will get your other 2 that I sent you.

I am glad your bee hive turned out so well and that you went to Uncle Orlos and had a good visit. The weather is very fine here and the mud is dried up so it is good marching and I can't tell what a week will bring forth. But I hope it will bring our company back to Vienna but I have but little faith and still I don't know but we will get back, time will tell.

It is curious what news you get about our skirmishes. We have not seen any rebs in arms yet. Well here it is Sunday morning and this letter is not finished. I am off guard at this time and been on Knapsack Inspection and mustered and the orders read to us were as follows. Some 6 regiments of Infantry and a Battery all our Division are to be ready to take the field on the morning of 13th with 40 rounds of cartridges in our boxes and 60 in wagons, which makes 100 rounds a piece. Also 7 days rations 3 of which shall be cooked.

It has been very nice weather 3 or 4 days past and the time has come to act. (You understand we are not ordered to march yet, but to be ready to take the field when called upon.) We may march tomorrow or we may stay here several days, there are some signs of a fight at Bull Run.

232

I suppose you have lots of Honey and Maple Sugar, I must close soon for I feel considerably tired for I slept only 3 hours last night, I want to sleep a little this afternoon. I will rite to Aunt Harriet as soon as I can get time. I must rite a few words to Mother. Your dream was quite annoying to you I suppose for the time being but I think you must have a woke before this time so it is all rite about the Southern Ladies. But I wish that some of your good dreams may come to pass and I think they will, don't you? Wife have faith and God will deliver us from the hand of the enemy. I can say that God has cared for me all my days and why should I fear to trust in him should danger stare me in the face, ever yours,

B. A. Cook

(written on the last page)

Mother, your kind letter was thankfully received and it will comfort me for several days to come with some other good letters that Louisa has written. I am sorry I haven't time to sit down and write a decent letter to you. But a few words from our friends does us much good sometimes. I expect my time for writing will be just as I can catch it after this. But I hope I can finish this letter the same week I commence it. If the boys go to school I don't see how you and Louisa can get along without one or the other getting a man to do the farming. Every thing is getting very high and some body has got to raise some thing or we will be as bad as they are in the South after a while. I hope a few months will bring peace to us for there is need of me with my little family.

Yours Truly Dear Mother

B. A. Cook

(written up the side of the letter)

I thank Mother Turrel for her kind wishes

Sugar

No Number Folly Island, S.C., November 12, 1863

Dear Louisa

I have a little while to rite before the mail goes so I will send you a few lines to inform you that I am well as can be and hope these few lines find you all in good health. *(illegible, but looks like)* For I have sent letters enough lately to cure you if there is any medicine in them. *(end of illegible portion).* I have no news to rite but I expect *(illegible portion).*

I dream of you every nite. Last nite we were out to *(illegible)* for a quarterly meeting and had a good time and that is no *(missing word).*

I long for the time to come when I can be by your side again for you are all to me. Oh what an earthly comfort a good woman is any your good letters is ever a *(illegible)* to me while deprived of your society. What a blessing it is that we can rite to each other.

I hope you have got wood this cold weather, we have had frost here this week but it is warm now. I guess you have had snow up your way by the feeling in the air here. I tell you I enjoy this way of soldiering as well as anybody.

I hear Steve is getting rite smart I hope he will return here soon. We expect the paymaster here soon but we may be disappointed. The health of the men is improving.

Tell the girls that I would like to see them and hear them speak and I would like to see them play as they used to. Wife you will excuse this short letter please and I will rite soon again.

Yours ever,

B. A. Cook

No. 88, Folly Island, S.C., November 19, 1863

Dear One

I must rite a little this morning before the mail goes. I ought to rote before but have been waiting for the mail which came last nite between 7 and 8 it brought me 3 letters from you. One mailed the 3rd, one the 4th, and one the 7th. I am glad you was as well as you was.

I hope Bill will cut you a good lot of wood. Yes it is time our place is doing better than Steve's, but I am *(illegible)* to hear that Kate has put all of Steve's wages to clothes. But we can afford it if they can. I am afraid we shall never see Steve alive, but hope for the best. I am glad your Sap(?) is all gathered. I am well and have spent in a little over a month $12.00 for I eat 5 or 6 apples every day they taste so good and have butter and cheese when I want it.

I got most out of money and got $2.00 yesterday which I have to pay $2.50 for after pay day but I don't want to hire more at that rate and I am going to stop spending so much money. If you have money you may send me $5.00 in greenbacks for that is preferable here. Likely I shall have to take all my pay in check next payday if I do I will send it home and then you can send me more money if I want it.

I will not forget the loved ones at home in prayer I assure you and you need not worry about me for I think everything will work out rite. You told me what Willy had told me concerning examination all very good and you know I am something of a lawyer

I have not had time to read your letters over this morning so as to answer them in full but will do it next time. I don't know what to tell you about paying that money to Brandt but I guess you can pay him some we can tell better after next payday. I think what you have then you can spare the most of it. George will furnish you some eatables this winter and I expect to furnish you with ten dollars a month this winter if it don't come till spring. They say the mail don't leave here today so I will have to wait till tomorrow so I can rite all I want to after dinner.

I have been over and seen Russ and he spoke of sending home for his folks and you putting up a box and send together for the expense will be less on one box than on two small ones. The express on a small box is $2.50 and on a good big one only $5.00. What ever I want in them is dried berries and fruit only for we have apples and some dried beef. If you can get it without too much trouble and some butter and honey or Maple Syrup *(illegible)* and they are not perishable.

I would not cook or bake anything to send for it might spoil before it gets to me. Butter is the main thing and if you could find any chestnuts or nuts of any kind send some along also. Now I have told you what to send and all this you have got to buy and it will put you to a good deal of trouble but get what you can and if Uncle George's folks come over to see you for Russ is going to rite to them about it. You can send together if not you can send when you get ready.

It is useless for me to say anything about the directions for they know at the express office what to put on, but I will put it down the boxes that have come here are directed as follows:

> Mr. --------------
> N.Y.S.V. 144 Regt. Co. ------
> Folly Island, S. C.

in care of Q. Master Gregory. You see I like to forget the N.Y.S.V. that must be in its place. Gregory is our quartermaster so when the box comes he will fetch it rite to us when it comes to the office.

I think you have done exceedingly well the year that is past and if you can't get your pay as you go along I will try and pay you when I get home. But one thing, do not work too hard or over do yourself for the sake of saving a little money. I am as anxious to get our debts paid as need be but I value health higher than property. You can pay debts as fast as you can get the money to spare but try and keep from $5.00 to $10.00 on hand so if we should need any we could have it.

If George will get you things you want this winter you will have your $10 per month to pay debts with or something else for I don't mean to spend more than $3 per month if I can avoid it. I am ashamed the way I let the money go the past month but it is gone so let her rip.

The election has gone bully in York State to good good. Yes I am an abolitionist I had rather stay my time out of 3 years and see the curse slavery abolished than to compromise with slavery in the States or Territories and get myself discharged tomorrow, For war will exist until slavery is done away with or steps taken to abolish it surely and forever.

I will rite more for I have the time and I can't improve it better than by writing to one who loves me. Yes there is warm loving hearts at home that would welcome me and I have thought strong of trying for a furlough but I have got to wait a while for there was 2 of our Co. went this morning.

Capt. Plaaskett got here yesterday nite from home he looks tough as a bear if he and the rest of the officers will try and get me a furlough I can have one if not I can't. If I apply for one I shan't expect to get it but I will try and if they don't give me one woe be unto them as you say.

So I have got all the stamps you have sent I got 5 last nite the letters you spoke of all rite. We have been very fortunate for everything goes and comes like clock work while others loose some of their letters.

It hasn't been cold enough to freeze here yet but it is quite chilly at nite and morning. Our Regt. went out on a three day scout they went onto some of the neighboring isles and waded through swamps and water and sand. They came back sorefooted and tired, they had a hard time of it.

Thomas Beavan one of our Co. was taken by guerrillas last summer and taken to Richmond got released and wrote to me but I hear since he went home on a furlough in time to vote. We were great friends and I would like to see him.

Friday Morning, the 20th. I have no news to rite only I have heard from Steve he says he is well but don't get his strength. Russ and I talked it over last evening he thinks his folks will come over to see you soon if they do, it will be all rite. Russ has wrote for the same things I have and when they get here what one don't have we will give each other.

I suppose Raymond has Maple Sugar if he hasn't Morehan has it at Deposit and granny Alexander has some good butter and honey. But it will be too much trouble for you to get all these things but what you can get handy get and let it go at that. You can send the articles I have mentioned in all that is from 5 to 10 lbs of each. Now I must close for it is time to pick up the mail. So be a good girl, yours ever.

B. A. Cook

No. 89, Folly Island, S. C., November 22, 1863

Dearest L

I seize my pen to converse with you this Sabbath afternoon. It is but a short time since I sent a letter to you Dear one. But I surely think you are in love with me and why shouldn't I not love you in return. Tell me if you can, why I believe I should love you if I had never seen you for your letters tell me there is true undying love within your bosom.

238

Yes love for me and how could I disregard that love or not love in return although I had never seen you. But thank heaven I have seen you and lived within the entwining influence of your love and companionship for years. But though the events of Providence we are separated but not lost to each others sight and we are anxious for the term of our separation to come to an end. But let us confide in One who has all power, the bugle blows for Preaching and I believe I will put on my Sunday coat and go now.

Dear wife I am at liberty to talk to you again before dark. I have been and gathered some more shells and shall get them home the first opportunity.

The Colonel is going to send some of our regt. home after recruits. 4 Commissioned Officers, 6 Sergeants, 6 Corporals, and 2 Privates, so you see the privates don't have much of a cite on that score. But I don't believe they will get many recruits.

In one of your letters you speak of our final separation on earth, yes that time will come without doubt one of us will be left in this cold world alone for a season without even a few kind lines from the others pen to cheer the drooping spirit. Alone did I say, where are those dear children of ours, why should we say alone. Are they not a blessing God has given them to us and I trust they will prove a blessing to us both in years to come. This is my prayer. Also that we may have an unbroken family beyond the river of Death, and I know you love them with a Mothers love this I have to comfort me while absent from them and you.

Perhaps all I have ritten you knew before and may think me foolish in writing this sheet. But I am writing as I feel and what I know, therefore let us thank God for the memory of the past and trust in Him for the future.

Louisa I am most sorry I said anything about your sending me those things for you have no way to get around and it will put you to so much trouble. I say again don't put yourself to much extra trouble to get any of those things. For you have enough to do without running after things to send me. It is most dark and supper is nearly ready. I suppose we have a cup of tea and bread for supper, so good nite my wife.

B. A. Cook

No. 90, Folly Island, S.C., November 25, 1863

Ever Dear One,

This afternoon I got 2 letters from you. One was mailed the 11th and the other the 17th. I was glad to hear you were all well and your letters found me the same. Your letters tell me I am loved by dear ones at home. All this I believe and my presence would add to your enjoyment very much, but I suppose we will have to do without seeing each other for a while yet. I expect to come to you one of these days. Then we will try and make up for lost time won't we?

I am taking comfort, but it makes me provoked to think how much money I have spent since the 15th of last month. I rote to you that I had hired 2 dollars. Well, that is most gone. I have 50 cts. left only and I won't hire any more . . . if I don't have it, I won't spend it.

You said in one of your letters that it was snowing, but your wood pile is small for winter. I hope you can manage to get a lot of wood cut ahead. It will burn much better, and you won't be bothered for wood as you were last winter. I am glad Mother and Mrs. Leonard are going to make you a visit. I hope you had a good time. You need not think that I suppose you can save much, for I know you need all I send to you, and I fear that won't make you comfortable this winter.

Charles Stiles got back today and some others that were home on furlows. I see a box that one man fetched that would weigh 3 or 4 hundred pounds if it had lots of good things in it. I see the folks are not all dead up in Delaware County yet and some of them have something to eat yet by the looks of things.

They are fixing things up here in camp just as though they intended to stay here all winter. I hope they will, but I would like to go north as far as Pennsylvania when spring comes. And I would like to stay here until I got ready to leave.

Mate must look funny with her hair cut so short and I guess she will make a good Johney. You say you have got the house all cleaned and ready for me, but I don't much expect to get there until I come for good. And that may be at the end of the war or the end of the 3 years, but I shall try for a furlow with scarcely any hopes of getting one. All Hancock can go out of our Company before anyone else can get a chance.

There have been several promotions of late to sergeants and corporals, but our officers prefer Hancock Thieves to decent men. The longer I am in this army, the more I am convinced that a decent man has no business here. The biggest devil is the best fellow, but they shall have their reward. God is their judge, not I.

I think the men that are at home are doing something the way the babies are shelling out. I hope they will bring them up rite. I am sorry Bill Early has got to come, for I think his Father needs him. I am glad Kate has heard from Steve. One that was there with him came back last night. He said he was quite smart.

I will stop writing for tonight and finish this before the mail goes in the morning.

Well morning come, but I can't see very well to rite. Everything is all tight this cool morning and it is Thanksgiving Day. It is to be observed here. We do no unnecessary work or drill today, and will have divine services. Oh I hope the many prayers will be answered for the restoration of peace speedily.

241

We will have fried pork and bread and coffee for breakfast I expect. I have a few potatoes buried in the sand in my tent, and I have baked a couple in the ashes to eat with my pork. So you see I will have a good breakfast.

Now Dear One, I have wrote all I know, but will write soon again. I hope this will find you all in good health and comfortable. So goo morning Wife and children.

Bishop A. Cook

No. 91 is missing

No. 92, Folly Island, S.C., November 28 in the evening

Dear Wife

I must tell you that I received yours of the 18th last evening and have had no time to answer it today. If I had it would not go until the 30th of this month but as I am going to leave camp early in the morning I must write a few lines.

We are going about 6 miles to Chio Island to help build a fort or some fortifications. We are to be gone 7 days so you see I may not get a chance to rite again this week. I have been on duty all this week. They say there is good water down where we are going and a nice camp. These islands are covered with troops.

You want to know if you shall take $100 for Jenny. I think she is worth $125 without doubt for stock is high like every thing else but to come rite to the point I guess you had better sell her for $100 or over than to run the risk of keeping her and a good note is just as good on interest as the cash.

You may depend hay and stock are both high as well as other things and those that have been home say that a good pair of oxen is worth 140 or 50 dollars and a good horse from 100 to 150 dollars but it is best to dispose of Jenny for what she will fetch and when I get home I will find something for a team.

It is raining and I wish I was with you beside the old stove. You will excuse me for writing so short a letter for it is the best I can do. I will rite again the first opportunity I am feeling quite well and am fleshy. The candle is most out so I must close and bid you good night Dear one from you S. Boy

B. A. C.

DECEMBER 1863

There are no references to December 1863 in the book

No. 93, Chio Island, December 4, 1863

Dear Louisa

This pleasant afternoon finds me well and I will pen a few lines and tell you of our journey here, etc. We started as I told you in my last letter and it proved to be a rainy day but we got here about noon and had to make shelter for ourselves the best we could so we first put up our rubber blankets on croches and poles for a shelter and threw under some brush which were all wet of course and spread one wool blanket on them to lay on then had two blankets over us for there is 3 of us sleep together and each had a blanket and rubber.

Well it ceased to rain before nite and cleared off so we had a chance to make some coffee for supper.

After supper we stood around the fires to dry our clothes and keep us warm as we could until roll call. Then we turned into our above mentioned bed and tried to sleep but we were forced to get up and build fires to stand around long before morning for it was freezing so the sand was froze and the water in my canteen hanging in my bedroom froze ice in fact it has froze ice here this week near half an inch thick. I think that is doing pretty well for the sunny South.

Reveille Monday morning came and we all went to work. Some on the fort and some at getting timbers and building bridges, well our rations ran short so the rest of us had nothing for breakfast Tuesday morning but pork and coffee, a rather poor breakfast. But I got some potatoes of the Sutter for post stamps so I made quite a breakfast and dinner and for supper I had 2 hardtack and a cup of coffee. But our rations came so that Wednesday morning we got 5 days rations and that is calculated to last us till we go back to camp.

We don't have to work more than 6 hours per day and half work at that but I don't like the plan of boarding myself half the time and get no pay for it. The fact is our officers have the commissary keep back report of our meat and coffee and rice and hoarding and get the money for it and call it company funds but *(illegible)* a bit of the funds has the company seen yet.

I guess if the truth was known we keep the officers in spending money and board than to part of the time but let them rip those there will be a time by and by if they don't render an account of what they are keeping from our company.

There was a National salute fired here and up to Charleston by all big guns last Tuesday for the success of our armies against the rebs. The news is that Grant has whippet Bragg severely also that Mead has gained a great victory over Lee and last night the news came that Burnside had whippet Longstreet and taken 5,000 prisoners. But this is too good to believe all at once but some of it is true.

No more today Louisa

B. A. Cook

No. 93 Continued, Folly Island, December 7, 1863

Dear Wife.

I seat myself to rite a few lines to you and let you know that we returned to camp yesterday (Sunday) all in good spirits and I got a letter from you that was mailed the 21 of Nov. I was glad to learn that Mother had the pleasure of seeing her 3 children together again. I wish I could of been with you. I think Nel W. done very wrong and I feel sorry for his parents but there is one thing to be considered that is the Soldier is bound and has no liberty but if he don't walk or speak and do *(illigible)* so he is punished and after he is kept so for one year give him his liberty and ten chances to one if he don't use i to excess and to his own injury, this is a fact.

I have expected to hear that those apple trees were injured but it can't be helped. The only way to save them is to keep a good fence around them and turn nothing in to the lot for it seems that every beast is inclined to destroy them if they can.

I hope you have sold Jenny ere this and you must do as you like about keeping the pig but you will have less trouble if you dispose of it.

Mr. Whitaker allowed what I rote to our folks about southern sympathizers was correct. So must every honest Man, you ask me to tell what I think of the was in every letter. Well I think the time is hastening when the rebellion will cease for the rebel army is very much demoralized and they have been whippet and drove so much that of late that they are sick of fighting and we have very cheering news of late and a few more victories will end the war.

I think you are a horse to travel from home to the river in so short a time, I guess you think I am making a pretty heavy draft on you for sending for $50 dollars and for the box to, but if I had thought I would of sent for a few pairs of suspenders and a lot of good pocket knives for I need a new pair of suspenders and a new pocket knife.

The Sutler charges for suspenders from 75 cts to $2.00 per pair the knives are the same price and the 75 cts. ones are not worth buying but you see the box will be on the way before you get this you see if I had a Doz. knives that would cost 75 cts, apiece up there I could sell them here for $1.25 or 50 each and then they would be cheaper than the Sutter sells them. If Russ and I get our box and stay here we will send for more things before winter is out. I tell you it is pretty cool here now days and the paymaster is here to. They say so we will probable get pay tomorrow. This will go in the morning. I will rite more tonite or in the morning no more at present, Louise.

B. A. C.

No. 94. Folly Island, S. C., Sunday December 13, 1863

Dear Wife.

The glory of my life I received 3 letters from you and a paper last Friday nite but haven't had time to rite until now. I cannot love or praise you too much for your good loving letters. I prize those kisses from my girls very highly. Tell them I have kissed their names in the letter and hope to return to kiss their dear little faces one of these days. I am glad, Wife, that your health is good, mine is good but my legs are not rite yet but I am on duty all the while. I came off guard this morning but I am hardy and fat for I eat plenty of apples for I got a barrel for $10.00 and it sets in my tent. I have sold some.

I think you have had care and trouble enough with Jenny and we had better dispose of her the first good opportunity. I think Mr. Kinion pretty sharp unless his colt and cow is something nice he didn't make you much of an offer. Russel Cook talks of buying her he is going to rite to his father to go and see her and buy her if you have not disposed of her if he thinks he can get work for a team this winter. Russ has got the cash at home to pay you for her or he will let you have a cow towards her. I told Russ I thought you would take $90.00 for her rather than keep her and it is better to sell her at some price than to keep her through the winter. So you had better make a bargain with Uncle George if he comes if you haven't let her go.

Well you can rite to Nel and answer his letters or any other soldiers letter for their letters are worthy of an answer if anybody's is.

Yesterday was a wet day but today is pleasant and warm so the flies fly around quite brisk in my tent this afternoon. I have read the paper and like those pieces you marked first rate. I will send it back one of these days.

I was surprised to see Thomas Beavans death poor fellow he suffered a great deal he was Steves and my tent mate all summer until he was taken prisoner and I hope it was under our influence that he gave his heart to God. He was a kind hearted man and I for one feel that I have lost a brother soldier and I am fearful that I shall never see steve in this world again.

For I saw a man last week rite from the hospital and he said he did not improve any and his Diarreaha was no better, and it is my opinion that it will wear him out in a few weeks at longest. Bit I hope for the best, this Chronic Diarreaha is almost incurable where it is long standing.

Can't you get anybody to cut wood? I hope if you have had a bee you got something done.

Oh I hope this war will end so I can come home and cut your wood next winter and then we will take lots of comfort. I will close for this time.

Dear Wife.

B. A. Cook

No. 95, Folly Island, December 18, 1863

Dear Wife,

I thought I would rite a few lines to that Dear One of mine and let her know I am strong and fine and doing well.

(illegible line)

is I don't have to go on picket or on guard duty but I have to go on dress parade. My legs gave and they put me on guard and other duty was more than my legs would stand. So I went to the Doctors and they marked me light duty. The head Doctor says he *(illegible)* to help my limbs but he thought they would get strong and well after a while. He told me to rub them thoroughly every day and at nite before I lay down so you see his prescription is not bad to take.

My barrel of apples is 3/4 gone and I got all of my money back but a dollar or so. I guess I will do well enough with them for what is left will bring 3 dollars besides what I eat. I have a half bushel of potatoes & had some for breakfast this morning with some fresh beef. Oh I live just as good as I want to all I lack is a little good butter and that is on the way, I suppose by this time.

I hope you will get rid of Jenny at some price then you won't have her to think about or care for. If you are out of money tell me and I will send some if I don't before I hear from you. I am sorry about that $5 but I was fearful that I wouldn't get my money payday but they paid every Unit in money after taking out my clothing and after I paid my debts I have only 11 or 12 dollars left. If you sent me $5 and I get it and you don't need money till next payday I don't know but I can let what I have to spare till next payday for 25 cts on a dollar. And you know that is better than having it at home doing nothing.

The health of the Regt. is good and there is a fair prospect of our staying here all winter. Christmas is to be observed here as a holiday and by all the soldiers here and I suppose we will have an extra dinner.

One of my tent mates that was on picket has been out about a month. Shot himself accidentally through the neck. He was getting onto a boat and hit the hammer of his gun so it went off, they say he is doing well and I guess he will recover. He is on board a hospital Boat where he has the best of care, his name is Thomas Cafferey.

I look for mail today but the mail don't go out till day after tomorrow. It is not much use for us to send letters only once in 8 or 10 days for the boat don't run only so often. So you see I got 3 letters from you the last mail and most every mail I get 2 letters from you. So we must rite when we have time and when we get a big letter *(illegible)* it.

I hear the rebs abandoned Charleston and are down at the mouth since Grant gained the late victory but before that they were heard by our pickets to play the tune called Dixie on the brass band and cheer and hurrah but now all is still.

Dear one I long for the time to come when I can be by your side and comfort you in your lonely hours. I suppose you see many lonesome hours for you don't have much to attract your attention to what I do.

For while I am writing this they are playing the Brass Band it sounds lovely. The 40th Mass Regt. has the Brass Band and they are in our Brigade and we are encamped side by side so there music is as good for us as for them.

You look outdoors and likely you won't see a human being but here if I look out any time of day I will see someone and likely a dozen. Yes there is something to keep a persons spirits up as long as he has got any. I never have had time to get homesick

(illegible line)

I long to be lodged in my quiet little home with those I love.

B. A. Cook

No. 65, (Note Number) Saturday December 19, 1863

Louisa

I will write a few lines today and let you know our mail has not come yet but we expect it tomorrow. My legs are about the same as they were yesterday. I had one of my double teeth pulled this morning it had been growling sometimes so now let it growl. You wanted to know if I had changed since you saw me. It is hard to tell but I think I am about the same flesh I was at Delhi. I am one year older and more beard on my face that is all. I guess, but you and the children would know me if you should see me anywhere and I think if I stay my 3 years you will find me nearly the same old fellow.

I expect you are getting young again you are certainly getting smart since I left home and I hope you will keep smart and have good health. I got a line from Steven yesterday he is no better he is confined to his room, he got a letter from one of Thomas Bevans friends informing him of his death so he sent it to me and rote some to me in the same letter to let me know how he gets along.

Sunday morning, December 20th, 1863

Wife, it was a pretty cold nite last nite so it froze ice most 1/4 inch thick. I suppose we are seeing about as cold weather now as we shall see here. There is a story in camp that we are to leave here this week but we don't know what to believe, we hear so much. I hope we can stay here all winter for we have got our camp and tents fixed up pretty good. But we generally have to leave as soon as we get fixed comfortable, but if we do move and have to march much they will find my legs won't carry me but if we go on Steamboat then I can go as well as anyone. My duty is very lite now all I have to do is to help clean out Avenue every morning and go on dress parade if I have a mind to, if not I can stay in my tent.

I intended to send this letter this morning but as near as I can learn the boat that carries our mail don't leave till Tuesday or Wednesday so there is no use sending it so soon. We will get our mail by Monday nite, I hope. Oh, my fingers are getting cold writing for we have no fire in our tents so I will wait till the sun gets up higher and warms the air before I rite more. Here is a kiss XXXX for you Lottie, M.C. and H.C.

Monday December 21st

Dearest L.

I am happy to tell you that I got a letter from you and it was a good long one to. I was much pleased with the contents, the $5 makes me over $15 for I had over $10. I think Grand Mother is very kind to me and hope we may both live so I can reward her for her kindness and Mother A. to for you. Say she sent me something and I got a letter from her to but she only said you was busy getting up a box to send me and Mrs. G. was very kind so tender her my thanks and tell her I think I will have to rite to her.

I am glad you got some wood cut at your bee. I wrote you about selling Jenny to Uncle George and I hope he will want her for he will use her well if he gets her. Aunt Rachel won't have to drive her if she drives all the rest. Oh she is a big thing ain't she but let her rip.

Russ and I look for our box this week for the Q.M. has sent to Beaufort for the Boxes for our Regt. But I am fearful our box hasn't got there on time to come back with them. If it ain't we wont get it in 2 or 3 weeks likely enough. I don't know as it will be possible to send that sack to Steve but I will do the best I can and that is all anyone can do. You didn't tell all you sent me but I suppose I will see it when it comes. You said you sent all I sent for. So I know pretty much what is in the box. It seems you haven't had much snow yet but some pretty cold weather. I hope your cold is well ere this, I will close for I have wrote all I can think of at present. So be a good girl gal till I come from your old boy

Bishop A. Cook

N.B. I don't hear anything about our moving very soon.

B. A. Cook

No. 96, Folly Island, S.C., December 27, 1863

Dear Louisa

This Sabbath afternoon finds me well trying to answer a letter I have just received from you, not numbered but dated December 15th. I was glad to get a letter from home, but was sorry to hear you had all been afflicted with bad colds. I don't wonder you was disappointed at so short a letter from me, but I believe I rote you the reason. If I remember right, it was the time I was going down to the other island.

As to the sick tent, I have been in no other than my own tent any of the time. I have not been in the hospital, but when I was not able to do duty, the Doc marked me quarters or lite duty. But now I am fat as a bear. One week ago I was marked quarters. You see, my legs ain't right if I go and lay on the ground one of these cold nights. It uses me up for a while.

You haven't rote anything to offend or discourage me concerning getting home, but you must know it takes time to do a thing good and one must not do it too fast. Now today I feel as well as ever I did, only a little stiff or older. Tomorrow morning I can go to the Doctor and get marked quarters, but you must not expect me home very soon to be too anxious about this thing. I will do the best I can and come honorably or not at all.

As to Gin, I have rote you before, if Aunt Rachel will give you $100 for Gin, take the 2 cows at 60, but the 40 in cash . . . but not her note. NB: if you come within 5 dollars of a bargain, don't let that stop a trade.

I hope your hog turned out well. I hope Wal and Elenora got a hold some where else besides the ears. And M.G. with her Mashein will accommodate A. W. Gates.

As to the war, I think look pretty good on our side. It is very hard in many places for the rebs to keep their men together, for they are bound to desert every chance they get. I think that what Abe said will be the means of bringing some of the states into the Union before spring. I heard that our Colonel offered to bet that our Regiment would be discharged in less than 6 months. I hope it will be so, but time will tell.

Now I will tell you how Christmas went off here. The camps of the different Regiments were decked with evergreens and no duty done that day. The officers got something to drink and had a jolly time of it. But our Captain did not forget Company F. He got a barrel of potatoes and 3 bottles of wine and 3 or 4 dollars worth of apples (the wine cost $5.00). We drew fresh beef,. so we had beefsteak and potatoes for dinner. We took up a collection sand got $5.00 and gave it to the Captain and he went and got 3 bottles more of wine and gave us. Then there was just a decent drink around for the Company. The suttler had some beer, but couldn't sell it to a private. He could sell it to the officers, so I told the Captain I wanted an order to get a canteen of beer. So he gave me one and I got my beer and gave 60 cents for it. Me and one of my tent mates drunk it up and called it good. In some of the Regiments they had foot races. The Colonel gave 5 or 10 dollars to the best runner, so there were lots of them running for it. On the whole, I enjoyed Christmas better than I did last year. I don't know how New Years will go off, but I hope our box will get here before then, don't you?

I must close for now my old gal. Your wish concerning our being as close as our names just suits me. Bully for you. I expect this will reach you about the 5th, so it is too late to wish you a Happy New Year, but I wish you well.

B. A. Cook

JANUARY 1864

No chronology in the book for this month

History Summarization Page 148

In January 1864, General Gillmore removed his headquarters from Morris Island and established them at Hilton Head, leaving General Terry in command of the forces surrounding Charleston. General Gordon was placed in command of the troops on Folly Island. Evidence of new plans and some expedition being fitted out was found in the withdrawal of troops from Morris and Folly Island and later it developed that Florida was to be the field of special effort. The Union element in Florida had exhibited so much activity it was thought by those in authority that the presence of a strong body of Union Troops might so shape events that this Union element could reorganize the political affairs of the state and bring it by the formal action of a legislature duly convened back into the Union again.

No. 2, Folly Island, S.C., January 6, 1864

Dear Louisa,

I seat myself to tell you of my good luck last nite. I got 4 letters. One from you, 1 from Al, 1 from Marcy Cook, and one from Chas. Dickinson. And today, Russ and I got our box and it is an old thrasher. I have got dried fruit enough to last a whole family all winter, and what a nice pail of butter. The cans of honey, both burst at the bottom, so they leaked a little. And there were some apples on the top of the box . . . . they were rotted considerably. But on the whole, the things come first rate and my share will last me a long time. I guess Mother meant I should have something good to eat. Oh what a good Mother and Grandmother shall not be forgotten when I am eating bread and butter and honey. I send you all my riten thanks and I hope to meet you all on the shores of time to thank and reward you.

It has been raining all the week so far and the rain is pattering on the tent this evening while I am trying to write. You must excuse this short letter, for if it goes in the morning, it won't be as long as No. 1 was that I sent yesterday.

Well, I am glad you have got some fresh pork. Your hog will help you a good deal this winter. Marion has been to buy you out. I declare. I guess he is going to get married, ain't he?

I want to see Emma too and kiss that little face. And I would like to be in my little home tonite with my little family. Not but what I enjoy myself very well here and am having a comfortable winter so far, but the truth is home is the place for me. For there is hearts that would be glad at my presence, and I know I should be a happy man if I am permitted to join my little family and live with them again. God grant that we may meet in our quiet home to praise Him together.

I hear nothing from Steven lately, but expect a letter soon in answer to one I wrote him. His sack of things is here and I will see tomorrow if there is any chance to send it to him.

All the stock you have is old Jerry, the red cow I got off Dan and the yearling you got off Dan, besides Jenny, the sheep, and calves. If you can get rid of Jin and have 5 cows next summer you will be in town.

I see in the Tribune that General Averel made a raid on the Baltimore and Tennessee Rail Road and done the rebs much damage.

He destroyed 3 depots, large stores of grain, and meat in the amount of 200.000 dollars. And he got out from among the rebs with losing only some 6 men which were drowned trying to cross a stream. One of the rebs got away and come over onto this island the other day. He said there is hundreds that would come if they could get a chance. He said they had to be careful and pick their men to put on picket next to our lines for fear of their coming to our pickets and giving themselves up. Bully for that. I must close, Louisa.

Yours with love,

B. A. C.

No. 4, Folly Island, S. C. , January 20, 1864

Dear Louisa,

It is more than a week since I wrote to you, for I have been on 4 inspections and on guard once within a week, and today we had review. All the troops on the island were out . . . 14 regiments and 3 batteries. We had to have our knapsack all packed and haversack and canteen, gun and equipment on our backs. Then stand in line or march from 9 a.m. until 12 noon, making 3 hours. I tell you my shoulders ached all over and my hand trembles so now I can't write straight. I will be on guard tomorrow I guess.

I had a letter from Aunt Harriet and one from Mother the last mail. She wrote of grandfather Cook's funeral and said you fell on the ice Monday and hurt your head, and Mert was with you. I have felt very anxious to hear from you. I am so afraid you are hurt so you won't get over it soon. I hope the next mail will bring a letter from you telling the particulars.

The sun shines warm today so sweat runs down our faces when we had our knapsacks on. I have one of *Leslie*'s papers and one *Harpers Weeklies* rolled up to send you. There are some good stories in them and the pictures are worth more than the papers both cost, that is 30 cts.

I have a good chunk of sugar yet and plenty of butter and some of most everything.

Thursday morning, the 21st. Last evening I received a long letter from you which gave the desired information concerning your fall. It must of been a pretty hard fall, but I hope this will find you all sound.

We have got to go on inspection again today. I don't go on guard as I expected. The weather is very fine now.

I have no money of any amount, but I expect payday here in about 3 weeks, and then I will send you all you want. Please state in the answer to this how much you will need for the next two months. If what money I have let this time does well, I will let some next time if I have it to spare.

Shit, I had to stop writing and go and backpack wood to the cook house, so this letter will be shorter yet for it has to go this morning.

I am surprised to think how fast our girls are growing. They will be young women in a short time. Excuse this. I will write soon again.

Yours with Love,

B. A. C.

FEBRUARY 1864

Olustee, Fla., Feb. 20th
On steamer *Delaware*, Feb. 23rd to Feb. 25th
Jacksonville, Fla., Feb. 25th to June 11th

History Summarization pages 148 to 153

Accordingly in the early part of February 1864, the troops
withdrawn from Morris and Folly Islands, were forwarded to
Jacksonville, Fla., where the army was organized under the
supervision of Gen. Gillmore, Gen. Truman Seymour being
placed in immediate command. As a feint to draw the attention of the enemy and prevent him from reinforcing the Confederate force in Florida from the troops in and around
Charleston, Gen. Terry received orders to make a reconnaissance in force toward Charleston by way of Seabrook and
John's Island. The skirmishing continued through the day resulting in killing several of the enemy and losing from the
Union forces one killed and three wounded, but there was no
general engagement. The next day the 144th was held in reserve and at night placed on picket line. Skirmishing was re-
newed on the 11th in which the Union forces lost four killed
and several wounded. On the 12th the entire force was withdrawn from Seabrook, the gunboats from Stono River covering the retiring movement with their fire. The entire force returned to camp on Folly Island. On the forenoon of February
23rd the Regiment embarked at Pawnee Landing on board the
steamer *Delaware* and bidding adieu to Folly Island, steamed
away southward. Our destination proved to be Jacksonville,
which place was reached about noon of the 24th. Although

there were evidences that war was in the land, Jacksonville showed more evidence of northern enterprise and thrift than any other place visited thus far in the South. Among the first things to engage our attention and demand our effort was the erection of fortifications that would command approaches to the town and to maintain a strong and efficient picket line.

No. 10, Camp near Jacksonville, Florida, February 24, 1864

Dear Wife,

I received the letter you wrote at Mother's the evening of the 22nd. We held that day for it was Washington's birthday. At dark we received marching orders. We packed up at 4 o'clock in the morning we started and went to the landing and got on board the steamer called the *Delaware*. We had a pleasant voyage.

This village has been quite a nice place, but fire has destroyed a large part of it. You will understand that this is in Florida and is ground lately taken by our forces. I have seen fruit trees in bloom today, so it is spring here. I expect we have got to drive the rebs or they drive us. Time will tell.

I was glad to get your short but good letter. It told me that I have a loving wife which is all the world tome. Your good letters are worth a pension to me.

I am in good health. There are lots of rebs here that have taken the oath of allegiance. Bully for them.

I will write soon again. I scribble these few lines thinking that they will go back on the boat that brought us here. I haven't time to rite more now.

Yours in love,

B. A. C.

No. 11, Jacksonville, Florida, February 28, 1864

Dear Louisa,

I am happy to tell you that I am well and in good spirits and am anxious to hear from home again. I am not out of hearing yet, although they can't take us much father. I wrote a line to you the 24th, the day we got here. Well, the 25th we went on picket and were relieved at night. The 26th we moved a short distance. The 27th we moved about one mile to this place. We are about 26 or 28 miles from the coast up the St. John's River. It is quite a nice country here but most of the people left the town before we got here. Those that are left seem to be pleased that we are here.

Yesterday, I saw several women and children, both black and white, come into town for protection. Most of them looked like the latter end of hard times. Some of them had old horses and carts with their goods in and they on foot. One cart had four pigs in it. There was a white boy with one cart and he said he was 15 years of age. I asked him why he wasn't in the Confederate Army and he said he wasn't old enough. An old wench spoke and said they would have conscripted him if we hadn't come just in time as we did. She said she hoped we would go out far enough to get her son. She said he was living with a lady here in town that had fled and took her boy with her.

There have been several black men come within our lines and some of them are barefoot and almost naked. They tell pitiful stories.

I saw a coarse, homemade cotton shirt that cost $8.00. Also a calico dress on a woman--I should think there was two breaths in the skirt and it cost $30.00. The rebs have no leather for shoes or harnesses. They make collars for their horses of corn husks and the bark of trees and they have to get along the best they can.

As to our position here, we have forts and rifle pits, so it will take a large force to drive us out. Besides, we have gunboats at hand if needed. Whether we shall advance and attack the rebs in their fortifications or lay here or be called to some other place is more than I can tell. I don't think they will attack us here, but quite likely we will advance strong handed and attack them in their fortifications.

It is warm as summer today. The morning of the 26th there was a white frost and the fire felt good after sleeping on the ground all night. I don't know but what lying on the ground will affect my legs so I can't march. They feel pretty stiff.

I have $11.00 in my pocket and have loaned $4.00, so you see I don't spend much money. When we left camp, I had quite a lot of berries. I took them to one of the clerks in the Sutlers Shop (a friend of mine) and gave them to him. He was bound I should have something for them so he gave me two cans of condensed milk worth one dollar. I sold one of them for fifty cents and bought a good supply of tobacco.

I haven't thrown away any of my cloths yet except my dress coat, one shirt, a pair of drawers and socks that were in the wash when we left. But, if we have to march much, I shall throw away half of what I have left if I can't sell it to some of the boys.

It seems to me as though it were June, for I feel just such weather as I am used to seeing in June. We have all got empty bellies and empty haversacks for this is the 6th day on four days' rations. But I guess we will get something tonight.

Now old gal, how often I think of thee when on guard, as I was last night. When all is still I can think of the good times we have had and think of the comfort of home with my kind wife and merry children. No more at present dear wife, L. M. Cook.

B. A. Cook

MARCH 1864

March 9th, President Commissions Grant as Lieut-General and General-in -Chief of all the Armies

History Summarization, page 154

The troops were stationed at various points in eastern Florida, sometimes only detachments of regiments being located at various posts. The service required was mostly picket duty with occasional raids into the surrounding country. On March 25th the 144th was embarked on the steamer *Harriet A. Weed* and moved down the river a few miles and debarked and in light marching order moved rapidly out into the country through the almost endless pine barrens; but the movement failed to disclose and enemy. One thing which marked our stay in Florida was our frequent changes of camp. Our last move brought us to a very pleasant one on the bluffs overlooking the St. John's River.

No. 12, Camp near Jacksonville, March 4, 1864

Dear Lousia,

The day I wrote to you last, the 28th of Feb., I went on picket at nite and came back to camp the 29th. We had a very good time, but as I told you before, our haversacks were empty. But there was a Sutler came along with a load of goods. He opened a barrel of cakes and sold some to us, so we felt better.

Our regiment mustered on the 29th for 2 more months pay. On the first of this month we all pulled up stakes and fell in behind our fortifications. There was considerable firing to be heard in front between the rebs and some of our mounted men who were trying to bring on a fite and get the rebs to pursue them until they came in range of our fortifications. But they didn't get the rebs to come.

The 2nd all was quiet. The 3rd I went on guard and our brigade moved in front of the fortifications again. Today we have been fixing our tents up in order. Oh this moving every other day I don't like. The nite of the 3rd our mail came here and I got 4 letters from you which I was glad to get. The last one told of your getting the check and that Kate was about to start out to see Steve. Poor fellow, I wish she may find him better than she expects.

I am sorry you have offended Mrs. Gates, but cannot help it as I know of. If you and Kate can hire that man you spoke of by the month, I think it would be a good notion. You have got to have someone to build some fence or the cattle will run where they are a mind to. If nothing happens, I will furnish you $10 per month as I did last summer. I don't expect you to save money or improve the place but if you can keep things together and not get in debt much, I will be satisfied. I knew when I left that every thing would go downhill, for it needs the labor and attention of a man almost continually to keep a small farm as it should be.

I am glad there are so many enlisting, but as you say, they ought to have been drafted instead of bought. Russel is in hopes that his folks will get Jenny and have a team. I think you are blessed with plenty of company at any rate. I have only 3 dollars, for I have let out $11.00 until next pay day. $2 to that Rosa and the rest to boys in our Company.

Why have you been afraid you offended me. I hope I haven't wrote anything to make you think so. If I have, I didn't intend to. But you will allow me to put in a few words for a joke won't you? No Lousia, I have no cause to feel offended at your conduct. I have every reason to respect you, but I must say I feel hard and curious toward you sometimes when I think of times that are past, never to return. I hope we may meet again in a few months. It don't seem possible that the rebs can keep an army together through another winter.

I must fix for dress parade, so no more at present. I will rite soon Louisa.

B. A. Cook

No. 13(?), Jacksonville, Florida, Saturday, March 12, 1864

Dear Lousia,

As I have a few leisure moments, I will converse with you. I received two letters from you the night before last and was glad to hear from you again.

Sorry to hear the sad news of Stephen's death and feel to sympathize with Kate. Stephen is the second one of my tent-mates that is dead. Thomas Bever was our tent-mate. Now there is no one in the regiment from our neighborhood except me alone. But Russ is here yet and there are several others that I think much of, for they are good boys.

James Broughton is my tent-mate now and has been for some time. we have fine weather and lots of the boys have been swimming today. Some have been fishing and caught catfish that weighed from 8 to 15 pounds. Yesterday, we moved camp a short distance. We are fixing up just as though we were going to stay here some time, but we may move in less than a week.

Russ got a letter from his father saying that he had taken the stock over to you and he seemed to be pleased with Jenny. He said that some of our good neighbors told him she was spoiled for she was balky. But he, Uncle George, thinks she will be a good beast to work. He thinks the we priced the steers too high and the sheep too low. I suppose the sheep are worth $5.00 per head for sheep are very high. You think they are small and so they are scrawny looking sheep. But they are a different breed from ours and have finer wool. I guess their fleece will weigh as much as our other sheep's fleece. I am sorry that the cow is farrow, for Russ and I supposed the cow was coming in but I guess Russ will make it right. I guess what stock you got is worth $70.00, ain't it? How many cows are coming in this spring, one, two, or three?

I hope you and Kate will hire Luther to work your places this summer and do things up right. If I had of known that you let Kate have your check, I could have sent you $10.00. But not knowing you were out of money, I loaned the $10.00 until next payday which, if nothing happens, will come the forepart of next month. But I suppose your credit is good, so you will not suffer if you are our of money.

I would like a dip of your maple molasses firstrate, but as long as I am well, I can eat hardtack and meat if I can get it. There has been little meat since we have been here, but we are getting more now. So we do pretty well. But I tell you a soldier ought always to have a little money for he can most always buy something to eat at some price.

I hope you won't work yourself sick agetting sweet this spring. You have trusted in God and prayed for my safety and He has preserved me thus far and is able to bear me up to the last. Let us praise Him. Those lines you selected are very applicable and we will apply them to ourselves.

Sunday the 13th. Well, another inspection is over and I will write a few lines to you again. I can't use the pen better than in talking to thee, the highest treasure on earth. But you are not the only treasure, for our little girls have a place in my heart. Yes, I love you all and am anxious to meet you all face to face. I trust in God that we will be permitted to meet in less than 2 years at any rate, whether the war ends or not, I don't think I shall reenlist if they give me $1000.00 and a furlow of 30 days, for I want to spend the rest of my days with my little family. Oh, it does me good to look at the pictures of our little ones. I say little, but I suppose Hat and Em think they are most as big as anyone and they are growing fast I suppose.

Now, Wife, do not overburden yourself with care for me, for I don't know as I am in any more danger than you are. The good Lord is able to protect me at all times and in all places. Therefore, trust me to His care in faith and if I fall, he will be your guide and protector.

Russ has been over here and made me a visit this afternoon. We have talked about the stock and horse, and he is bound to make it all right if the cow doesn't come in.

It is very warm today. I have no news of importance from this part, so I will close for this time hoping to hear from you soon again.

Ever yours, Lousia,

B. A. Cook

No. 14(?), Florida, March 18, 1864

Dear Louisa,

It is with pleasure I seat myself to scribble a few lines to inform you I am well and received a letter from you yesterday. I am always glad to get a letter from you for it assures me that I am not forgotten by the one I love. I also got one from Elizabeth Cook. She writes good letters for a young girl. I am glad you have got your stock all right and have got rid of Jenny for it is not as risky property as the horse.

I think Mrs. Gates must have been cramped to act so about her turn at the funeral. But she is selfish like a great many others, so let her rip. You must not speak disrespectful of her at any rate for if you and she can't agree, then let her alone and be careful what you say.

Yes, I am willing you should trade anything in the shape of steers for heifers if you can trade to suit yourself. I am glad if that cow I got off Dan is so nice.

I was on guard yesterday and last night. We have got to go to work and build arbors in front of our tents. Likely by the time we get fixed, we will have to move, but there is no use caring whether we move or stay for we have got to do as we are ordered, hit or miss.

The city here when we came appeared to be deserted, but it is pretty well populated now. The people have come in from rebellion every day. Some days a dozen come in at a time. they say there are hundreds that will desert the rebel ranks the first chance they get. We have got lots of stores and groceries. A school for the colored children has started and business is quite brisk. The weather has been frosty for 3 or 4 nites past. There is some talk that we wont to get paid next month for our payrolls are not made out. If this is the case, we wont get our pay until June, then it will be near the 1st of July before I can get it to you, but it will be 4 months pay. You can get along and get what you need someway I suppose, and wait for the money. But I had rather get the money every 2 months so you can have it on hand.

I want to write 4 or 5 letter but I can't get time unless I adopt the plan of writing short letters. I believe I have wrote all I know of importance.

You spoke about getting a sewing machine. If you can manage to get one to suit you, I am willing. You spoke about selling a watch if you could towards getting one. You spoke as though you had 2 watches, but I don't remember whether I left 1 or 2. I know I gave you a watch and if it is not spoiled you must keep it. But if you have another watch, do what you please with it. Or if that one is spoiled, do what you please with it.

Who lives on the old place of Aunt Harriet's? Are those new steers pretty well matched? If they are small, they will grow to be worth $100 if they are matched.

From Your Soldier in Love,

Bishop A. Cook

APRIL 1864

April 8th and 9th, Sabine Cross Roads, La.

No mention in book of any action during the
Month of April.

No. 15(?), Headquarters, Jacksonville, Florida, April 8, 1864

Dear Louisa,

I feel it my duty to pen a few lines to you today as it is the only
means we have of talking to each other. I am happy to inform you
that I am well and sincerely hope this will find you the same. I expect the mail here tomorrow and suppose it will bring me a good
letter or two.

I have wrote to Esq. Moses concerning what I wrote you about in
my last and expect to hear from him in a few weeks. I hate to raise
a row with the heirs, but right wrongs no man . . . ask and ye
shall receive. I intend to ask them for nothing but what is right and
if they feel disposed to do the fair thing, they can easily settle the
matter without contention.   But if they don't feel disposed to do
anything for me or my heirs, then if the law will give up anything, it
is best to have it.   For we need all that belongs to us if we live to
raise our girls. And if we don't live, it is necessary they should have

something to clothe and school them. It seems to me that I feel more concerned about the welfare of my children since I am where I cannot see them than I did when I was with them. Oh how I long to be with you again, but I thank God that they have a kind mother whose guiding hand I hope may guide them until they are capable of guiding themselves. I am not permitted to assist you, but I hope we will all be together in a few months. I have not much hope of the war ending before my time is out which will be in less than 18 months. I will not re-enlist for I believe it my duty to be with my family after the 3 years are up. Not but what my patriotism is as good as ever, but I think when a man situated as I am serves 3 years it is time to step out and quit soldiering a while and let some one else have a chance.

We are expecting the Paymaster here any day and I would like to see him first rate for when he comes I expect to get near $40. What the boys owe me beside what Russ will give me . . . and I don't know how much that will be . . . but if I have good luck, I can send you enough to pay Brandt. Likely it will be some time before Kate will get the money to pay you. Therefore, I will be advise you to get as much money together as you can when I send you some and go and buy what you have got to buy through the summer as far as your money will go. Let the debts stand, for I think the price of most everything you have to buy will get higher during the summer. This is a hint and I may be wrong, so you do as you like.

As near as I can tell ny Uncle George's letter, Jenny was poor and covered with lice, so it is no wonder that folks wouldn't give a very big price for she did not look very flattering. Now I mst go to work on my gun.

Sunday the 10th . . .

Now Sunday inspection is over I will try and write a little to my kind wife. I am getting anxious to have the mail come for I want a letter. Our Sutler got here last week and he has some good butter for 50 cts. a pound. Thomas Whitaker is Chief Cook and Baker and he bakes some of the nicest bread I ever eat. So you see, I fill myself with good bread and butter and coffee. We eat all together in our cookhouse where we have 2 long tables with seats on each side. Our tables are set with tin plates and cups so we eat like gentlemen, and we black and brush and scour up so nice we are gentlemen to look at. But, if we should get aboard of the rebs, they wouldn't think up very gentle.

Sunday evening . . .

I am in my tent alone at present. Some have gone to the church to meeting and some are singing here in their tents. All seem to be happy. I ask myself how is my little family. Is Mother sick or is she sitting writing to Pa or is she reading or putting the children to bed. I can but think some of these things are being performed if Mother is well, but I may be far from the mark. Mother may be confined to her bed, or some of the children may be sick and she standing over them, but I will hope for the best.

Well, it will soon be rollcall and I have got to fix for bed soon, but I will tell you before I stop that I love you. How much I cannot tell, but the Lord knows I cannot love thee too well. The bugle blows for rollcall so good nite dear one.

Monday eve the 11th . . .

Dear Louisa,

I have been at work today building a fort and when I came to camp I found 3 letters for me. One from you, one from Al, and one from Hannah G. I am sorry you were in so low spirits, but I hope you feel better ere this. I was glad to hear you were all alive. Your letter finds me well and in bully good spirits.

You must pay but little attention to what those little women say about you. Say as little about them as possible except to me and if they say too much they may get their ass in a sling. But they will soon cool down if you pay no attention to them.

I hope you will have good luck lambing this spring. what has become of Luther? Is he going to farm it for you and Kate or has he left? I hope you and Kate can get someone to work your farms this summer. The girls have bad colds you say, I suppose they get wet feet for it is sploshy and wet under foot. The health of the regiment is good but the weather is quite warm.

If George settles up this spring, I think he is doing pretty well.

Your new sheep cause you some trouble, but if you get a piece fenced and put them in, I guess they will stay. Sheep are the best stock you can keep. I know you need me very much, and I would gladly come to your fond embrace and assist you but cannot at present. Well, we have had rollcall and I have got to go to bed and in the morning go on guard. So I will have time to write no more, but will soon again.

From your true lover,

B. A. Cook

No. 21(?) On Picket near Jacksonville, Florida, Sunday, April 18, 1864

Dear Louisa,

I must write you a few lines and let you know that yours of the 1st is at hand. I received it last night. It found me well.

I learn that our Emma is very sick. Poor girl, how I wish I was there to assist you in taking care of her. What troubles we are subjected to in this world. I think Buddy will do all he can to save her and I think he will cure her, but it may be otherwise. How kind our Mother is--she is always at hand to do everything for us.

Oh how much good it does me to read that Emma wanted to say her prayer and to pray for Pa. May God bless and preserve her and may we all be permitted to meet again in our home. But if we do not meet on earth, let us try for heaven.

I am fearful that some of the rest of you will get sick. Can't you get shoes so your feet don't get wet every time you go outdoors? You know it won't do to go with wet feet.

I got a letter from Charles Dickinson. He inquired about you and Mother. He is well.

You have a very correct opinion of Mr. Jenson. There is a good deal of coffer about him. So much that he is good for nothing in the Union ranks and I don't believe he would be in the reb ranks. He is a ignorant, superstitious, quick tempered man. I would warrant that if you disagreed with him, he would get mad. He has a brother with us here now that is off of the same piece. The other day at the table he said he wished the niggers were all in one big fort with powder enough to blow it up and he would like to touch a match to it.

Our Regiment moved camp today. I was on picket so I had but little to do about moving since we take our things with us when we go on picket. There is some talk that we are to have horses to ride. Several Regiments have left here for the Army of the Potomac or elsewhere. I can't tell whether we shall stay here this summer or go back to Virginia.

You ask what I thought about getting home. If I remember, I told you in my last letter that I had made up my mind that the war would probably last my 3 years out, and I am bound to stick by Uncle Sam that length of time. If I am alive, then I think I will be free. No, you have never said one thing that discouraged me. The best way is to be a man and do duty like one. When I was sick on Folly Island, I wasn't a man then. So you must make some allowance for what I wrote then. I guess all will come our right.

I don't believe I can stand it to ride a horse if I get one.

This is a very nice day and how I wish I was in your presence. But let us do the best we can, and month after month will slip away and we can meet. How thankful I am to you for writing to me so often. I should have written to you before, but I am on duty nearly every day so I hardly get time to clean my gun.

I will write to Mother as soon as I get a chance. Tell my little girls I think often of them and want them to speak a word to Pa every time you write. And like my little Emma, pray to God for me. Poor girl, how she must suffer and yet with all her pain, Pa is not forgotten. How much I think of their likenesses. How good they look to me. And my Wife, how glad I am that you got them and sent them to me.

If we ever get paid again, and I can get my face taken, I think I will send it north to some of my friends. I have to get my paper and to-bacco off the Sutler on tick now for it is over 2 months since we got pay. But if they don't pay, I guess we can get along 17 or 18 months longer and not starve.

Yours in love,

                                    B. A. Cook

MAY 1864

May 5th, Naval Battle with Ram Albemarle
May 5th to 7th, Wilderness, Va.
May 5th to 9th, Rocky Face Ridge, Ga.
May 8th to 18th, Spottsylvania, Fredericksburg
      Road, Laurel Hill and Ny River, Va.
May 12th to 16th, Fort Darling, Va.
May 13th to 16th, Resaca, Ga.
May 16th to 18th, Bermuda Hundred,
      Va.
May 16th to 27th, North Anna River,
      Va.
May 25th to June 4th, Dallas, Ga

History summarization pages 159-162

In the early part of May the recruiting officers sent north
some months before, rejoined the regiment and with them
came some forty recruits. On May 13th Col. William J.
Slidel, appointed by Governor Seymour to command the
144th appeared and took charge of the Regiment. On the
21st of May, Gen. Gordon commenced a movement intended
to capture a body of the enemy, reported to be making a raid
on the east side of the St. John's. A detachment of two hundred men from the 144th under command of Col. Slidell was
embarked on the transport, *Houghton*, and under convoy of
gunboat *Ottawa* and an armed steam launch, the *Columbiana*,
moved up the river to Picolata where we were reinforced by

Col. Beecher's regiment of colored troops and a detachment of the 157th N.Y.V. making our force seven hundred. For the next day's march a good guide was needed and Gen. Gordon asked one of the residents who seemed to be quite intelligent to perform this service for us. The man refused all offers and slighted all commands to do this duty. At length the General riding close to the man to make further effort heard the whispered words: "Take me--tie me by force". The Gen. understood that this man was being watched and that any service which he should render to the Union cause of his own free will would be at the sacrifice of his life. The day's march brought us to a crossing of Haw's Creek. The route was through pine woods and over monotonous flat country that kept the soldier constantly puzzling with the query "What do we want this forlorn, forsaken section of the country for anyway?" On the 24th our detachment, under command of Major Rice, commenced its return march to Picolata. This march proved to be one of the most severe that the 144th ever had a part in. It was very warm and the march of the day before had resulted in a large number of blistering their feet. Coming to a water sink we were directed to fill canteens as we would not reach water again for several hours. The feet of many of the men were covered with raw sores and they made their way in great pain. The next morning's march brought us after a few miles to a stream of water. What a rush was made for it! What delight, what comfort, to drink, to wash, to bathe the tired sore limbs in the cool, cleansing water. We reached Picilata in the afternoon of Thursday, May 26th, sore and tired. On the 28th the steamer, *Mary Benton*, came up and conveyed the detachment to Jacksonville. This expedition proved to be our last in Florida.

No. 23, Jacksonville, Florida, Sunday, May 22nd, 1864

Dear Wife,

I am well and get relieved from guard this morning and am at liberty to answer your letter which I received the 20th. I am sorry you are having so much trouble, but I don't know as I can stop those Scrapegraces from talking. But their talk is of little account anyway . . . farther than they will have to answer for their idle words You write that you have fears that I will believe that something is wrong. I will relieve you of those fears by saying I never had reason to distrust your faithfulness to your marriage vows and further I believe your love for me and respect for me and yourself would prompt or cause you to shun any temptation that Man or Men could put before you. Yes, you would lose your right hand rather than be untrue to me. I say this for I believe I know you to possess that decision of character and pureness of mind which Women rarely possess. And further I believe you to be as virtuous as myself and I know that I would suffer a loss of limb rather than prove untrue to you. Yes, all others I forsake and ever shall if I keep my senses.

You have heard of love powders. I don't think they are properly called for they ought to be called devilish powders for some devils in this Regiment have told of using them and accomplishing their design. The powder consists of nothing more or less than the Spanish Fly made fine and put into candy or anything so that it is taken into the stomach. It has such affect on the system that they come down at once and have no desire to resist. But woe be to the devil that would give it to one of my daughters for I would shoot him I believe. Now Wife, you were in trouble when you wrote the letter I am trying to answer. Therefore you are excusable for addressing me My Dear Absent Friend for I claim to be nearer than that. I feel for you in your lonely troubled hours. But you must learn that no one has anything to do in this world but what they are talked about. And as you have to be both Man and Woman, you can but expect that people will spend a double portion of their invaluable breath about Lousia, or the Widow, or Cook's Wife, or whatever they please to call you. Especially such Slinks as Aaron Travis, who would enlist and get the bounty and then lay and grunt around pretending to be sick and wouldn't do anything. So of course he got his discharge as he intended. I hope I may never stoop so low as to swindle money from my government in any such shape as that.

Now Louisa, I fear you have made Kate too good a friend for your own welfare, but maybe it is all right. But I tell you to make a confidant of no one but ourselves. Then when they get mad, they have nothing to throw in your face. I must say Kate has shown herself a silly creature in marriage. I am afraid she will feel like wearing that black dress and bonnet in remembrance of her wedding day before she has lived with him 2 years. But I hope not for I wish him well.

I am sorry you have made up your mind to tell Luther he must not come there any more without bringing his wife. He may think that if you are so afraid of him as that, he won't come at all. But I hope he will help you in getting the spring work done. And I wish he would take the place and stock at some rate for a year or longer if he likes and relieve you. Then you could go and live with Mother, or stay there just as you liked or could agree. Then you would have nothing to look after but yourself and children and that is enough. Luther is just the one to take the place for he wants a home for himself and wife. And he can do well to hire it, for he can have it reasonable if he will take it. We won't quarrel about the price for he can pay the rent in butter and such things as he would have to spare. The increase of stock he could have . . . such as lambs and calves. I would of spoke of this before if I had known that he had his wife up there. Now you must do as you think best, but you know you can't go to the river to live without getting someone to live on the place and take care of the stock. And I know it is wearing you out to have so much to do, but we will do the best we can and I guess we will come out all rite.

I got the *New York Herald* of the 14th and it tells of 8 days of hard fighting in the Army of the Potomac. Some of the regiments that left here a few weeks ago have had some fighting to do. If we had not been left here, we would have seen some fighting too, but we have been a lucky Regiment so far. Last night at 12 midnight an order came for our regiment to draw 5 days rations and 60 rounds of cartridges and be at the dock in one hour. So off went the most of the Regiment up the river on the steamer. They were to report at Pickalatka (*sic.*) some 17 miles above here. If I had not been on guard, I would of went I suppose.

It seems that General Grant is pressing the enemy hard at all points and Lee was forced to retreat with fearful losses. I hope the next news we get will be that Grant has pursued him so close that both forces have got inside the fortifications together. If this were the case that both Armies were on a foot race for Richmond together, the big guns at Richmond would be of no use for they could not fire on our men without killing their own men. I have reason to hope that Richmond is ours before this. But if it is not ours, Grant will have it before next Fall if he has to dig them our as he did at Vicksburg. We fired a salute here of 40 guns on the 18th on hearing of Grant's success.

I have got no letter from Moses yet. If you go to Deposit, I wish you would see him and see if he got the letter I wrote him. If he didn't, I will write again and send it to you and you can send it to him. I had a good letter from H. L. Greenmun. She spoke of you and Kate and she said if you were sisters you could not think more of each other. I pity Emmy for those swellings must have been very painful. Kiss them all for me. I have written all I can think of. It is very warm. I am sweating sitting in the shade, the coolest place I can get.

Yours ever,

B. A. Cook

No. 24, Jacksonville, Florida, May 31, 1864

Ever Dear One,

It is with pleasure that I seize my pen to let you know that I am well and got lots of letters last nite. Three from you and a line from Chas. G. Esq. He said you had requested him to make out a deed for Mr. Leonard. He said I would have to sign and acknowledge it myself or give someone I could trust the power to do so for me. He said that the deed would have to be acknowledged in York state. Well, all this I knew before and I would as soon give the Power to James Leonard as any man, but that wouldn't work for he is to receive the deed.

I think I had better give Henry Brunning the power of attorney, and yet I hate to put him to the trouble. I suppose Mr. Leonard wants his deed and he should have it. But if I were to make out a form giving anyone the power of attorney there is no Justice or Civil Officer here to go before to acknowledge it. The contract is just as good as a deed when paid up and receipted for it holds the giver and his heirs or assignees responsible for a deed. So if I should die before my term of service is out, you could give the deed. But I think if I live to see fall, I shall try pretty hard to get a furlow and come home. Then I will try to get things in shape.

Well, you will think this is a business letter I guess, but I tell you I was glad to hear from you and my little ones. And to hear you are well and that you and Mrs. G. are going to have Lute to do something for you in the way of farming. What you can raise you won't have to buy and a dollar is worth only 50 cts. for it won't buy as much as 50 cts. would 3 years ago. But we will try and get along another year some way. You said you got your check cashed but didn't get home with the first cent of it. You done rite and I wish you had had 3 such checks to spend. It was the best thing you could do to get flour and things as you did.

I think I wrote you that the regiment had gone on a journey up the river. They were gone just one week. They traveled over 100 miles and encountered no rebs. They marched 35 miles one day, but when they halted at 10 o'clock at nite, they were scattered along the road for several miles. They got tired and lame and couldn't keep up. The reason they went so far was to get water. They got none that day, only what they had in their canteens, but they got out all right. The journey didn't amount to much for they didn't capture anything, only what fresh meat they wanted to eat and some sugar. I came off guard duty this morning and am trying to talk to you dear One. What a privilege it is to tell the girls that kiss was gladly received. Oh how I long to clasp those little Dears in my arms, and the big Dear too.

B. A. Cook

JUNE 1864

June 1st to 12th, Cold Harbor, etc.., Va.

June 5th, Piedmont, W.Va.

June 9th to 30th, Kenesaw Mountain, etc., Ga.

June 10, Brice's Cross Roads, Miss.

On steamer *Mary Benton,* June 11th to 12th.

Hilton Head, S.C., June 12th to June 27, 1865.

June 15th to 19th, commencement of Siege of Petersburg, Va.

June 17th to 18th, Lynchburg, Va.

June 19th, capture of the Alabama.

June 22nd to 23rd, Welden RR. etc., Va.

History summarization pages 162 and 163

This expedition proved to be our last in Florida. Gen. Birney was returned to the command of the district on the 6th of June, taking Gen. Gordon's place and about this time Gen. John G. Foster came into the command of the Department. Among the first results of this change in command was the ordering of the 144th to Hilton Head, S.C. On the 10th of June the steamer, *Mary Benton,* carried the regiment down the St. John's and the next morning found us safely conveyed to the dock at Hilton Head, which proved to be our permanent camping place during the remainder of our sourjourn in the south.

No. 25, Jacksonville, Florida, Sunday, June 5, 1864

Dear Old Gal,

I am happy to pen you a few lines this afternoon and inform you that I am in good health. I am happy to learn by your late letter of May 24th that you and the children were well and that you had got some potatoes in the garden, for they are next to the staff of life.

We have news that General Grant is closing in on Richmond and the rebs begin to tremble. I say long live Gen. Grant.

I am sorry you blistered your feet walking to Mother's to see that thing. It is not a picture but you may see something of my looks about it after all. I am sorry you were disappointed in the fact that I didn't send it several days after it was taken, consequently I have caused Mother and you some anxiety. I perhaps ought not to of wrote Mother about it until I sent it.

In my letter of May 31st I wrote you we were going on a raid. Well, that evening we drew 2 days rations and got in line and stacked arms and broke ranks. We were to be ready to fall in at any moment, so we lounged around until near midnight when we fell in and left camp. After moving about a mile, we stacked arms and lay down until break of day. Then we started forward without taking breakfast. We did not see much sign of rebs, so we halted long before noon. It was exceedingly warm. We got some coffee and about noon moved on, hearing once in a while a few shots fired on either side of the road by our skirmishers. They didn't fetch in any dead rebs and I have my doubts whether they saw any rebs. But some told of seeing 6, some as high as 30, and others saw 60. And here we were after them with 12 hundred men and several pieces of artillery besides a force of 6 or 8 hundred that was to come from another way. Well, at 5 o'clock we found ourselves connected with the last mentioned force. So we encamped for the nite near where some reb cavalry had been stopping. Well after supper, pickets were detailed to send out for the nite, and of course I was one of them. Well, about 11 o'clock there was 8 or 10 guns went spang,

spang about 80 rods from where I was posted. I knew it was on our line, but I didn't know what to make of it. It routed the whole camp for they were up in arms in 2 minutes, but no more guns fired. We soon learned that it was some of the colored pickets that had heard something and fired at the noise. But I did not learn that they hit it. Well, in the morning some of our cavalry advanced and the guns began to pop again and it lasted near half an hour and I supposed we were going to get a little fite. But no, Gordon must have us retreat and I don't think there were 200 rebs there. He acted as though he wanted to run us all the way to camp (15 miles), but it was so very hot that the men could not stand the double-quick long, so they took it a little slower.

A few of our cavalry and some 2 companies of our infantry made a stand after retreating some 3 miles and Mister Rebs made their appearance for a fite. We were then in the advance for camp, a mile and a half away, but we could hear the firing quite plain. Our boys soon gave them enough so they did not choose to follow them any farther or at least keep in company with them. We stopped to get dinner and rest and those that the rebs tried to scrape acquaintance with joined us again. Then we waited about an hour but no rebs came. Finally we moved on for camp where we arrived about 5 p.m. having accomplished nothing except one of Gordon's marches. He marched several of our men to death last year and I felt bad when I heard he was in command of us this year. But thank God, he, General Gordon was relieved of his command last nite and Gen. Birney has taken command here.

The other day Gordon marched and kept us exposed to the hot sun until near one fourth of the men fell out of ranks, for they could go no further. I saw some of the colored soldiers that fainted and fell like logs to the ground. The doctor took charge of them and got them into an ambulance for camp. I fell out myself after I got in sight of camp for I had no water in my canteen and I was very thirsty and the heat of the sun affected me much. Our Regiment was going at the rate of 4 miles per hour. So I sat myself down and let the Regiment pass, what was left of it. Many had fell out by the wayside. I was close to a good spring so I washed my face and took off my things or equipment and cooled off before I went to camp. Now I have given you a memorandum of the 1st and 2nd days of June 1864.

Now the 3rd day I lay in camp and got rested. The 4th I went to town on guard or Provo as we call it and this morning returned to camp and went on Co. inspection this afternoon. It is raining and I am in my tent writing to thee Wife, the joy of my life.

I hope Gen. Grant will have good success and may his plans all work so that U.S. will let me come home this fall to live with you. Oh it seems as though if I could get my eyes on your form I would never let you get out of my sight. I am glad you are getting to be a good boss. I would like to have you here to boss me a while. Can you form any idea what you would set me at first. What say You? Now I have run this our quite lengthy, but you can read it in 2 days if you can't in one.

Dear Louisa, in remembrance of better days than these, I subscribe myself your affectionate husband.

Bishop A. Cook

JULY 1864

**July 1st to 31st, series of engagements in front of
Petersburg, Va.**

(While the permanent camp of the 144th was at Hilton
Head, S.C., until it was ordered North to be mustered out, the
Regiment was absent on a series of expeditions and the several
camping places follow).

On steamer *Mayflower,* 1st to July 2d.
John's Island, S.C., 1st camp, July 2nd and 3rd.
John's Island, S.C., 2nd camp, July 3 and 4th.
John's Island, S.C., 3rd camp, July 4th to 5th.
John's Island, S.C., 4th camp, July 5th to 9th.
     July 9th, John's Island, S.C.
John's Island, S.C., 5th camp, July 9th to 10th.
Hilton Head, S.C., July 10th to Nov. 28th.
     July 12th, Fort Stevens, Washington, D.C.
     July 20th, Peach Tree Creek, Ga.
     July 22d, Atlanta, Ga., (Hood's 1st Sortie)
     **July 23rd to 24th, Kernstown and Winchester,
        Va.**
     **July 28th, Atlanta, Ga., (Hood's 2d sortie at Ezra
        Chapel).**
     July 28th to Sept. 2d, siege of Atlanta.

History Summarization pages 165-169

From the time of its capture to the end of the war Hilton Head became the military center of operations in the South. It was the depot of supplies and so the distributing center for the department and for a large part of the time this was the head-quarters of the General commanding the department. The introduction of the 144th to the place was marked by the most severe rain storm accompanied by thunder and lighting that the Regiment had known in all its experience in the South. It had just reached the grounds selected for camping, with only a few tents in place when the storm came down completely deluging the camp and the unsheltered soldiers. In a few days the camp was in shape and the Regiment doing duty as guards in various parts of the island. Company B, was sent to the south part of the island, Co. G. to the west and Co. F on dock guard and H, I and K on fortification guard. Later Co. D and K were detailed for Provost guard at Provost barracks and E to garrison Fort Wells.

On the evening of July 1st, the expedition left Hilton Head, or as much of it as had gathered there. The next morning we were just entering Edisto Inlet and about sunrise the *Mayflower,* the transport conveying most of the 144th tied up to a rude dock on Seabrook Island and very soon we were on shore. As soon as we landed skirmishers were thrown out and after an advance of about five miles some Rebel cavalry appeared in our front and occupying the same works where they were found in February. They retired as we advanced and we occupied the works. It being low tide no difficulty was experienced in crossing from Seabrook to John's Island. Company F was advanced as skirmishers and soon drew the Confederate fire from some cavalry waiting in a piece of woods.

The 4th of July, 1864, will be remembered in the history of the 144th as one of the warmest days in the service. There was no special incident in the day; but the intense heat and the stifling dust and intolerable thirst marked it. Our march was along a narrow road with high hedges of wild plum on either side into which the sun seemed to be focused like a search light, while the sand dust, ankle deep, would rise just above the hedge, marking all the line of our advance to the enemy, and then settle back upon us as we sweltered along.

An advance of only four or five miles was made during the day.

The next day's march was made with constant skirmishing on the advance line. Several of our cavalry were wounded and some of the infantry. A member of Co F of the 144th was among the wounded.

On the morning of the 6th word came from the advance line that the enemy had planted a new battery during the night within about three hundred yards of our picket line. This battery made its presence known very soon after daylight by opening a savage fire on the picket line and sharpshooters. During the forenoon Jessie Baxter, of Co F came in with a thumb badly lacerated with a shot and soon after Sergt. Seacord of Co E was wounded in the arm.

No. 29, Hilton Head, S.C., Sunday, July 3, 1864

Dear Wife,

I am pleased to tell you that this day finds me a liberty to pen a few lines to a loved one who will never forget me. As I have time, I will tell you a little about things here.

In the first place, this is on an island about 15 miles long and 12 miles wide and it is pretty well populated with colored people. They raise lots of things to sell. They come into our camp with potatoes, cucumbers, squash, turnips, and peaches. And watermelons will soon be ripe. We pay 10 cents a pint for huckleberries and the same for a cucumber, and 30 cents for huckleberry pie. We get butter in town for 55 cts. and lemons are a dollar a dozen and white sugar 30 cts.

Now I will tell you something else about the 28th of June. We got orders to draw ten days rations for all the troops here. So the rations were dealt our on the 30th and we were mustered for 2 months pay, May and June. We had to put our rations in our knapsacks. Well, I was ready to go, but early in the morning of the 1st I found I had a good deal of pain in my bowles and I had to go to the sink quite often. So I went with the sick to the doctor and he felt my pulse and asked me what the trouble was. I told him and he gave me a great big pill of opium and said it would stop the pain and it did after a few hours. He marked me quarters, so I did not try to go on the expedition.

They all went in the afternoon of the 1st. The 2nd I was on guard at the commissary tent, but I could sit down and guard it. Today (the 3rd) I have been to the doctors for I don't have much appetite to eat and my bowels are rather loose. I have got some codfish and potatoes I want to cook for dinner. Oh if you had the potatoes and fish to cook and fix up with milk and butter, it would be good. But for me to boil it in water, it won't taste very good without a good gravy on it. But I can't get things today to make gravy or butter to eat on it, so I will do the best I can.

You ask about Bill Garlow. He is the black sheep of Company A. He is in the guardhouse or punished for something every few days, but he has gone on the expedition now. Josh Leonard is corporal in Company K. His health is good.

We have pretty warm weather. We can go to the dispensary and get ice water to drink. We have a report that Buauregard is taken at Petersburg with 15,000 men, and Gen. Grant is between Petersburg and Richmond, and our expedition has captured the reb General that was in command at Charleston. They took him on James Island in 2 lines of earthwork. But how much of this is true I cannot say. I wish it mite all be true.

I have sent for the N.Y. *Weekly Tribune* for a year so I expect I will get the news every time the mail boat comes. That is every 8 days. There are 2 steamers running regular between here and N.Y., viz the *Fulton* and *Arrago*. The *Arrago* is due here tomorrow (the 4th) and I expect she will bring some mail from you. She will stay here 3 or 4 days to unload, then start for N.Y. again and take our mail north. So you see I am writing 4 or 5 days before I can send it off, but it is the first chance I have had since I have been here to write a full letter to you Louisa.

B. A. Cook

Continuation of 29, Hilton Head, S.C., Wednesday, July 6, 1864

My lovely Louisa,

I have got no mail yet for the *Arrago* didn't come as expected. She was ordered to some other port. There was a boat come and fetched some mail, but it left N.Y. some 3 days sooner than the *Arrago* would have done. So you see it cut us short of mail. I am feeling pretty good about now for my appetite is good. Yesterday I washed 30 pieces (shirts and drawers). We had a thunder shower the 4th and it cooled the air. I have heard nothing to be depended upon from our expedition but I am thankful that I am not with them. Let them be where they will. Well, it is almost breakfast time, so I will stop for now.

July 7. This morning I am well and on guard. I feel a little concerned about you for there has come 3 dribs of mail and none for me. But I guess it is on the way. Last nite I dreamed I saw you and you had your head tied up. You had been hurt or was sick. I must hear from you soon.

Our Regiment is on Johns Island, 5 miles from Charleston. I suppose they are hanging around there to get a chance to steal something from the rebs. A young fellow just from the North reports a great drought and nothing growing. He says on the 20th of June the meadows were only good pasture and he read in a paper that the wheat was nothing out west. If this be the case, you had better pay no debts, but get 3 or 4 barrels of flour on hand so you won't starve next winter.

There is going to be a great time if this war don't end in the course of a year. But I think there won't be much fiting after this 1864 is out, but no one can tell. If we live to see the end, then we will know more about it, won't we. Oh how I long to be free and go home to all that I hold dear on earth.

Well, Dear One, I have only 14 months to serve after this one is gone, so let us take courage. I have a letter wrote to send to Mother and Aunt Harriett when this goes. Mother said in her letter that they could not raise much to eat this year. I hope your grass will be pretty good so you can get the barn full. Then you will be all right for I will try and send home $12 a month or more hereafter. I hope to hear from the $30 I sent in a few days, for I should hate to have it lost. A dollar aint worth as much as it was 3 years ago, for it won't buy near as much of anything. It takes $2.10 of greenbacks in N.Y. to buy a gold dollar. So it goes.

Yours with all love,

B. A. Cook

No. 31, (No number 30), Hilton Head, S.C., July 20, 1864

My Good Wife,

I must write a few lines to you so far away and tell you that I love you. But this is no news to you Dear One. I long for the day to come when I can fly to your arms to be torn from them no more so long as we live.

I have not had very many letters the 3 weeks that is past, but I hope to get more hereafter. The P.M. was here and paid us last Sunday. I will try and send you $30. I will send a $20 in this and probably $10 in the next. I have heard from the $20 I sent before, but the $10 I have not heard from yet, but expect to when the next mail comes.

Now you want to know how my health is so I suspect. Well, I am going to the Doctor every morning yet, for I am troubled some with the piles and have the diarrheas some yet. But I am a good deal better and if I get no new attack I will be fit for duty in a few days. But the time goes off pretty well, Now, if I could only get a letter from you every 3 days, but that can't be for we don't get mail from the North so often.

Well, I suppose everything is getting so high you can't buy much with what money I send you, but it will help some. And if you raise some potatoes and garden trash, it will help, and if you have any-thing to sell you will have to ask two prices for it in order to get what it is worth. Your butter and wool will help you very much.

I paid 30 cts. for 6 eggs this morning and boiled them and 3 of them were rotten. Cow's grease is worth 60 cts. a pound and you would go without butter before you would eat it, for it is far from being good. You must have some new swarms of bees before this time. Ant it is time to commence haying, but I don't know as you have much hay to cut. Oh, it seems as though I hadn't heard from you in 2 months.

Saturday, July 23rd. My health is still improving. I have been to the doctor this morning and he marked me quarters. Bully for Doctor Brice. Doc. Oliver Bundy is at Jacksonville, Fla. I believe he is Medical Director for that district.

I went to the landing or dock yesterday and got 2 watermelons for 50 cts. and fetched them to camp and sold one for 35 cts. Then I sold half of the other for 25 cts. I was going to eat the other half but it was not ripe, so a fellow wanted it for 25 cts. and he got it. So I got 85 cts. and give 50. I don't know but I will go again to-day.

This is crooked writing for the wind blows a gale all the time and the old tent shakes, so I can't write straight. The sand flies like snow. There has 2 mails come and no letter for me. I don't know what to think of it for the last I got from you was mailed the 30th of June. I got the first *Tribune* this week. I wrote you I was going to take it for a year. Our company is building a barracks to live in if we stay here. We have had but 2 hot days in 2 weeks.

I hear that Charles Wever was killed. What a slaughter there has been in the Army of the Potomac. Grant has got them in a tite spot and I don't see how they are going to get out unless they starve out, Grant will dig and fortify so they can't fite out. The rebs had write a time on their raid into Maryland, but I haven't heard whether they got back safe or not. I hope to hear the Hunter and Seigel have given them what they need.

Yours with all love Dear Wife,

B. A. Cook

AUGUST 1864

August 14th to 18th, Strawberry Plains, Va.
August 18th to 21st, Six Mile House, Welden R.R. Va.
August 25th, Ream's Station, Va.
August 31st and September 1st, Jonesboro, Ga.

No history summarization identified for August 1864

No. 35, Hilton Head, August 24, 1864

Dear L,

I seat myself to answer your letter of the 5th. It found me well and all rite. I can say that as long as I get news from home that things are going half way right, and you are all well, I feel as contented as most anyone can taking all things into consideration. But after all, there is no place like home and I know that my reception there would be highly gratifying to all concerned. I am bound to get a furlow if possible, but whether I succeed or not remains to be seen. I am glad the people are so kind to help you in your haying and I hope your potatoes will be a good crop for I want a few of them to eat with that chicken pie.

I am sorry little Mate is suffering with a cough. Have you tried nettle root tea? You recollect the other girls once had a bad cough and that helped them. I hope she will soon be better. There is a death in most every letter I get and it sometimes seems to me that if we all live to see the end of another year, and live together all rite and sound, it will be a miracle. Oh, won't we be happy if the good Lord spares us to live together with our loved children. Poor Mant, I pity her. I tell you Mr. G. has acted no part of a man and I hope Mant can live to see him rewarded for his false and selfish love.

I have nothing to write concerning things here. Only that our Colonel has gone to Washington and our Regiment is at work every day at the fort. I am on guard today and the mail closes at 4 p.m., so I must hurry this letter. We will muster the last of this month and I guess I will get pay the 15th of next month. The watermelons are about played out, but peaches and apples are ripe and in market. Wm. Garlo is on guard today. Russ is well and intends to get a furlow this fall. I hope we can get together. I think Jenson sticks pretty well, but he is worth just as much to government there as here I think, so let him go it.

I have time to write no more for I must go on guard soon.

Yours in love,

B. A. Cook

(A separate note inserted)

Good morning wife. I feel pretty well,. How do you feel? Yes, if I was aware before I came that I would have to stay so long, I would of stuck by you awhile before I left. It seemed that this war must close in a year, but there is a chance to fight another year if they are mind to. Good bye, for the mail goes.

B.A.C.

No. 36, Hilton Head, S.C., August 28, 1864

My Own Dear Wife,

I will try and write a few lines to you this Sunday afternoon and tell you some of my foolish thoughts last nite when I was on guard. I thought how happy I should be if I was at home with my little family. I thought how my girls looked when I left them and how they would look and act now if I where to come home. And how you and I would act if we got together and how the place must look now. And of the chickens and honey you have got for me to eat if I come on a furlow. And I thought how I would eat mush and milk if I were at home, for it is over a year since I have had any new milk.

I think you are doing first best with things at home and if we all have our health to live together after our debts are paid and the war ended, we can go it in good style and take comfort. But we must not count chickens before they hatch. I suppose if I live one year and one month from today, I will be of age again or a free man. Then I will serve you and you me, then get away trouble. Oh wife, I cannot tell how much I love you. But you know that I have loved thee long and well. Rest assured my love has not decreased for you are my true and lovely wife and God knows I would not be otherwise than true to you.

We were on guard every other day and night. It keeps us busy to keep scoured up and a fellow feels dull. Last nite I got only 4 hours sleep and some nites I don't get 2 for the musketoes (*sic.*) and fleas are so intimate one can't sleep if he gets a chance to lay down.

Wednesday, August 31st, 11 a.m. We have been mustered this morning so in a few days we expect our $32. I got 3 letters from you yesterday. The latest was mailed the 20th. You have not spoke of getting the $20 I sent in No. 31, but you seem to be flush with money. I am glad to hear you have got done haying and are going to get the orchard fenced. Good, for it is too bad to have those apple trees destroyed. I want you to write how full the barn

299

is, but I hope I can come and see how full it is before winter. You ask if you shall nit me some socks. No, I get government socks for 32 cts. and they will do me. I don't know as I want anything sent from home this year for we can buy anything to eat here except new milk.

I am sorry Mant Lake is no better. Where did Mate get the houping cough? I am glad your potatoes are nice. I hope I can come and dig them for you. I don't see how Jenson stays there so long, but let him rip.

You dreamed of killing 2 rattlesnakes. I dreamed of killing one of the largest snakes I ever saw. It was the color of a streaked snake and I thought I killed it very easy, for I surprised mister snake and hit him on the head with stick.

After Dinner. We had stew for dinner. Potatoes and a little pork and after it was cooked put in a few slices of bread to soak up the juice.

The rebs are attracting the attention of our outpost by shelling them.

(This was the end of the page and letter was not signed, so we can assume that there was a continuation that can't be found.)

SEPTEMBER 1864

September 1st to October 30th, In siege of Petersburg, Va.

September 2nd, Fall of Atlanta, Ga.

September 16th, Sycamore Church, Va.

September 19th and 22nd, Winchester and Fisher Hill, Va.

September 26th and 27th, Pilot Knob, Mo.

September 28th and 30th, New Market Heights, Va.

History Summarization, page 178

On the 20th of September, two hundred Confederate officers, that had been confined at Fort Pulaski, were brought to Hilton Head and placed under the care of our Regiment. Before they came their camp had been laid out and A tents set up. As the prisoners filed by our camp, most of our men were on hand to note what sort of men these visitors were, and yet, as they passed no taunt was uttered or aught but courteous greeting given. More than that, since it was late and the men seemed tired and worn, our cooks on their own motion went at once to their cook houses and prepared coffee and carried it out to the prisoner's camp. At this time Lieut-Col. Lewis was absent with a recruiting party at the North. The efforts of this recruiting detail had been very successful. About two hundred recruits for the 144th reached Hilton Head, on the 22nd of September, and by the 6th of October, enough had arrived to fill the Regiment up to its maximum of one hundred men to each company, leaving several hundred for assignment to other organizations.

No. 37(?) Hilton Head, S.C., September 1, 1864

No Opening

I have no news to write only I am on guard duty and last night I sold my watch for $28 cash in hand. The money will come good to speculate on between this and payday. The weather has been very warm here but it is some cooler today.

I hope Wallace Early will get out of service safe and sound. I hear that Squire Layne was taken prisoner. Day before yesterday was your birthday and I would like to of been there and went blackberrying with you. But my dear gal, all our wishes cannot be granted in war times, but I hope the war won't last much longer. I think the election will either close the war soon or extend it to the extermination of the South. Old Jeff says they must have independence or extermination, and I think if the war is carried on 2 years longer, the latter will be their portion. It seems that the war can't last a great while for everything is getting very high and the country is flooded with money. We seem to be drifting into the same channel the rebs were in two and a half years ago as to price of goods and provisions.

You ought to spare the lives of all the sheep that are fit to live for they are the standby. If you dispose of stock, let Jerry go for what she will fetch.

If I have time, I will mail a paper for you. The mail closes soon and I must wind up by saying I love you as ever and hope to hear of your health and prosperity often. Tell Mother and all of our folks that I will write soon as I get time.

Bishop A. Cook

No. 37, Hilton Head, S.C., September 10, 1864

Dear Louisa,

I seat myself to answer 2 letters that I received from you. One was mailed as late as Sept. 2nd. Oh you are a good gal to write such good long letters to me. You tell of dark and lonely days which I doubt not you see many of them during my absence. But Dear One, hope on there is better days coming.

We have very flattering news from all points. Sherman has driven the rebel army from Atlanta and cut their army in two, Faragot has taken Fort Morgan, the last fort in the way of getting to Mobile. We may soon hear that he occupies Mobile. General Grant is after the rebs around Richmond. They begin to see that Grant is there for something besides butting his brains out against their fortifications as they predicted. It seems that Grant has taken possession of the Weldon Rail Road. The rebs have tried to drive our men and failed. I suppose our men are throwing up earthworks so it will be held at all hazards. Then Richmond is nearly cut off or in danger of coming short of provisions.

You say Charles is going to be a soldier. Well, let them all come and we will soon overpower the rebs and there will be no draft. So I guess Almus will be left to look after you and Mother. So I guess you will get along and stick with here another year if I come home and see you a few days.

Our Colonel got back last nite from the North. The party that went home recruiting are getting lots of recruits, so I expect our Regiment will be filled up this winter.

Dear Lousia you say you are short about 4 tons of hay, so if we can get rid of Jerry the hay will come out about even. I think you and Em done well killing snakes in the cellar. I don't see what they were in there for. I don't think the letting of those bees to Mary will amount to much. Well, I will try to do well by our bees if I get home to take care of them. I suppose you like to hear me talk about coming home. I like to think about coming and like to dream of being there, but I may not get a furlough after all.

September 11, Sunday after dinner

I seat myself to finish this for the mail will go tomorrow I suppose. Well, old gal, they say Sherman is giving the rebs fits or something worse. He has chased them to Macon, Ga. and drove them from there. It seems he has them completely routed and I hope he can bag the greater part of their army. The report is that the rebs have evacuated Petersburg and if things work well the rebellion will be crunched in 2 months for our armies are everywhere successful of late.

I hope you can get someone to cut a lot of wood before winter so you won't suffer for wood. Mrs. Gates is getting good ain't she. You said you expected her and Mary G. on a visit . . . these women are quite changeable.

B.A.C.

This one is uncertain but it appears to have been written at Hilton Head in the fall of 1864

I dreamed last nite that I was in bed with you and you asked me if I didn't want some. Of course I did and made a move to roll over and awakened and found no wife, so I had to do wanting one. That is the way it goes, but I hope it won't always be so, don't you? We will want to make up some lost time when we get a chance.

I have bought another watch for 15 dollars. I owe here now 33 dollars and have 45 coming pay day besides my pay. I don't expect to get the whole that is coming to me this payday. I let Joe Rose have $5.00 and he has gone to the hospital, so I shant get that next payday. But I guess I can send you $20 when we get our pay and still have enough to get home on if I get a furlough. I calculate to make enough besides my wages to take me home on a furlough. I have made more than my wages amount to in the month that is past, but I have been unwilling a good part of the time. I have bought everything to eat and it takes the change to buy things. Apples are 5 cts., butter 60 cts., potatoes 5 cts., per lb. 3 griddle cakes with butter and sugar are 25 cts. You can go into a saloon and eat for 75 cts., or a dollar, but I don't go in as heavy as that for I can't afford it. Everything is getting so high.

The war will soon end I guess. I suppose about this time you see frost, but we see none here. Russ expects to get a furlough before lone. I guess there will be a good many furloughs given in the regiment if nothing turns up and we stay here this winter. I shall speak to the Captain about one again before long. There will be furloughs given in less than a month and I want to be among them. I think very likely he will send some ahead of me, so then I can't go until they return. But I want to come to you before cold weather so I can fix fence or dig taters. If I get a chance to come at all I will be thankful, won't you?

Now tell the girls that I think often of them and want to see them. I dream of seeing them, but awaken far from them. I have wrote a letter to mother.

I will close by saying yours ever,

B. A. Cook

OCTOBER 1864

October 5th, Allatoona, Ga.
October 7th to 13th, Darbytown Road, Va.
October 16th, President issues call for 300,000 men
October 19th, Cedar Creek, Va. ("Sheridan's Ride")
October 27th, Hatcher's Run, Va.
October 27th and 28th, Fair Oaks, Va.
October 28th, Destruction of Rebel Ram, *Albermarle*, by
Lieut. Cushing

History Summarization, page 180

On the 25th of October, the recruiting party reached the Regiment and Lieut-Col. Lewis at once assumed the command, and soon after receiving his commission as Colonel of the 144th.

No. 41, Hilton Head, S.C., October 19, 1864

Dear Louisa,

I take up the old pen to inform you of the news of the day. The Captain's family have come down to spend the winter I suppose. He has a very nice little boy and girl. He can keep his family cheaper here than at home for he will draw his provisions of the government. I hear the Captain says he means to have all the old soldiers go home that have not been.

Well, the Paymaster is here and I have my pay in my pocket, and the largest bill is five. I want to send you $20 if I can get some larger bills to put in this letter.

My health is better, but I am not on duty yet. I have had 2 ague chills but I have no shits at present. I got a letter from you yesterday stating that you had a bad time with your teeth. I am glad you got the old thing out.

I was sorry to hear Amanda was dead, but death is in the land. One of our recruits is to be buried today, and I don't know but 2. The soldiers are voting here for all sorts, but very few for Mc. Abe is the man. I hear we Pennsylvania men are going to get a chance to vote.

We have some pretty cool nites. I have drawed another woolen blanket so. I slept comfortably last nite. I dreamed of you. I thought we were in bed together. Well anyway, I have got to wind this up so this can go this mail. I expect I have got to go on fatigue, but I shan't do much.

I can't get anything bigger than 5 to send unless I get it downtown. Russ is not sure of his furlow to go on this boat. I guess I will put 2 fives in this and send it and the same in the next letter for I don't like to make them too bulky.

I wish I had time to write more. If the boat don't go too soon, I will write another letter to accompany this.

Yours in love Louisa,

B. A. Cook

No. 42, Hilton Head, S.C., October 20, 1864

Dear Louisa,

I will try and scribble a few lines for your edification and I hope I may learn that they find my little family all well. I have got a ten dollar bill to put in this letter. Both letters will go on one boat I expect, and if I was going on it how pleased I would feel.

I traded watches today and got a splendid watch. The watch I have got is worth 25 or 30 dollars and it cost me less than 15 dollars. I am glad Al got clear. There are 2 men in the guard house for getting drunk and I am afraid there will be more in if they don't look out. But let them rip.

All the new recruits most are out of money. Two or 3 have tried to get some off me, but I have got to keep all the money I get but what I send you, for if I ever get a furlow I want a little money to get home with. I hope we will get pay again in about a month.

I wish I was with you. I could talk more than I can write. But rest assured, I love you and love to read your good letters. I think sometimes my letters are not very interesting, but I have not been able to write every time as I would like to, but you will make proper allowance.

I read a letter from Dan Low's wife. She allows that is it quite a job to drive business alone, but she thinks she will get broke in after a little. She wrote of all the deaths. She is quite a writer and a pretty smart woman I guess.

The weather is quite cool nites and mornings, but it warms up in the middle of the say. I expect to hear of snow soon up north. I would like to get there before snow does, but I guess snow will visit you first.

The girls are not learning to write to Pa much. If they are, I can't see it. Some are getting boxes from home. I had some cake that came in one yesterday.

Yours with all love,

Bishop A. Cook

NOVEMBER 1864

November 8th, Lincoln re-elected President
November 14th, Gettysburg Monument Dedicated
November 28th and 29th, Spring Hill and Franklin,
Tenn.

November 28th to 29th, on steamer *Sylph*
November 29th to December 1st, Bolan Church,
S.C.
November 30th, Honey Hill, S.C.

History summarization, pages 181 to 192

For some time Chaplain Fullerton had been broken in health
and unable to perform the duties incident to his office and in
Nobember he resigned his office and went North to recuper-
ate. A successor was appointed, but was never mustered into
service. Political news from the North began to ferment in
the camp as the time of a Presidential election, 1864, drew
near. Special interest was awakened among the soldiers in
this Presidential election because of the privilege which had
been extended to those of the Empire state and many others
also to send home their votes. The sentiment of the soldiers
was largely for Lincoln and all efforts to stampede them for
McCllelan because he was an old soldier, failed. The day after Thanksgiving sixty rounds of cartridges were issued to the
men and on the 28th orders were issued directing that every
man should be provided with five days' rations in haversack
and be ready to report at the dock early in the afternoon. By
four o'clock in the afternoon the Regiment, with the exception
of Companies D and K, on duty in the Provost Marshal's barracks went on board the steamer *Sylph*. The casualties of the

144th in the Battle of Honey Hill were ten killed, fifty-two wounded, a number mortally, and two missing, supposed to have been killed since no word was ever heard from them.

No. 43(?), unnumbered, Hilton Head, S.C., November 4, 1864

Dear Louisa,

I write today to tell you that I am pretty well and helping to attend the sick. Yesterday we carried everything out doors onto the piazza, even the sick that were not able to walk, and scrubbed the floor. I am pretty stout and might go to the convalescent camp, but the ward master says he wants my help here a few days. I fare well for grub. I get everything I want except butter and potatoes. The butter I buy, but the potatoes I can't cook. We get a few once in a while at the dining room.

I wrote in my last that our Regiment were to go on an expedition. They went and quite a number of them have returned wounded. There is some 9 or 10 killed out of our Company (F) that I know of. How many have been killed since I have heard from them I can't say for they were still fighting at last accounts. There were some 200 wounded brought here in one day and nite. That about filled all the wards, for the whole hospital holds about 400 patients. Among the wounded of our Co. I have seen Benjamin Falkner (wounded by explosion of shell) and E. L. Thomas (by balls, one in each arm and in one leg), both of Hancock. George White lost one leg and I am fearful will lose his life. There are several others of our Co. here, some with wounds in their hands, one with the end of his thumb shot off, one with a hole through his hand.

The 144th N.Y. and 25 Ohio suffered severely. I understand they lost heavily in officers. James Mc., Lieutenant in our Co. was killed and Plaskett is supposed to. He was Major. James Nutt was our orderly all summer and was made Lieut. a few days ago. I understand he is killed.

As I wrote in my last letter to you, I was one of the lucky ones this time, for if I had been able to went, I should of been hit most likely and mite of been killed. After all, I am no better than the rest to be shot at. I suppose that men never walked up before a thicker shower of bullets, shot and shell than our men did to take a battery from the rebs. But all to no purpose, for there was a bush fence growed full of vines 10 feet high.

November 6. I seat myself Dear One to finish this letter and tell you that the old boat brought me a letter from my old gal who is ever punctual to write, and one from Mr. Beavin. The old gentleman is bound to correspond with me and says I must come and see him if ever I get home. I am glad to get Chatles' address and to get an invitation to your bee, and to hear that you are all well, and are like to have a few yards of woolen to cover your nakedness.

I am sorry to disappoint you and the girls by not coming home, but be patient, 9 or 10 months will soon pass and I don't know but I shall pass most of it in the hospital or some other good place if I keep my senses. I have told you that I was helping in the ward to take care of the sick. Well, it is rather unpleasant to be in the sick room of 30 or 40 patients sick with fevers and diarrhea and have to carry shit and empty spit boxes. These things are to be done by somebody. Monday nite I set up the after part of the nite and attended to the wants of the whole ward, but we have water and vessels and everything handy here. Last night one of our patients died of fever. I had quite a turn of the belly ache last night and didn't sleep much, for I had to get up too often. But my bowels are quiet this forenoon. The Dr. says I must keep quiet. He is giving me tincture of iron to give me blood and strength. It will do me good to stay here a spell I think, for we have a very clever Dr. and I like the beds here first rate.

November 7. We are doing pretty well here this morning and hope you are the same. I saw Russel yesterday. He said you seemed to be doing pretty well and was expecting me home every day. It is rather bad that you should be disappointed, but it cannot be helped. Some of our boys got back from home just in time to go into the fite and are here now badly wounded. One of them is George White. His leg is off above the knee. Another has a severe would in the shoulder. I had rather not go home until the expiration of my term of service than to get served as they did. Russ got back too late to go, so he was lucky once in his life.

He says you have a nice pair of steers if they were small, but he didn't speak very highly of Jenny. He said she had been sick and wasn't worth more than 60 dollars. He seemed to talk as though he got a rather a poor bargain. I am sorry the colt turned out so, but it can't be helped. I suppose you are satisfied with the trade ain't you? Is the cow worth much or like to be? When I get home, if I think Russ got too bad a bargain, I will give him something to make it rite.

Now I will tell you something about the hospital. It is 4 long buildings setting with the ends together forming a square yard inside. The 4 buildings are divided into 6 wards, viz. A, B, C, D, E, and F. Some of the wards are longer than others. E is the one I am in now. It is a small ward with only 28 beds. The beds here are all one man beds. Some of the wards have 56 beds.

Now old gal, lest I weary you, I will stop for this time, but not until I tell you I love you.

B. A. Cook

No. 44, Hilton Head, S.C., November 5, 1864

Dear Louisa,

It is with pleasure I address you in answer to your letter of Oct. 23rd. I am getting strong. Was on guard yesterday. It is pretty cool weather here as well as up there.

I am sorry Mother is so rebellious, but she is old and set in her way, and there is no use of talking to here to get her to change her mind. I don't know but I have wrote something to her that displeased her for she don't write to me any more, but let her rip. You can't depend on E. Cook to do anything, he is so fickle. I suppose Russ is at home about this time and will be over to see you soon.

You are making preparation for my reception, but you must be patient for it will be some time yet before I get there. They are all diving for furlows and the Captain don't know which to send first. But he told me today that he meant all the old soldiers should go home this winter. If they do, I shall probably be among them if the Lord is willing.

If you have good potatoes, it is a very fine thing. I am glad if Harriet is better. I hope she will outgrow it entirely. I suppose you are spinning about these days. Well, that is the way to cover the back when others fail.

Our Chaplain is going home for good and we will hardly miss him for he is a little flat thing.

There is no prospect of our leaving here very soon and I don't care if we stay here our time our if we don't bet discharged, which I hope may be the case, for I hope the war will soon end. If it don't stop in 3 or 4 months, I think it will last a long time. But thank the Lord, I hope 10 or 11 months will find me a free man.

How are you Louisa and my little girls and all the rest of the good folk? You don't get very long letters from me for I am lazy and today my fingers are getting cold, and I have no fire to set by. You see we soldiers have to take it just as we can catch it and make the best of it. But I have stood it 2 years and I hope to stand to get a discharge and get home to my Dear Wife and children.

Oh, we begin to count the months of our separation. Keep trust in God and all will be well, and the few months will pass away and bring us together to enjoy the comfort of our life together. I am glad you feel so strong and have such good courage. May the good Lord give you strength and sustain you in your hardships. I must close or the mail will close this out.

Yours in love,

B. A. Cook

No. 45, Hilton Head, S.C., November 13, 1864

Dear Louisa,

I seat myself to inform you that I got a good letter from you yesterday. One of the girls are sick you say. It seems that there is a good deal of sickness up there as well as here. I was glad you got your money straight and had got the potatoes near dug, and have enough to last you if they don't freeze. The swelling of your stomach is an old complaint and I suppose is troublesome, but you must be careful and not work too hard. Do take care of your health old gal.

I suppose that 10 dollars a month don't keep you out of debt, but we will do the best we can this year and if I get home and have my health, I will soon put things all rite if we are a little in debt.

It is the hour for church and the brass band are playing a very nice hymn tune. The voters here from Scott were 22. 18 for Lincoln and 4 for McClellan. That was good voting. We hear that Lincoln is elected and the Pirate Florida is captured. We also hear that Grant has got the last railroad at Richmond fortified. If that should be the case, the rebs are pretty tite up, but it is good to believe. I suppose you don't hear much about Jenson lately, for he keeps dark if he is around there, the miserable old coward.

We are getting pretty cool weather here and I suppose you have snow up there to look at. I expect to get up there to see snow one of these days, but the best of all will be to see you and my children, and spend a few nights with them. But you need not look for me till about New Year. I guess that will about fetch me home.

If I had Charles' address I would rite to him. You say you got a letter from B. A. Jennings and they think Steven is lost. He may be a prisoner or he may be killed, but I hope he will turn up rite yet. H. Dickinson is very sick you say and Amelia won't have a doctor. I suppose she thinks she has more skill than a Doc, and I hope she has skill enough to cure him at least.

Wife, when I look back and see how many happy Sabbaths we have spent together, how I wish to be with you today. But month after month passes away and I hope we may all live to spend many happy days together hereafter. We live in hopes of seeing better days after the war, which I hope is near to an end. But we can't tell how long it will last. Time will tell.

Yours ever,

B. A. Cook

No. 46(?), Hilton Head, S.C., November 21, 1864

Dear Wife,

I will try and answer your kind letter of the 11th. I have to tell you that we have 200 rebel officers here to guard. Some of them say they are glad Lincoln is reelected.

I think you are pretty smart to get your fleece spun beside doing your other work. Well, I have just filled myself with codfish and potatoes and butter. You see I come pretty near boarding myself for I can't eat the meat and other rations for my appetite is not very good.

I got a letter from Mother and Hat. I was surprised to see Hat write so well. I could read it rite straight along. She can write to Pa when she has a mind to.

I have just got a handfull of chestnuts from one of the boys that got a box from home. One man got a firkin of butter. I suppose he will sell it out at 70 cts. a pound. It is raining today and the boys have to guard the rebs. The rebs can lay and sleep in their tents and out boys have to stand in the storm to guard them. But I don't do duty any more. I have done 2 days duty in about 2 months. So you see I am soldering about these days and they mite as well let me go home and soldier it awhile. If they don't, it will be but little duty they will get out of me for the 10 months to come. That is the way my back sticks up.

I have got to put this up in a hurry so it can go this mail. Excuse this short thing Dear Wife. I will commence sooner next time and write more. I will write to Mother and Hat. The orderly is very kind to me. So much for him.

B. A. Cook

DECEMBER 1864

Boyd's Landing, December 1st to 6th
Devaux's Neck, S.C., December 6th to January 1st, 1865
December 6th to 9th, Devaux's Neck, S.C.
December 10th to 21st, Siege of Savannah
December 15th and 16th, Nashville, Tenn.

History summarization, pages 200 to 208

On December 4th the 144th and one other regiment with a section of artillery, all under the command of Col. Lewis, were sent out to examine the strength and surroundings of a Rebel fortification on Bee Creek, some three miles north of our encampment. As a result of this reconnaissance the entire Brigade was moved out the next day with intent to take these works by assault: but just as the formation for the attack had been made, a Union prisoner captured by the Rebels at Olustee, made his escape from the enemy and came running into our lines as we were waiting the order to advance. This man reported the works as very strong and well manned with three masked batteries in position to do very great damage to the attacking force. As a result of this communication the troops were withdrawn without loss and returned to camp. The 144th casualties in a fight were three killed, and twenty-four wounded. On the 14th word reached us that General Sherman had captured fort McAllister and the investment of Savannah was complete. The good news was voiced to us all the way from the Landing by a continuous roll of cheers as the news ran from camp to camp.

319

No. 49, Hilton Head, S.C., December 14, 1864

My own Dear Wife,

I must say a few words to you and let you know that I am feeling pretty well, and got a letter from you last night. Oh, how much good it does a "feller tu git" a letter from his old gal. What a fine thing it is to hear from each other if we can't see each other. But I hope the day is coming in less than 10 months that we can see each other and not be parted very soon. I am pleased to think you had such fine luck getting wood. You are not friendless and I hope never will be.

It has been some time since we got pay and I have spent $20. It costs me 50 cents a day, but I am so I can eat most everything. It won't cost me much. The last of this month there will be 4 months pay due up, and I hope it will come in a pile about the 10th of next month. If it does, I hope to send you $50 that will help you to get through the winter.

I have not seen Russ but once since he came back. If I go back to the Company I shall want a little box from home to taste of. I will let you know in time so you can send it before warm weather comes. I shant dare get much good things on hand for fear we have to move and I can't carry it with me.

I hope you and the children will keep warm this winter. It is warm here today. The flyes are nimble as can be. But the nite of the 12th was freezing cold. It was about as cold as any nite we had last winter and I hope we won't have any colder this winter.

They say Sherman is up to Savannah and has taken the city. But I guess he hasn't got the city yet, but it won't be long before he will have it anyway. Then he will be after Charleston, then down foes the Confederacy. Bully for Sherman. He is the man to make the rebs hunt their hole. Well I have wrote quite a lingo and it is about time to stop.

But Jenson the old shit is there yet. It beats all how he acts. One thing, don't you make up to friendly with Kate or have much to do with her.

Tell my little girls I would love to see them. Russ said I would not know my girls when I got home. But I guess I will know them it I don't see them until next fall. Give my respects to the good folks.

I remain yours ever,

Bishop A. Cook

JANUARY 1865

Hilton Head, S.C., January 1st to February 2nd
January 13th to 15, Fort Fisher, N.C.
January 18th, Charleston evacuated

History summary, pages 209 to 211

Soon after the return to Hilton Head the 144th was ordered to furnish guards to relieve a detachment of an Illinois regiment, in guarding a camp of some eight hundred rebel prisoners. Orders of retaliation had been issued directing that these prisoners should be treated as our own men in Andersonville were being treated. The soldiers of the 144th were often brought face to face with the suffering inflicted upon and endured by Union soldiers at Andersonville and Salisbury, in the person of escaped and paroled prisoners, and had often heard from their lips of the suffering inflicted, and indignities practiced upon them, and if feelings of resentment and retaliation could have been awakened and made permanent the circumstances were favorable.

No letters dated in January exist.

FEBRUARY 1865

On steamer, *Ann Marie,* February 2nd and 3rd
Edisto Island, S.C., February 3rd to 4th
Gov. Aikin's Plantation, S.C., February 4th to 5th
> **February 5th to 7th, Dabney's Mills and Hatcher's Run, Va.**
On steamer *Cosmopolitan,* February 5th to 7th
Folly Island, S.C., February 7th to 8th
Cole's Island, S.C., February 8th to 9th
> **February 10th, James Island, S.C.**
On transport steamer, February 10th to 12th
On transport steamer, February 13th to 17th
Graham's Creek, S.C., February 17th to 19th
Bull's Island, S.C., February 19th to 14th
Mt. Pleasant, S.C., February 21st to 22nd
> **February 19th, Charleston occupied by U.S. Troops**
Charleston, S.C., February 21st to 22nd
On march from Charleston to Strawberry Ferry, S.C., February 22nd to 26th
St. Stephen's Station, S.C., February 26th to March 2nd

History summarization, pages 211 to 219

Early in February, the 144th was sent with the 32rd U.S.C.T.
on an expedition to Edisto Island to make examination of Re-

325

bel occupation and fortifications. On February 2, we went on board the steamer *Ann Marie* and going up to Beaufort were joined by a transport having on board the 32nd U.S.C.T. We continued up Beaufort River to the Coosa, then down the Coosa into St. Helena Sound, then up Edisto River to South Edisto Island when we debarked and marched inland until a stream was reached with the bridge removed. After reconnoitering in the vicinity we marched back to the landing. Tuesday morning, February 6th, the steamer brought us into Stono Inlet, and we disembarked on Folly Island where we bivouacked and had our last experience with the Folly Island sand storms, endured so many times before. We remained on Folly Island until the night of the 9th when we were moved across to Cole's Island. After all the force had been concentrated on James Island it was moved up the island until the enemy's pickets were driven into a line of earthworks. It was determined to take the works by assault and the 144th and 32nd U.S.C.T. were designated for this purpose. The time from the commencement of the movement to the conclusion was about fifteen minutes: but in that time the 144th had lost one killed and twenty-five wounded, one mortally, and this out of two hundred twenty-five men, which represented the strength of the Regiment in action. Companies D and K had been left at Hilton Head on special duty, besides a number of men on guard duty and detached service. Among the wounded were Capt. Witter H. Johnston of Co. F and Lieut James Nutt of Co. B, both valuable officers. We had barely lain down on the night of the 18th when word was brought by dispatch boat announcing that Charleston had been evacuated. In a few moments the camp was wide awake and loud and continued cheers evinced the joy awakened by the good news.

No Number, Hilton Head, S.C., February 21, 1865

Ever Faithful Wife,

I received your kind letter yesterday. It told me you were all on your taps which I was very glad to hear. I am well and am living on top of the heap, for my box got here the 18th right side up, and it's just as nice as can be. Your cake is very good, but as you say, Mother's cake is ahead for it is the richest thing I ever eat. I can eat but a small piece at a time. The sausage and cider applesauce is splendid and so is everything, even the tobacco Al sent. I will think of him every time I take a chew. I let Russel have one of the cakes of sugar for $1.00 and the round cake and a chunck of beef for another dollar, and I gave him some of the blackberries.

I am afraid we will have to move before I get through my box, for I shouldn't wonder if we went to Charleston or some other place in a few days. The report is the rebs have left Charleston and two companies are in Fort Sumter and the rest of our Regiment is in the city of Charleston.

We hear that Sherman has got Branchville and Columbia, the capitol of S.C. It seems the rebs are leaving their strongholds and fleeing before our armies. I think there are indications of peace and I hope it will soon come. The story that the rebs had offered to lay down their arms and come back into the Union is not so I guess. When that comes there will be no more fighting.

You and I often wish we were in some place where the winters were not so tedious. I often think if I live to get home and can sell out, I will go to some country where we won't see 6 months of winter in a year.

We can go to Iowa, Missouri, of Nebraska, but it is quite an undertaking to move so far into a new country. We will talk about that hereafter.

I am sorry your wood pile is low, but I don't think the folks will let you freeze. But you must have wood, let it cost what it will.

We have rough weather here but no snow. Oh how tedious and dreary the days are to you when your loved one is so far away, and you have to face the wind and snow and endure most everything. But Dear One, the winter will soon be gone and then things will look more cheerful. And when fall comes I hope to be with you and our children to cheer and relieve you of some cares. The Lord has been very good to us thus far and we will trust him still, for his mercy endureth forever.

I was one of the escorts to convey the remains of 3 soldiers to their last resting place yesterday. They died in the hospital.

No signature

MARCH 1865

Monk's Corners, S.C., March 3rd to 5th
March 4th, Second Inauguration of President Lincoln
Strawberry Ferry, S.C., March 5th to 9th
Calais, S.C., March 9th to 22nd
Charleston, S.C., March 10th to 22rd
March 19th to 21st, Bentonville, S.C.
Hilton Head, S.C., March 22nd to June 27th
March 25th, Fort Steadman, Va.
March 26th to April 9th, Siege of Mobile, Ala.
March 31st, Boydton and White Oak Roads, Va.

Historical summarization, pages 224 and 225

The movements of the 144th from Charleston to the Santee River and return, covered the time from February 22nd to March 10th, 1865 and were not marked by any matters of special military interest. The itinerary of this march is in part as follows, February 22, left camp near Charleston, February 26th to March 3rd, Monk's corners, March 6th, Strawberry Ferry, March 9th Calais on Wando Creek, March 10th in camp at Oak Grove near Charleston.

No number, United States Sanitary Commission, New York City, March 21, 1865

Dear Wife,

I am well, but feel much displeased at staying here so long when I could have been with you. Al and I went to see Aunt Harriet for the cars were behind time. She seemed much pleased to see us. We got up at 1/2 past 4 and went to the depot, but the train did not come until 9 a.m. We didn't get back here until 9 in the evening. So you see I am spending twice the time here that I did at home and it don't set good on my crop. It cost twice as much to come back as it did to go. I had to pay full fare of $5.85. If I had known when we got here that we were to stay so long, I would of went back home again if I had the money. But I was short of funds and expected to leave every day. I hope I will leave tomorrow the 22nd.

I went to Barnums Museum Saturday afternoon and I saw 30cts. worth. I would of given a good sum to had you and the girls with me. I know they would have been highly entertained. Last evening I went to the theater and saw 35cts. worth to laugh at. Besides I saw the world rolling around and saw the Heavens open and the angels going to and fro.

Now Dear Lousia I have told you all and no doubt you wish you had been with me and so do I. But I cannot take half the comfort here that I could if I were home. How bad I feel that I have to stay here when I could of been at home. But Dear Louisa, I trust the following 6 months will roll away and roll us to each others embrace. Ever Yours,

B.A. Cook

APRIL 1864

April 1st, Five Forks, Va.
April 2nd, Fall of Petersburg
April 3rd, Occupation of Richmond
April 6th, Sailor's Creek, Va.
April 7th, Farmville, Va.
April 8th and 9th, Appomattox Court House, Va.
April 9th, General Lee Surrenders
April 15th, Flag raised on Sumter
April 15th, President Lincoln Assassinated
April 17th, Moseby Surrenders
April 26th, General Joe Johnston Surrenders

History Summarization, pages 239 and 247

In accordance with an arrangement between Commissioner Ould of the Confederate Government and Commissioner Mulford of the U.S. Government, Major Thompson, Provost Marshal-General of the Department of the South, met an officer of the Confederate Government, under a flag of truce, near Savannah, Ga., and it was then agreed between the two men that 5,000 of the Union prisoners then in Andersonville, Ga., should be sent to Darien, Ga., and exchanged. But transportation in Rebeldom was limited and it was found after this agreement had been entered into that so large a number could not be sent at one time. So a further understanding was had, that the U.S. Government was to establish a camp at Darien, Ga., under a flag of truce and prisoners be sent in detachments until the whole 5,000 were sent. From this place they were to be sent, as fast as transportation could be obtained to points North, where they might be furloughed and sent home. Captain Frank B. Hart with his Co. G of the 144th was detailed as guard for the parole camp.

No number, Hilton Head, S.C., April 14, 1865

Dear Louisa,

I set me down to write an answer to yours of April 2nd and tell you it found me well and in good spirits. I am glad to hear you are getting warm weather and the grass is growing. I hope you have got a few hundred of hay from Uncle Brainard's and can save the lives of all the cattle and sheep.

We have fine weather here and the war news is very favorable. General Grant gained Richmond on my birthday as you have probably learned. Major Anderson is to replace the flag on fort Sumter that he was forced to pull down 4 years ago today. We are waiting further news from Virginia with great anxiety. If they can only bag Lee and his army, we will be all rite. But I fear he will get out someway. I cannot see how he is to get supplies, and yet if he had supplies, it seems we have cavalry forces enough with the aid of our infantry to harass him to death and take his army in a few days.

There is much talk about peace negotiations. Jeff will give up everything if he and his imps can be restored to citizenship (the old skunk). He dug out of Richmond 2 or 3 days before the army left. He is sure to keep a proper distance from our army. It looks to me like after he was forced to leave the Capitol, he then sent to Abe looking for peace on the above terms. But when he was in Richmond in his easy chair, he would not think of peace or union, but would suffer annihilation before subjugation.

If a man was to commit murder, it would be very natural for him to bid defiance to the world as long as he was sure he was out of reach of the authorities. But when he finds he is cornered, he is more humble. But does he come forward and say . . . gentlemen, I will come back and be a man if you will restore me to citizenship? No, if he did he would be called insane, and one might suppose Jeff was a little that way. If it was not that the innocent have to suffer with the guilty, I would say follow Jeff to annihilation. But to stop the effusion of blood and the sufferings of those that are human, I say Peace on honorable terms. And I think we shall soon have it, the way things shape at present.

I am glad Charlie is all right and wish he was here with me. We got no pay yet, but I can get what I need and be trusted until pay day, and hope you can too. We will have quite a pile of money when it does come. I don't care if we don't get pay till May, and then get 8 months pay.

I think Mrs. Turrell must be sick indeed to ask you to help her clean house when you have so much to do at home. Well, you can tell her you have all you can do at home, if she don't know it already.

I think there is someone in the north to make babies the way they are shelling out this spring. I guess one don't make them all though, for there seems to be quite a difference in size.

No signature.

MAY, JUNE AND JULY 1865

May 4th, President Lincoln's funeral at Springfield, Ill.

May 10th, General Jones Surrenders

May 11th, General Jeff. Thompson Surrenders

May 13th, Last Skirmish of the war at Palmetto Ranch, La.

May 23rd and 24th, Grand Review, Washington, D.C.

May 26th, General Kirby Smith Surrenders

On steamer *Fulton*, June 27th to 30

New York, N.Y., June 30th to July 1st

On N.Y. Central R.R., July 3rd to 4th

Canandaigua, N.Y., July 4th

Elmira, N.Y., July 4th to 13th

Between July 4th and 13th the 144th was mustered out of service.

History summarization, pages 253 to 259

The order for the muster-out of the Regiment was received at Regimental Headquarters on the 7th day of June: but the company officers had commenced work on their muster-out rolls and they faithfully continued that work until Thursday the 15th of June. It was Monday, June 26th, 1865, when we bade farewell to Dixie. As we rested "in place" near our old camping ground with all our movable goods in knapsacks, waiting for final orders, there was one characteristic scene which comes back vividly--the swarm of negroes despoiling our vacated camp, and especially when loaded with impedimenta of all sorts, carefully poised upon the head: boards, kettles, straw ticks, cast off clothing and all variety of left behind things. We reached New York on Thursday, the 29th and late in the afternoon the Regiment found itself the guests of the 71st N.Y.S.M., and comfortably quartered in their barracks, where we remained until the afternoon of the next day. Friday evening found us aboard the John Brooks enjoying the beautiful scenery of the Hudson. A good breakfast, provided by the citizens of Albany awaited us. The afternoon of July 4th found us on the cars running down the Chemung valley, with colors flying, making the echoes ring with soldier cheers. Elmira reached, the work of mustering out was begun and one by one the companies were paid off and as fast as paid made their way back to the homes in Delaware county and elsewhere. During the time of waiting the officers made their home in the Hathaway House.

APPENDIX

These are parts of lettersand written by Bishop to people other that Louisa.

Camp Bliss, December 19, 1862

Dear Mother, Brother and all concerned,

I seat myself this morning to tell you that that long looked for letter arrived last nite. It done me good to hear that you are all well. I began to think that you were sick that you did not write but the Lord favors us all with health. I have had a very

missing pages

Virginia when I was on picket I went to a house a short distance from where we were stationed and got the lady to make us some mush and let me have a quart of milk when the time came that the mush was done I got one of my mates to go with me to help eat it. We had all we both could eat, 10 cts for the milk and 15 cts for the mush. It was the best of anything I have eat in Virginia. I miss the butter and milk I tell you and I suppose you know how to do without milk too. well I have been out on drill and returned to converse with you a little more before

missing pages

and set our cloth tent on top it makes more room and very comfortable with the brick fireplace we have erected in one end of the

337

tent we can do our own cooking but the company cook does the most of our cooking at present we have enough to eat at present and have had thus far such as it is but I think I lived as well at home, but I did not expect as good fare as I get when I enlisted. The time passes away much faster than I expected. christmas is most here then New Years Day. But Government has forgot to pay us I guess. I got our of money and sent home and got $2.00 to last till payday and have got to make it last

missing pages

reinforcements before he attacked then had to fallback after loosing several thousand men it was useless for him to attack them after giving them so long to receive him. I think if this wa is ended by fighting it will be sometime before it ends. I think Lincoln in his message opened ground so that if congress takes the rite steps and our army are successful this winter I think the war will end in 6 months. I just shook hands with G. V. Whitaker he said he see Louisa the other day and she was well I told him I heard he was at Kingston and intended to come here from Philadelphia. He said he did but it was so cold he went home and found no snow and all of a sudden he started and come here to see the soldiers. He brought some tobacco and give us, the old fellow is clever. I don't know but he will come and stay with us tonite as two of our tent mates are on picket. We have a spare bunk we got some boards and made a platform up from the ground and lay a blanket on them and lay on them and have two blankets over us, my hips

missing pages

I have improved all the time I could get today and this evening it is now 6-1/2 o'clock you are pardoned twice over for not writing sooner. I suppose you are full of business as well as I. I have wrote to Louisa once this week and must write again. My little girls talk about me a good deal and are anxious to have me come back. I suppose you are tired of trying to read this so I will close. We have freezing nites but it thaws a little daytime. I think it will storm soon but we are comfortably situated.   Accept this from the old boy.

B. A. C.

Suffolk, Friday Morning 24th

All quiet this morning a rainbow in the sky as it rained a little.

Officers are:
1st Lieutenant Crawford Luis
2nd Lieutenant William B. Luis
1st Sergant James Mack
2nd sergeant John Whitaker and so on down

E. W. G. is reduced to the ranks.

Oh, I found my knapsack all rite when I got here.   James Gould took care of it for me.   He is a good fellow.   Some of the boys told him to leave it for he couldn't carry it.   But he hung to it and I will reward him for it.   His brother Wm. is made corporal.

P.S.   John Barlow of Co, A is reduced to the ranks, he was 1st Corporal.

Bishop A. Cook
the old soldier Boy

SERVICE RECORD

The service records of Private Bishop Cook are entered on a series of forms which I have condensed. The forms are headed C, 144, NY

August 13, 1862

Bishop A. Cook Co. F, 144 Reg't N. Y. Infantry.

Appears on the company Descriptive book of the organization named above.

Description

Age 31 years; Height, 5 feet 8 inches; Complexion, Dark; Eyes, Gray; Hair, Auburn. Where born, Tompkins N. Y. Occupation, Lumberman.

Enlistment

When August 13, 1862. **Where** Hancock, NY **By whom** Wm. Plaskett; term 3 years.

E. R. Thompson **(Copyist)**

September 27, 1862

Bishop A. Cook, Pvt., Co. F, 144 Reg't N. Y. Infantry Age 31 years.

Appears on Company Muster Roll of the organization named above. Roll dated Delhi, N.Y. September 27, 1862. Muster-in to date September 27, 1862.

Joined for duty and enrolled:

When August 13, 1862
Where Hancock
Period 3 years

O. T. Taylor **(copyist)**

July & August, 1862

Bishop A. Cook, Pvt., Co. F. 144 Reg't NY Infantry.

Appears on Company Muster Roll for July & August 1862, **Present.**

Kelly **(Copyist)**

October 1862

Bishop a. Cook, Pvt., Co. F, 144 Reg't NY Infantry.

Appears on Company Muster Roll From roll in 2nd Aud Office from enlistment to Oct. 31, 1862. Present or absent, not stated.

Remarks: Received one months pay 13.00.

O. T. Taylor **(Copyist)**

November & December 1862

Bishop A. Cook, Pvt. Co. F, 144 Reg't NY Infantry. Appears on company Muster Roll for Nov. & Dec. 1862 **Present.**

O. T. Taylor (Copyist)

January & February 1862

Bishop A. Cook, Pvt, Co. F, 144 Reg't NY Infantry. Appears on Company Muster Roll for January and February, 1863. Present or absent Not stated.

O. T. Taylor (Copyist)

March & April 1863

Bishop A. Cook, Pvt., Co., F, 144 Reg't NY Infantry. Appears on Company Muster Roll for March & April, 1863. **Present.**

Bishop A. Cook, Pvt., Co. F, 144 Reg't NY Infantry. Appears on special Muster Roll for Dated April 12, 1863. **Present.**

O. T. Taylor (Copyist)

May & June, 1863

Bishop A. Cook, Pvt., Co. F, 144 Reg't NY Infantry. appears on company Muster Roll for May & June, 1863. **Present.**

O. T. Taylor (Copyist)

September & October 1863

Bishop A. Cook, Pvt, Co. F, 144 Reg't NY Infantry. Appears on Company Muster Roll for Sept. & Oct., 1863. **Present.**

Kelly (Copyist)

November & December 1863

Bishop A. Cook, Pvt., Co. f, 144 Reg't NY Infantry. Appears on Company Muster Roll for Nov. & Dec., 1863. **Present.**

Kelly **(Copyist)**

January & February 1864

Bishop A. Cook, Pvt, Co. F, 144 Reg't NY Infantry. Appears on Company Muster Roll for Jan. & Feb., 1864. **Present.**

Kelly **(Copyist)**

March & April 1864

Bishop A. Cook, Pvt., Co. F, 144 Reg't NY Infantry. Appears on Company Muster Roll for Mar & Apr, 1864. **Present.**

Kelly **(Copyist)**

May & June 1864

Bishop A. Cook, Pvt., Co. F, 144 Reg't NY Infantry. Appears on Company Muster Roll for May & June, 1864. **Present.**

Kelly **(Copyist)**

July & August 1864

Bishop A. Cook, Pvt., Co. F, 144 Reg't NY Infantry. Appears on Company Muster Roll for July & August 1864. **Present.**

Kelly **(Copyist)**

September & October 1864

Bishop A. Cook, Pvt., Co. F, 144 Reg't NY Infantry. Appears on Company Muster Roll for Sept. and Oct., 1864. **Present**.

A. J. Robbins **(Copyist)**

November and December 1864

Bishop A. Cook, Pvt., Co. F, 144 Reg't NY Infantry. Appears on Company Muster Roll for Nov. and Dec. 1864. **Absent.** **Remarks:** *In Genl Hosp Hilton Head, SC*

A. J. Robbins **(Copyist)**

Bishop A. Cook, Pvt., Co. F, 144 Reg't N.Y.V. Appears on **Hospital Muster Roll** of USA General Hospital at Hilton Head, SC, for Nov. & Dec. 1864. Attached to hospital November 27, 1864. How employed patient. Last paid by Maj. Rucker to Aug 31, 1864. Bounty paid $25; due $75. Present or absent? **Present.**

F. E. Parks **(Copyist)**

No specific date

B. A. Cook, Pvt., Co. F, 144 Reg't New York Inf. appears on **Returns** as follows:

Febry 1863--On duty at Wood choppers camp, Arlington Mills Va. commenced January 28, 1863.

March 1863. Absent on detached duty at wood depot, Vienna, Va.

November 1864 to February 1865. Absent in Genl Hospital.

O. T. Taylor **(Copyist)**

January & February 1865

Bishop A. Cook, Pvt., Co., F, 144 Reg't NY Infantry. Appears on Company Muster Roll for Jan. and Feb., 1865. **Present.**

A. J. Robbins **(Copyist)**

Bishop A. Cook, Pvt., co. F, 144 Reg't, N.Y.V. Appears on **Hospital Muster Roll** of USA General Hospital, at Hilton Head, SC for January and February, 1865. Attached to hospital November 27, 1864. Returned to duty Feby. 1, 1865.

Meaher **(Copyist)**

March & April 1865

Bishop A. Cook, Pvt., Co. f, 144 Reg't NY Infantry. Appears on company Muster Roll for March and April, 1865. **Present.**

A. J. Robbins **(Copyist)**

June 1865

Bishop A. Cook, Pvt., Co. F, 144 Reg't NY Infantry. Appears on **Co. Muster-out Roll,** dated Hilton Head Is., SC June 25, 1865. Muster-out date June 25, 1865. Last paid to August 31, 1864.

Clothing Account Last settled August 21, 1864. Due soldier $34.30.

Bounty paid $25.00; due $75.00

Remarks: Due US for Musket and accouterments six (6) dollars in accordance with telegram from Washington DC dated Washington DC June 10, 1865.

A. J. Robbins **(Copyist)**

PENSION RECORDS

The following are a series of legal papers concerning a pension paid to Bishop Cook's widow after his death.

The covering paper identified these records as, Box #34389, Certificate No. 194164, Louisa M. Cook, Bundle #20, No. 261945, Acts of July 14, 1862, and March 3, 1873

Louisa M. Cook, Binghamton, N.Y., Broome County. Widow of Bishop A. Cook, Private Co. "F", 144 N.Y. Inf. Vol.

Died Jan. 18, 1874 of Disease.

May 1, 1880. Virgil Hillyer (Clerk)

Application filed: March 23, 1880.

Attorney: George E. Lemon

P. O. Present

War Department
Adjutant General's Office

Washington April 15, 1881

Respectfully returned to the Commission of Pensions. Bishop A. Cook Company "F". 144 Regiment New York Volunteers, was enrolled on the 13th day of August, 1862, at Hancock, and mustered in Sept. 27, 1862 at Delhi a private & reported present to Oct. 31. 1864. Dec 31, 1864 in Genl. Hospital, Hilton Head, S.C. Feb. 28. 1865 present. April 30, 1865 present. Mustered out with Co. June 25, 1865.

Assistant Adjutant General

Declaration for Original Pension of a Widow
Child or Children under sixteen years of age surviving.

MUST be executed before a Court of Record or some officer thereof having custody of the Seal.

State of *New York*
County of *Broome*

On this 9th day of March A.D. one thousand eight hundred and eighty, personally appeared before me, Dep. Clerk of the Supreme Court, a court of record for the County and State aforesaid, Louisa M. Cook, aged 44 years, a resident of Binghamton, Broome County, New York, who being duly sworn according to law, makes the following declaration in order to obtain the pension provided by Acts of Congress granting pensions to widows, to wit:

That she is the widow of Bishop A. Cook who volunteered under the name of Bishop A. Cook at Hancock, N.Y. on the 13th day of August A.D. 1863 as a Private in Co. F, 144th Reg't.. N.Y. Inf. Vols. of the war of 1861-1865 who died after his discharge of disease contacted in the service on the 18 day of January A.D. 1874.

That she was married under the name of Louisa M. Alexander to said Bishop Cook on the 10th day of July, A.D. 1853 by Rodney S. Rose at Hales Eddy, N.Y. There being no legal barrier to such marriage; that neither she nor her husband had been previously married that she has to the present date remained his widow; that the following are the names and dates of birth of all his legitimate children WHO WERE UNDER SIXTEEN YEARS OF AGE at the father's death, to wit:

> Mary E. Cook, born July 1859
> Ella L. Cook. born July 1866

That she has not in any manner been engaged in, aided or abetted the rebellion in the United states; that no prior application has been made.

She hereby appoints, with full power of substitution and revocation, George E. Lemon of Washington, D.C. her true and lawful attorney, to prosecute her claim. That her Post-Office address is Binghamton, Broome Co., N.Y.

> (signed) Louisa M. Cook

Also personally appeared J. W. Large residing at No. 100 in Oak Street in Binghamton, N.Y. and E. P. Barton residing at High Street in Binghamton, N.Y., persons whom I certify to be respectable and entitled to credit, and who being by me duly sworn, say were present and saw Louisa M. Cook the claimant sign her name to the foregoing declaration; that they have every reason to believe, from the appearance of said claimant and their acquaintance with her, that she is the identical person she represents herself to be; and that they have no interest in the prosecution of this claim.

> (signed) 1. J. W. Large
> (signed) 2. E. P. Barton

Sworn to and subscribed be fore me this 9th day of March A.D. 1880.

(signed) Chas. F. Tupper
Deputy clerk in and for
Broome County, N.Y.

AFFIDAVIT

State of New York
County of Broome

Louisa M. Cook of Binghamton in said county, being duly sworn, says: That in her claim No. 261,945 as widow of Bishop A. Cook late member of Co. F, 144 N.Y. Vols that she is unable to furnish a record of the death of her late husband, Bishop A. Cook (other than the affidavit of the attending physician and neighbors and friends) for the reason there was no public or other record of his death to her knowledge.

That her residence in 1864 was Scott Township, Wayne County Pennsylvania and her Post Office address Hales Eddy, Delaware County, New York until October 1865 then her residence was Harmony Susquehanna County, Pennsylvania and Post Office Address Louisburg Susquehanna and Starrucca Wayne County Pennsylvania until 1874. Since 1874 and to the present time 1881 her residence and Post Office address has been Binghamton, Broome County, New York.

Deponent further says that her post office address is Yale Box 102, Binghamton, Broome County, N.Y.

Signature Louisa M. Cook

Subscribed and sworn to before me this **13** *day of* **May 1881;** *and I further certify that said* Louisa M. Cook *is a credible witness, that his foregoing affidavit was fully read to or by him before execution, and that I have no interest in the prosecution of this claim.*

Lyman M. Sherwood, Notary Public,
Binghamton, Broome County, N.Y.

AFFIDAVIT

State of New York
County of Tioga

Charles E. Whitaker of Berkshire in said county, being duly sworn says: That He was a member of Company F of the 144 New York vols and remembers well one Bishop A. Cook a member of Co F of the 14 New York Vols and is personally knowing to the fact, was present at the time, and saw said Bishop A. Cook when he was while in line of duty taken sick at Hilton Head, South Carolina on or about the 25th day of November 1864. That said Bishop A. Cook was sent to Hospital at Hilton Head, S.C. and that he saw said Cook in said Hospital and that said Cook's disease was disease of the lungs.

Deponent further says that he has no interest in the persecution of this claim, and that his post office is Wilson creek, Tioga county, N.Y.

(witness) George G. Kimball   *(signed) Charles E. Whitaker*

Subscribed and sworn to before me this **19th** *day of* **June 1880;** *and I further certify that said* Charles E. Whitaker *is a credible witness, that his foregoing affidavit was fully read to or by him before execution, and that I have no interest in the prosecution of this claim.*

A. M. Kimball
Justice of the Peace

AFFIDAVIT

State of Pennsylvania
County of Susquehanna

David Fancher of Harmony is said county, being duly sworn says; That he was a member of Company F, of the 144th N.Y. Vols and remembers well one Bishop A. Cook a member of company F of the 144th N.Y. Vols and is personally knowing to the fact and was present at the (time) and saw said Bishop A. Cook when he was while in line of his duty taken sick at Hilton Head South Carolina on or about the 25th day of November 1864. That the said Bishop A. Cook was sent to the hospital at Hilton Head, S.C. and that he saw said Cook in said Hospital and that said Cook's disease was disease of the lungs.

Deponent further says, that he has no interest in the prosecution of this claim and that his post office address is Montrose, Susquehanna Co., Pennsylvania.

Signature Silas D. Fancher

Subscribed and sworn to before me this **3rd** *day of* **August 1880;** *and I further certify that said* David Fancher *is a credible witness, that his foregoing affidavit was fully read to or by him before execution, and that I have no interest in the prosecution of this claim.*

George B. Ward
Justice of the Peace

AFFIDAVIT

State of Michigan
County of Manistee

Mary C. Garlow of Manistee, Manistee county Mich. is said county, being duly sworn says; That she was present at the time and is personally knowing to the fact that Mrs. Louisa Cook, wife of

Bishop a. Cook gave birth to a female child (which was named Mary E. Cook) at Scott, Wayne County, Pennsylvania on the 26th day of July 1859 that Doctress Polly Barton the attendant physician at said birth is now deceased.

Deponent further says, that she has no interest in the prosecution of this claim, and that her post-office address is Manistee, Manistee County, Mich.

Witnesses
Fred Springborn   Mary C. Garlow
Hannah Springborn

Subscribed and sworn to before me this **7th** *day of* **June 1880;** *and I further certify that said Mary C. Garlow is a credible witness, that her foregoing affidavit was fully read to or by her before execution, and that I have no interest in the prosecution of this claim.*

Frank Bull
Justice of the Peace

AFFIDAVIT

State of New York
County of Broome

Mercy D. Alexander of Binghamton in said County, being duly sworn says; That she was present and personally knowing to the fact that Mrs. Louisa M. Cook wife of Bishop A. Cook gave birth to a female child (which was named Mary E. Cook) at Scott, Wayne County Pennsylvania on the 26th day of July 1859. That doctoress Polly Barton the attendant physician at said birth is now deceased.

Depondent further says, that she has no interest in the prosecution of this claim, and that his post-office address is Binghamton, Broome County, N.Y.

Signature Mercy D. Alexander

Subscribed and sworn to before me this **5th** *day of* **August 1880;** *and I further certify that said* Mercy Alexander *is a credible witness, that his foregoing affidavit was fully read to or by him before execution, and that I have no interest in the prosecution of this claim.*

Lyman M. Whitworth
Notary Public
Binghamton, Broome Co., N.Y.

AFFIDAVIT

State of Pennsylvania
County of Susquehanna

Martha Cook and Bethania Stevens of Harmony in said County, being duly sworn says; That they were present and are personally knowing to the fact that Mrs. Louisa M. Cook wife of Bishop A. Cook gave birth to a female child (who was afterward named Ella L. Cook) at Harmony, Susquehanna County, Penna. on the 26th July 1866. That doctoress Polly Barton the attending physician at the time of said birth is now diseased.

Deponant further says, that he has no interest in the prosecution of this claim and that his post-office address is Harmony, Susquehanna Co. Penna.

F. C. Cook   Martha Cook
                              Bethania Stevens

Subscribed sworn to before me this **6th** *day of* **May 1880;** *and they further certify that deponents are credible witnesses that the foregoing affidavit was fully read to or by him before execution, and that they have no interest in the prosecution of this claim.*

Less S. Page
Justice of the Peace

AFFIDAVIT

State of New York
County of Tioga

Rodney S. Rose of Candor in said County, being duly sworn, says; that He as a Methodist minister united in marriage Bishop A. Cook and Louisa M. Alexander at Hales Eddy, Broome County, New York on the 10th day of July 1853.

Deponent further says, that he has no interest in the prosecution of this claim and that his post-office address is Candor, Tioga county, New York.

J. W. Parmalee   Rodney S. Rose
Witness

Subscribed and sworn to before me this **29th** *day of* April **1880;** *and I further certify that said* Rodney S. Rose *is a credible witness, that his foregoing affidavit was fully read to or by him before execution, and that I have no interest in the prosecution of this claim.*

J. W. Parmalee
Justice of the Peace

AFFIDAVIT

State of New York
County of Broome

James Stone and Ezra B. Barton of Binghamton in said County, being duly sworn, says; That they have been well personally and intimately acquainted with Louisa M. Cook widow of Bishop A. Cook late a private of Co. F, 144 N.Y. Vols and are personally knowing of the fact that said Mrs. Lousia M. Cook has not remarried since the death of her husband Bishop A. Cook 18 January 1874 but still remains his widow. That they are personally knowing to the fact that Mrs. Lousia M. Cook has not abandoned the support of her family and has always been a loyal woman and good citizen to the government of the United States. That they are personally knowing to the fact that said Bishop A. Cook did not leave any children under sixteen years of age other than Mary Cook and Ella Cook at the time of his death aforesaid.

Deponents further say that they have no interest in the prosecution of this claim and that their post-office address is Binghamton, Broome county, N.Y.

James Stone
Ezra B. Barton

Subscribed and sworn to before me this **1st** *day of* **May 1881;** *and I further certify that deponents are credible witnesses and that their foregoing affidavit was fully read to or by them before execution, and that I have no interest in the prosecution of this claim.*

Lyman A. Sherwood
Notary Public,
Binghamton, Broome Co. N.Y.

AFFIDAVIT

State of Pennsylvania
County of Wayne

Daniel Utter, M.D. of Straucca Borough in said County, being duly sworn says; That He was called upon in the month of September 1865 to give medical treatment to Bishop A. Cook a recently discharged soldier. That after the necessary examination he found him suffering from bronchitis and disease of the lungs. That said Bishop A. Cook informed him that he had been afflicted with said disease while in the United States service to which he ascribed his present difficulty. That he did not give continuous treatment but did act as the family physician of said Bishop A. Cook, and did at intervals each year prescribe for and treat said Bishop A. Cook from September 1865 to 1874 that said Cook was not free from said disease of the lungs and bronchitus from 1865 to 1874 and was in the opinion of the deponent fully three-fourths disabled from manual labor by reason of said bronchitis and disease of the lungs from 1865 to 1874. That he was attending physician and that said Bishop A. Cook died at Harmony, Susquehanna County, Pennsylvania on the 18th day of January 1874 and that the sole and immediate cause of said Bishop A. Cook's death was bronchitis and disease of the lungs.

Deponent further says, that he has no interest in the prosecution of this claim and that his post-office address is Straucca, Pa.

Signature: Daniel Utter, M.D.

Subscribed and sworn to before me this **14th** *day of* **May 1880,** *and I further certify that said* Daniel Utter, M.D. *is a credible witness, that his foregoing affidavit was fully read to or by him before execution, and that I have no interest in the prosecution of this claim.*

N. M. Benedick
Justice of the Peace

AFFIDAVIT

State of Pennsylvania
County of Wayne

Daniel Utter, MD. of Straucca in said County, being duly sworn, says; That he was physician attendant upon Bishop A. Cook from September 1865 to his death 18 January 1874 as stated in his affidavit given 14 May 1880.

That on or about April 1873 said Bishop Cook became much worse and was not able to perform any labor whatever only get out of his room and house occasionally and that on or about Sept. or Oct. 1873, said Bishop A. Cook was confined to his house and bed did not to this deponents knowledge again get out.

That said Bishop A. Cook was during his treatment from Sept. 1865 to 18 Jan. 1874 troubled with bronchitis and disease of the lungs but from April 1873 the disease of the lungs became fully developed with occasional hemorrhage and that in the opinion of this deponent the sole and immediate cause of said Bishop A. Cook's death was disease of or consumption of the lungs said Bishop A. Cook died 18 January 1874 at Harmony Penna.

Deponent further says that he has no interest in the prosecution of this claim and that his post-office address is Straucca, Pa.

F. A. Benedick   Signature: Daniel Utter
Witness

Subscribed and sworn to before me this **19th** *day of* **May A.D. 1881;** and I further certify that said Daniel Utter, M.D. *is a credible witness, that his foregoing affidavit was fully read to or by him before execution, and that I have no interest in the prosecution of this claim.*

N. M. Benedict J.P.

Letter on Letterhead

W. J. & F. W. Welsh
Attorneys
Rooms 8 and 10 Strong Block

Binghamton, N.Y., April 20, 1896

S. E. Nichols,

Dear Sir:

In relation to the claim of Louisa M. Cook, pensioner under certificate No. 194,164, issued to Louisa M. Cook as the widow of Bishop A. Cook, rate $8 per month. Mrs. Cook died March 29, 1896, just a few days before her quarterly pension became due. We have the voucher which you sent her to be executed. Her daughter Mrs.. Hattie M. Large has been appointed administratrix of her estate. There is but very little estate left. Will you send me proper voucher to be executed by the administratrix for the pension to the time of the death of the pensioner, which I understand she is entitled to, although I do not know much about these matters.

Respectfully yours,
W. J. Welsh

This letter stamped

Received April 21 1896, U.S. Pension agency, Buffalo, N.Y.

INDEX

The following index is made up of the names that Bishop mentions in his letters. there is some variations in spelling, etc. I have tried to cover them all but I don't know how much success I have had.

A

Alexander, Almus, 12, 19, 46, 61, 119, 185, 188, 223, 303

____, **Charley,** 143, 180, 185, 187, 196

____, **Mercy,** 114, 117, 353, 354

Ames, Gen., 194

Anderson, Maj., 332

Austin, Maj., 194

B

Barlow, John, 339

Barton, Ezra, B., 349, 356

____, **Polly,** 353, 354

Beavan, Thomas, 166, 171, 238, 249, 252

Beecher, Col., 280

Benedick, N. M., 357, 358

Benedict, F. A., 358

Bragg, Gen., 8, 85, 246

Brainard, Uncle, 12, 21, 43, 225, 332

Brunning, Henry, 284

Bull, Frank, 353

Burnside, Gen., 20, 24, 28, 29, 44, 45, 70, 75, 246

Butler, Gen., 89

____, **Bradford,** 194, 195

Burrows, Palmer L., Capt., 63, 68

C

Casey, Silas, Brig., Gen., 1, 56

Christensen, E., Maj., 1

Cole, John, Lt., 63, 118

____, **Alfred,** 97

____, **Charles,** 98, 141

Cook, Al., 17, 20, 25, 102, 114, 115, 164, 166, 175, 180, 181, 207, 257, 275, 309, 327, 330

____, **Charles,** 98

____, **Elizabeth,** 269

____, **George,** 31, 187

____, **Harriet, (Aunt),** 18, 86, 91, 123, 145, 164, 176, 179, 189, 233, 259, 271, 315, 330

____, **James,** 3, 17, 20

____, **Orlo,** 97, 225

____, **Ruth,** 74

____, **Russ(el),** 20, 21, 31, 39, 45, 53, 74, 115, 173, 187, 189, 236, 238, 248, 249, 253, 257, 266, 267, 268, 269, 274, 298, 305, 308, 313, 314, 315, 320, 321, 329

____, **Martha,** 354

____, **F. C.,** 354

Curtis, Gov., 162

D

Davis (Jeff), 100, 118, 302, 332, 333
Dickinson, Charley, 3, 39, 166, 257, 277
____, Thurston, 188
____, Hattie, 39, 91, 317
_____, Wesley, 18, 39, 71, 91
Dix, Gen., 128, 144, 174

E

Early, Nelson, 184
____, Bill, 241
____, E. W., 137, 181, 188, 302
Ellsworth, 105
Evans, Bill, 30, 146

F

Fagen, Andrew, 27
____, Curtis, 15
Falkner, Benjamin, 312
Fancher, David, 352
____, Silas D., 352
Fish, William, 161, 194, 206
Fletcher, 151
Foster, John, G., Gen., 169, 285
Fullerton, (chaplain), 311

G

Gardinier, Dan, 3

____, Jacob, 197
Garlow, Bill, 189, 292
____, Elias, 67, 71, 76, 191
____, John, 18
____, Mary, 352, 353
____, Mrs., 53
____, Pete, 43
____, Steve, 5, 41
Gates, Mrs., 24, 40, 49, 266, 270, 304
____, Mr., 35, 89, 255
Gillmore, Gen., 189, 210, 257, 261
Gordon, Gen., 169, 170, 257, 281, 279, 285, 287
Grant, Gen., 142, 144, 152, 162, 167, 189, 190, 246, 251, 265, 282, 283, 286, 288, 292, 296, 303, 316, 332
Green, Col., 96, 110
Greenman, Mrs., 24
____, Charles, 30, 65

Gould, James, 7, 34, 38, 44, 49, 67, 92, 216, 339
____, William, 7, 34, 38, 44, 49, 67, 935
Greely, 37
Gregory, Col., 227, 236

H

Hathaway, Charles, 60
Hart, Frank B., Capt, 332
Hillyer, Virgil, 347

Nutt, James Major, 312, 326

P

Page, Les S., 355
Parks, Silas, 7
____, F. F. 345
Parmalee, J. W., 355
Peck, Gen., 128
Pemberton, Gen., 144, 189
Plaskett, Capt., 4, 5, 79, 136, 154, 210, 312, 341

R

Reynolds, Elijah., 24, 31, 191
____, Benjamin, 140
Rice, Calvin, Maj., 149, 280
Robbins, A. J., 345, 346
Rose, Joe, 21, 304
____, Rodney S., 349, 355
Rosencrans, Gen., 142, 182

S

Schlager, Brandt, 51, 58, 97, 107, 132, 139, 146, 158, 159, 172, 187, 211, 235, 274
Serryne, William, 182
Seymour, Gov, 227, 279
____, Truman, Gen., 261
Sherman, Gen., 182, 303, 304, 319, 320, 327
Sherwood, Lyman M., 351, 356

Slidell, William J., Col. 227, 279
Springborn, Fred, 353
____, Hannah, 353
Squire, Mr., 172
Stegel, Gen., 28
Stevens, Bethania, 354
Stone, James, 356
Steinrod, William, 144
Stiles, Charles, 220, 240

T

Taylor, O. T., 342, 343, 345
____, Bill, 211
Thomas, Bowl, 219
____, George, 34, 61 172
____, Will, 39
____, E. L., 312
Thompkins , Mr., 35
____, Arthur, 151
____, Leroy, 220
Thompson, E. R., 341
____, Maj., 331
____, Jeff., Gen. 335
Travis, Aaron, 48, 82 118, 281
____, Sol, 197
Tupper, Charles F., 355
Turell, Granny, 187
____, Mrs., 27, 30, 333
____, Mr., 23, 62

U

Utter, Daniel M.D., 357 358

W